Also by Welles Hangen

After Nehru, Who? (1963)

THE
MUTED REVOLUTION

THE
MUTED
REVOLUTION

EAST GERMANY'S CHALLENGE

TO RUSSIA AND THE WEST

BY

WELLES HANGEN

■

NEW YORK : ALFRED · A · KNOPF

1966

Library of Congress Catalog Card Number: 66-19379

THIS IS A BORZOI BOOK
PUBLISHED BY ALFRED A. KNOPF, INC.

Manufactured in the United States of America

First Edition

TO MY WIFE

Preface

∎

THE PURPOSE of this book is to describe East Germany as
it actually is and not as its apologists or adversaries would
have us believe. I regard this little-known country—what one
writer calls "a white Tibet in the heart of a wide-open world"
—as one of the most important in Europe and indeed in the
world. I have tried to give as graphic a picture as possible of
East Germany today and especially the growth of an embryo
national communism among its ruling elite, a development of
potentially epochal significance in all future efforts to decide
the fate of Germany and Central Europe.

Most books on Germany are really about Berlin or the
Federal Republic of West Germany, but Berlin is not Germany, and Bonn's claim to represent all Germans is as shaky
in fact as in law. There are indeed two German states and, increasingly, two mentalities. Neither can be realistically ignored. In this book I have devoted considerable attention to
policies and prospects in Berlin and West Germany, but my
main focus has been on the lesser-known element in the German equation—East Germany.

I first visited the communist part of Germany in 1955 as
a *New York Times* correspondent. Later, as Bonn bureau chief

of the National Broadcasting Company, I made more than a dozen trips to East Germany, ranging the length and breadth of the country from Marienborn to Frankfurt-on-Oder and from Rostock to Chemnitz (rechristened Karl-Marx-Stadt). The communists no longer fear foreign visitors and their need for hard currency is so acute that they even issue entry visas at the frontier. My wife and I talked to hundreds of East Germans from charwomen to the chairman of the Council of Ministers. When we traveled together we drove our own car and roamed the country for the most part without a guide. At other times I went on formal journalistic expeditions with an escort appointed by the East German authorities. No matter how or where I traveled, I found the same somber, brooding land beginning to grope its way out of misery and chaos; seventeen million talented, industrious Germans beginning to forget their disgruntlement and take a defiant pride in their achievements under communism or, as many would say, despite communism. Above all I found a communist party whose heirs are beginning to think and act like Germans as well as communists.

This book is a collection of vignettes of East German life. I have also included sketches of Bonn and Berlin. This is in no sense a history of the German problem or a scholarly dissection of the East German state. Nor is it a connected narrative of my time in Germany. Rather it is a highly selective culling from the myriad impressions one gets when he travels through the fragmented parts of Hitler's old Reich today. I have included chapters on what I consider the most important elements of East and West German government policy, but I have not tried to cover everything or to follow a strictly logical progression from one topic to another. I have dwelt on things that seemed striking or significant and left the rest aside. Each chapter is largely self-contained because each is based on my investigation of a particular area of German life.

I am indebted to the many Germans—East and West— who unselfishly shared their experiences and expectations with me, providing the essential material for a report like this. The

German Information Center in New York, and especially Mrs. Godenschweger, were of invaluable help in furnishing documentation and photographs to illustrate the text. I am also indebted to the librarians at the Council on Foreign Relations. In writing this book I have drawn frequently on the work of Dorothy Miller and other analysts of Radio Free Europe as well as Carola Stern's biography of Ulbricht and her recent analysis of relations between German and Chinese communism. The first part of my chapter on Dresden is based in part on David Irving's moving account of the destruction of that city.

I am grateful to Professor Roland Warren of Brandeis University, who made available material gathered during his time in Germany. Professor Melvin Croan of Harvard offered helpful criticisms at several stages. My thanks also go to the National Broadcasting Company which enabled me to spend the last two years as its correspondent in Germany. The NBC News Bureau manager in Bonn, Frau Wanda Mencke-Glueckert, was of enormous help both during my time in Germany and afterward. Naturally, none of the persons or institutions who contributed to this book bears any responsibility for the conclusions reached or factual errors that may have crept in.

As usual, my most heartfelt gratitude goes to my wife, who found time to read and improve the manuscript as well as type it in final form despite her preoccupation with a new member of our family.

WELLES HANGEN

New York
July 1966

Contents

Illustrations

THE
MUTED REVOLUTION

■

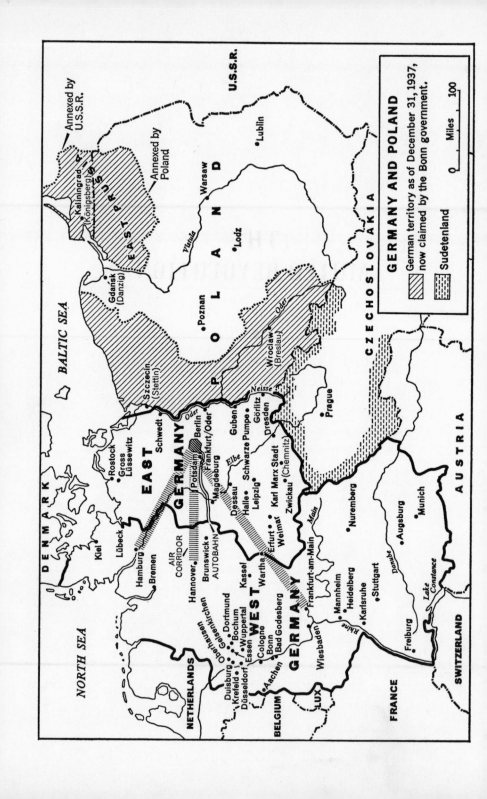

GERMANY AND POLAND

German territory as of December 31, 1937, now claimed by the Bonn government.

Sudetenland

Miles 0 100

Annexed by U.S.S.R.

Annexed by Poland

U.S.S.R.

Lublin

Warsaw

Vistula

Lodz

Gdansk (Danzig)

EAST PRUSSIA

Poznan

P O L A N D

Oder

BALTIC SEA

Szczecin (Stettin)

Wroclaw (Breslau)

Neisse

CZECHOSLOVAKIA

Schwedt

Oder

Berlin

Frankfurt/Oder

Guben

Görlitz

Dresden

Prague

Rostock

Gross Lüssewitz

EAST

Potsdam

Magdeburg

Schwarze Pumpe

Karl Marx Stadt (Chemnitz)

AUSTRIA

GERMANY

Elbe

Dessau

Halle

Leipzig

Zwickau

Lübeck

Kiel

DENMARK

Hamburg

Bremen

AIR CORRIDOR

Brunswick

AUTOBAHN

Kassel

Wartha

Erfurt

Weimar

Main

Nuremberg

Augsburg

Munich

Hannover

WEST

Frankfurt-am-Main

Danube

NORTH SEA

Oberhausen

Gelsenkirchen

Dortmund

Bochum

Wuppertal

Duisburg

Krefeld

Essen

Düsseldorf

Cologne

Bonn

Bad Godesberg

GERMANY

Mannheim

Heidelberg

Karlsruhe

Stuttgart

Lake Constance

NETHERLANDS

Aachen

Wiesbaden

Rhine

Freiburg

BELGIUM

LUX.

FRANCE

SWITZERLAND

(1)

Shaking the Temples
of Certainty

∎

A T *ABOUT TEN O'CLOCK* on the morning of December 3, 1965, a heavy-set, balding man entered the office of the Chairman of the State Planning Commission in communist East Berlin, pulled a revolver from his desk drawer, and killed himself. Ten hours later ADN, the official East German news agency, moved a brief medical bulletin reporting that Dr. Erich Apel, forty-eight years old, "took his life in an uncontrollable reaction following a nervous breakdown." It said he had long suffered from "circulatory disorders." The following morning Apel's black-bordered obituary appeared on page one of *Neues Deutschland,* central organ of the East German Socialist Unity (Communist) Party, beside a posthumous tribute from the Central Committee of the party, the National Council of the National Front, the State Council, and the Council of Ministers of the German Democratic Republic.

"His tragic death," the statement said, "took him from us in the midst of a fruitful creative work." It praised Dr. Apel's "tireless and self-sacrificing work in the service of the party of the working class and the German Democratic Republic."

Monday, December 6, was a national day of mourning in the communist part of Germany. Erich Apel's body lay in state at Central Committee headquarters. Walter Ulbricht was the chief mourner at a ceremonious state funeral attended by high-ranking leaders of the party and government. Premier Willi Stoph eulogized Apel's services in reforming the economy. Then the body was taken to the crematorium at Berlin-Baumschulenweg and the ashes buried in the rigorously simple manner prescribed for dialectical materialists. Unfortunately, no way was found to inter Dr. Apel's political legacy. Even before he was buried, this began to plague Ulbricht and the other aging oligarchs who rule East Germany. It will keep plaguing them until they too are in their graves and a new generation of communists has come to power in the far-off land between the Elbe and the Oder.

Amid the pomp and platitudes that marked Erich Apel's passing, several important facts were left unmentioned: above all, the conclusion a few hours after his suicide of a five-year Soviet-East German trade agreement providing for a major expansion of exchanges between the chief trading nations in the communist world. East Germany promised to deliver more than 300 sea-going freighters and other vessels to the Soviet Union at 1949 prices, at least 30 percent below what they would fetch on the world market. More than 200 East German chemical plants were to be furnished at similar bargain prices. Russia would get pipes from East Germany at 40 percent off. In exchange, Ulbricht's state agreed to buy an additional 36 million tons of Russian crude oil for almost twice the world market rate, pig iron at a markup of more than 85 percent, and 31.5 million tons of Soviet coal on equally disadvantageous terms. East Germany committed itself to buy 4 billion East marks (one billion dollars) of "machines and installations," for which Moscow could evidently find no other market. The East Germans also undertook to purchase some 24 Soviet passenger planes to meet the needs that East Germany's own aircraft industry had sought to supply until it was throttled in its cradle by Moscow. Total Soviet-East German trade by 1970 would amount to 60 billion East marks (15 billion dollars), an increase of about one fifth over the 1961–5 level. Moreover, the agreement was said to include a secret protocol requiring East Germany to make up shortages in deliveries previously promised Russia. Apart from its extortionate terms, the trade pact irrevocably tied East Germany for the next five years to the floundering Soviet economy. It also threatened to undo the "new economic system" launched by Dr. Apel and kindred spirits in the East German party. As Chairman of the State Planning Commission, Candidate Member of the Politburo, and Deputy Prime Minister, Erich Apel had fathered the most far-reaching program of economic rationalization ever attempted by a communist regime. He had introduced the profit motive and elements of a market-oriented system of production and distribution that had already achieved what many considered an economic miracle in East Germany. The revolution in industry was beginning to rouse the East German countryside out of collectivized stagnation and to encourage new ferment among intellectuals and artists.

Frightened by the pace of change and the growing diffusion of power in the economy, Ulbricht re-established nine economic ministries with financial control over industry a few days after Apel's suicide, but he left the most important reforms intact.

Erich Apel was that most dangerous foe of the Stalinist order in East Germany: a communist who put East Germany's own interests above those of the Soviet Union. The story of his death begins in September 1965 when he arrived in Moscow with Ulbricht and a large East German delegation to discuss a new trade agreement with the Soviet Union. The Russians were more implacable than usual. It had been a bad year for them. The harvest was poor. Industry was operating at a loss. American bombers were hammering Moscow's ally North Vietnam while China accused the Soviet leaders of scheming to divide the world with America. The men in the Kremlin demanded that the East German comrades answer the call of the socialist motherland by sending her essential machinery

and chemicals at huge losses to themselves. At the same time
the Russians insisted there be no reduction in prices of Soviet
raw material exports. When the argument waxed hot, the Soviet negotiators produced detailed evidence that the East
Germans had consistently fallen short on their deliveries to
Russia because they had diverted Soviet raw materials for the
production of finished goods exported for hard currency to the
West. Walter Ulbricht feigned ignorance of the whole business. Alfred Neumann, then Chairman of the National Economic Council, a body subordinate to the State Planning
Commission, managed to evade responsibility. According to
Stephan G. Thomas, one of the best-informed German authorities on communist affairs, Apel was made the scapegoat. He
was held personally accountable for making up the deficit in
East German exports to Russia and was ordered to sign the
new trade accord. But no agreement on details was reached
in Moscow, and after the East German delegation returned
home, negotiations dragged. Finally, in a gesture of despera-
tion the powerful First Secretary of the Soviet Communist
Party, Leonid I. Brezhnev, flew to East Berlin at the end of
November to give Ulbricht an ultimatum. It would be interesting to know what was said at their meeting. The upshot was
predictable. The seventy-two-year-old German *apparatchik*,
who had spent his adult life in Moscow's service, capitulated
on all counts. Brezhnev departed on the morning of November
29. On the same day the Soviet Foreign Trade Minister,
Nikolai S. Patolichev, arrived in East Berlin to collect the
spoils. But Apel continued to resist. On the morning of December 3 the Soviet delegation announced it would brook no
more delay; it demanded that he sign the draft trade treaty by
11 a.m. that day. During a recess in the talks Alfred Neumann
is reported to have told Apel on behalf of Ulbricht and the
entire Politburo that he must sign without further ado. A
violent argument ensued. At about ten o'clock Erich Apel was
dead.

A few hours later Neumann and Patolichev signed the
draft agreement in the presence of Willi Stoph, Chairman of

East Germany's Council of Ministers. That evening the Soviet ambassador in East Berlin gave a reception attended by Ulbricht and members of both delegations. ADN reported that the atmosphere was cordial.

Apel had taken care not to die politically intestate. Whether he left a formal testament is still unclear, but word soon reached West Berlin about the real reasons for his suicide. The information made clear Apel had been in good health and exposed the magnitude of Ulbricht's hypocrisy. Above all, it shed new light on the struggle between the old guard and the young communist cadres in East Berlin, presaging new storms to come. Erich Apel was not the first East German communist to choose death rather than sell out to the Russians. Nor is he likely to be the last. Almost exactly eight years before Apel killed himself, Gerhart Ziller, Economic Secretary in the East German party's Central Committee, committed suicide in the same way and for many of the same reasons. Whereas Ziller was denounced as a member of an "anti-party" subversive group, Apel was given a state funeral. Dissenters can no longer be automatically labeled disloyal.

The remarkable thing about Erich Apel was how much he had in common with his contemporaries in the East German party. Born in 1917 in the backward province of Thuringia (now part of East Germany), he was fifteen when Hitler seized power. After attending primary school and becoming an apprentice toolmaker, he took a degree at the engineering college at Ilmenau. He served on the Eastern front during the war. For him, as for so many other young Germans, the path to communism led through a Russian prisoner-of-war camp. Apel remained in the Soviet Union until 1952, helping to reassemble German plants dismantled as reparations and pursuing the study of engineering and Marxism-Leninism. After his return to East Germany he rose quickly through the ranks of the Ministry of Heavy Machine-Building but did not consider it necessary to join the East German Communist party until 1957 when he was already in charge of the ministry. By February 1958 Apel was head of the Politburo's economic commission. He became a Candidate member of the Politburo and a Full member of the Central Committee and also received his doctorate in economics by mid-1961. In January 1963 at the SED party congress that approved the "new economic system" Apel succeeded the doctrinaire Karl Mewis as Chairman of the State Planning Commission and Deputy Chairman of the Council of Ministers. Ulbricht gave him a surprisingly free hand in weeding out party hacks in economic positions and bringing in young, technically qualified engineers. By trampling on vested bureaucratic interests, the new planning chief antagonized many of the old guard and even colleagues on the State Planning Commission. He finally clashed with Ulbricht himself by asserting the primacy of East German interests over those of the Soviet Union.

Ulbricht is quite willing to dupe, but not defy, the Russians. He considers himself an international civil servant of the communist movement, whose headquarters, as far as he is concerned, is still in Moscow. Since 1945 he has been posted in Germany, but he has served with equal diligence in Prague, Vienna, Paris, and Moscow. He is the interchangeable *apparatchik* par excellence. Whatever he really feels about his seventeen million subjects, Ulbricht is realistic enough to know that they would never accept him in the raiment of a national communist. His personal power, perhaps his life itself, depends on Soviet backing. Most other German communists who took refuge in Stalin's Moscow after Hitler came to power and returned in the wake of the Red Army are in the same predicament. As the Red tide recedes from Eastern Europe, Ulbricht and the coterie of Moscow émigrés are being recognized as the fossils they are.

Erich Apel was no fossil, and he knew it. He dreamed of creating a national communist state in East Germany based on rational economic principles. He was also aware of the need for political reform. Shortly before his death Apel reportedly discussed with Professor Robert Havemann an article in which the former East Berlin university chemistry teacher called for more freedom in East Germany, including a parliamentary opposition. Whether Apel himself would have gone this far is open to doubt. In any event, he found himself increasingly at odds with the SED's old guard. Far from regarding the Russians as his only support, Apel came to consider them a menace. He never believed being a communist required renouncing one's nationality.

If Erich Apel had been unique and all other East German communists like Ulbricht, there would be little point in a book about East Germany. The country would indeed be the outsized concentration camp pictured in West German propaganda. Change, except on the purely technical level, would be unthinkable. East Germany would enter the European scene only as an object, a piece of Stalinist ice impervious to warm currents from East or West. But the fact is that Erich Apel was not unique. Some of his fellow technocrats have already attained positions of importance; others are waiting impatiently to inherit power. They are committed to make communism work in their part of Germany. In this they have the active cooperation of many younger East Germans, both in and outside the party, who increasingly identify their fortunes with those of the German Democratic Republic.

The mechanical reunification of Germany by free all-German elections is now a chimera. The Soviet Union would go to war rather than permit it. The West is similarly pledged to defend the noncommunist part of Germany. To "neutralize" a reunited Germany means denying the most numerous and technically advanced people in Western or Central Europe any effective part in the affairs of their continent. It would be easier to square the circle. Germany's future will be decided in the framework of the two German states that now exist. This is not to say the situation is static. While each side repeats the old slogans, things are changing in both East and West Germany. Vast disparities remain, but both German states are now stronger, more self-confident, more assertive. They are reacting to what Chancellor Erhard meant when he told the West German Bundestag that "the inner cohesion of the two big power blocs has loosened, both in the West and the East." Bonn is unwilling to remain a second-class member of NATO while continuing to make a larger contribution to the alliance than any other member except the United States. The search for a West German role in nuclear strategy reflects uneasiness on both sides of the Atlantic about Bonn's ultimate course. Under intense external pressure the government of the Federal Republic has agreed to continue the legal pursuit of Nazi war criminals until 1970, but it has bluntly declared that the post-war era is over and that Germans are no longer on probation.

Similar stirrings are apparent in East Germany. Apel's suicide was a dramatic example. There are many others. Moscow can no longer count on automatic East German acquiescence. The comrades in East Berlin insist on being treated on a par with other Eastern European communist parties. East German spokesmen no longer hesitate to lecture the Russians in public. In private they are outspoken in their resentment against Soviet policies. Less than a month after Ulbricht visited Moscow in September 1965, East German officers commanded a Soviet Army division for the first time in a major tactical exercise by Warsaw Pact forces. The East German communists can take a tougher line with Moscow because they are stronger at home. Before the Wall was built through Berlin in August 1961, East Germany was losing as many as two thousand people a day. Entire apartment buildings were vacated overnight. The first thing every factory manager did on Monday morning was to find out how many workers had fled during the weekend. Officials reckoned they would lose at least twenty percent of every medical graduating class. The drain of teachers left hundreds of empty classrooms.

The torrent has now been cut to a trickle. Chances of escaping across the Wall are estimated to be one in nine. Factory managers now know how many work benches will be occupied on Monday morning. By stabilizing the labor force, the Wall has enabled the communists to consolidate the economy. Ordinary East Germans now realize they must make the best of things where they are. Voting with their feet is out. They

now vote with their hands, not in the sham elections organized
by the communists, but by working to produce the goods
East Germany so desperately needs. More production helps
to narrow the disparity between living standards in East
and West Germany, reducing the pressures that originally
caused the exodus. East Germans are beginning to speak what
one former *New York Times* correspondent calls "the language
of awakening pride."

Such in outline are some of the tremors being felt today
on both sides of the Wall. They have already shaken the temples of certainty in East and West Germany and sent shock
waves as far as Moscow and Washington. Only a major earthquake could make the two German states one today. But if
both are still around after another generation, they may find
they have more in common with each other than either has
with its present allies. The resulting dialogue among Germans,
long championed by the Soviets, could lead to the nearest
approximation of German unity likely in this century. Before
then, however, the Russians might have concluded that a German communist is little better than a German capitalist.

Maxwell Anderson said names were invented "so that we
might walk without fear among things known." Today, among
things German, names themselves arouse fear and anger. The
federal German government in Bonn denies the legal existence
of anything called the German Democratic Republic, objects
to the term "East Germany," and insists on calling it "the Soviet Zone," "the Zone," or even "Middle Germany" (with the
implication that the Oder-Neisse territories and East Prussia
acquired by Poland and Russia at the end of the Second World
War are really Eastern Germany). This usage is generally followed in the West German press, radio, and television and by
almost all politicians in the Federal Republic. The East German communists insist their state must be called the "German
Democratic Republic" (GDR) or its German equivalent,
"die Deutsche Demokratische Republik" (DDR). They
and many ordinary East Germans object to the term
"Zone" almost two decades after the founding of an ostensibly

independent state between the Elbe and the Oder. America, Britain, and the Scandinavian countries avoid taking sides in the war of nomenclature by using the relatively apolitical "East Germany." In this book I shall be using these terms interchangeably since they all denote the same place. Another label that will crop up frequently is "SED," standing for the "Sozialistische Einheitspartei Deutschlands" (Socialist Unity Party of Germany), the name adopted by the German communist party in April 1946 after it swallowed the Social Democratic party in the Soviet Occupation Zone. All power in the SED is wielded by communists, so I shall use the terms "SED" and "East German Communist Party" or "East German communists" interchangeably. The tiny West German communist party, outlawed since 1956, still calls itself the "Communist Party of Germany" (KPD), but it now operates out of East Berlin as an appendage of the SED.

By whatever name it is called, there is a communist state on German soil today whose gross industrial production ranks fifth or sixth in Europe, after the Soviet Union, West Germany, Britain, France, and possibly Italy, depending on the indices used. Since 1964 East Germany claims to have exceeded the highest prewar (1936) industrial production of Hitler's Reich, which was four times as large and had almost four times as many people. This is disputed by some West German economists, but the UN Economic Commission for Europe accepts the East German figures. In per capita chemical output East Germany boasts it is second only to the United States. Official statistics show that, on a per capita basis, the DDR produces more cement than Britain, more steel than Italy, and more electricity than France, Italy, or even West Germany. East Germany accounts for more than one third of the world's lignite production and operates the world's only lignite coke works at the huge Schwarze Pumpe complex near Cottbus. The country is also a leading producer of machine tools, optical goods, office equipment, railway cars, and ceramics. In the communist world East Germany ranks first in industrial output after the Soviet Union. It is Moscow's main trading partner, supplying about one fourth of all Soviet imports and the bulk of the machine tools, ships, and chemical plants and equipment that the Russians obtain from abroad. Although more than half of East Germany's trade is with the Soviet Union, exports carrying the label "Made in DDR" now reach more than one hundred countries located on every continent.

Economic strength, albeit achieved at the expense of its own people, is what has enabled the East German regime to win increasing recognition outside the communist world. Eight days after the DDR was founded on October 7, 1949, Finland became the first noncommunist state to sign a trade agreement with East Germany. The DDR still has no embassies outside communist countries, but it has consulates or consulates general in eight nonaligned African and Asian states, and official trade representatives in Britain, France, Italy, Belgium, Holland, Austria, Denmark, Norway, Sweden, Finland, Greece, and Turkey. Since East Germany has no diplomatic relations with Western countries, trade agreements with them are usually concluded between the respective Chambers of Foreign Trade. Exchanges with the West have increased irregularly during recent years. The East Germans are eager to expand such trade, but their commitments to Russia and the other Eastern bloc countries as well as payment problems have hampered this effort. In Guinea, Burma, Egypt, and a few other Afro-Asian countries the DDR has furnished technical advice and credits for the purchase of East German machinery and equipment. Such ventures in foreign aid are usually coordinated with other bloc countries, especially the Soviet Union. Students from ninety-four countries, mostly Asian, African, and Latin American, are currently reported studying at East German universities and technical schools.

The DDR's biggest stride toward recognition came when official East and West German delegations attended the 1959 Big Four Foreign Ministers' Conference in Geneva on an equal footing and sat at an equal distance from the main conference table. Four years later the United States and Britain agreed to open the Partial Nuclear Test Ban Treaty to "all states" despite bitter objections from Bonn. The DDR was one of the first to sign.

Early in 1965 Ulbricht was invited to make a state visit to Egypt. The trip failed to produce full diplomatic relations between Cairo and East Berlin, but it set off a chain of events that eventually prompted ten Arab states to break relations with West Germany. It was a dividend the SED chief had probably not expected.

Ulbricht is by no means the only East German who travels abroad in pursuit of recognition for the DDR. East Germans now belong to more than 250 international organizations dealing with everything from philately to railroads. Every time an East German delegate takes the floor at an international conference he is expected to open with the words "On behalf of the delegation of the German Democratic Republic."

Sportsmen fulfill the same purpose. By dint of professional-type training, "amateur" East German athletes have set 45 world records and 28 European records for the greater glory of the DDR. In 1963 the DDR team won the world handball championship in Switzerland, and an East German teacher holds the world title in toboggan racing. At the 1964 Tokyo Olympics an East German captained the all-German team for the first time, and henceforth the DDR will be represented by its own Olympic team. East German sports associations are now affiliated with 44 international sports federations. Only the International Riding Society (Reiterverband) still excludes DDR sportsmen. The East Germans also go out of their way to attract international athletic competitions. More than 35 world and European championships have been decided in the DDR in the last fifteen years.

The Leipzig trade fairs every spring and fall are the regime's chief economic showcase. Among the 10,500 exhibitors from 70 countries who displayed their wares at the spring fair in 1966 were 40 American firms and hundreds of West German concerns. Leipzig is still not the international crossroads it was before the war, but it now attracts more than 90,000 foreign visitors twice a year and nearly matches West Germany's Hannover fair in size.

The SED's success in putting the DDR on the map is all the more remarkable in view of the fact that the former Soviet Occupation Zone is a completely artificial entity without precedent in German history. This truncated torso cut from the old Reich is no larger than Ohio and numbers barely 17 million people compared with West Germany's 58 million. At Yalta the Big Three decided that the Soviet Occupation Zone should embrace the provinces of Saxony, Saxon-Anhalt, Thuringia, and Mecklenburg and parts of Brandenburg and Pomerania. This area includes the heart of old Prussia. To this has been added the former Soviet sector of Berlin embracing one third the population and less than one half the area of the old Reich capital. Before the war the area now included in East Germany produced less than three percent of Germany's iron and hard coal and less than six percent of its finished steel. East Germany's only abundant raw materials are lignite, potash, and uranium. Crude oil, cotton, iron ore, and virtually all other raw products must be imported. When the Russians refused to treat Germany as an economic unit, they cut their occupation zone off from its natural trade and communications with West Germany. Not a single German river or major canal runs exclusively through the DDR. Autobahns and trunk rail lines still run from east to west, not north to south. The Soviet Zone economy would, therefore, have suffered severe dislocations even if it had sustained no wartime damage. In fact, the devastation was appalling. Dresden was razed, Leipzig decimated, and Chemnitz all but obliterated. The three Allied Zones were also hard hit, but the 1948 currency reform and massive American aid set them on the road to recovery before the end of the 1940's. Balked in their effort to take reparations from current production in West Germany, the Russians ruthlessly looted some 70 billion marks of reparations from their own zone. It has been estimated that the reparations burden per capita in the Soviet Zone was almost two hundred times what it was in the Allied-occupied area. In his study "The Second Germany

—a State that should not be" Ernst Richert says that the East Germans could not really begin rebuilding their shattered economy until about 1955, when dismantling ceased and limited Soviet credits were granted. West Germany had a head-start of at least seven years.

Although Magdeburg, Leipzig, and Chemnitz were traditional manufacturing centers, it is not true, as often asserted in Bonn's propaganda, that East Germany includes the "industrial heartland" of the old Reich. The Silesian coal basin is now in Poland. And West Germany's Ruhr is again the largest metallurgical center in Europe. On the other hand, East Germany did inherit Mecklenburg and Thuringia, historically two of Germany's most backward provinces.

It is probably true that had the Soviet Zone not already been economically debilitated, the communists would have made it that way in their postwar zeal to smash the old order and install a one-party dictatorship. But the point remains that what we now know as East Germany was an uneconomic remnant of empire that has managed to become the world's tenth largest industrial power despite the rapacity of its conquerors and the blunders of their German proconsuls. The real economic miracle, as the East Germans are fond of saying, is on their side.

The DDR's only really important resource is people; people are also its greatest weakness. East Germans, being Germans, work hard even if they are politically disaffected. They generally dislike the communist regime but have such ingrained Teutonic respect for authority that they often shrink from exercising what modest rights they are now accorded. Many may dream of escaping across the Wall, but few will risk running afoul of the SED in their factory or collective farm. To overcome "negative attitudes," the regime knows it must raise living standards by increasing production. But to produce more requires more productive use of tools or more workers to operate them, or both. The "new economic system" for which Erich Apel gave his life is a bold attempt to put East Germany's industrial tools to better use. No system has yet

been devised to find more workers. On the contrary, the DDR
is one of the few countries in the world whose population has
declined steadily since the war. It fell more than a million and
a quarter in the decade 1950–60. Even the Wall failed to stop
the downtrend. On the basis of calculations he has made, Ernst
Lemmer, Bonn's former Minister of All-German and Refugee
Affairs, estimates there may now be even fewer than 16 million
people in East Germany. Most other observers are inclined to
accept the figure of 17,011,931 given in the DDR's 1965 statistical yearbook. The war has left a large surplus of women. For
every 100 men there are 119 women. Women now make up
46 percent of East Germany's labor force. The age composition
of the population is even more unfavorable. For every 100 East
Germans of working age there are 73 children and old-age
pensioners. The proportion of elderly people is twice what it
was in prewar Germany. As one East German official puts it,
"Our population profile is concave; we have big bulges at the
top and bottom and a very narrow midriff where people in
their productive years should be. Thanks to the war, we are
missing seven age groups in that section." The burden of gov-
ernment-financed pensions and medical care is so heavy that
Ulbricht now allows East German men over sixty-five and
women over sixty to travel West with the clear understanding
that they will not be missed if they choose to stay away. "For
us," one East German woman told me, "life begins at sixty."

The most alarming thing from the regime's point of view
is the continuing decline in the birth rate. With fewer than five
births a year per thousand population, the DDR now has the
fourth-lowest birth rate in the world. Hungary has the lowest.
The DDR is the only Eastern European country that has not
legalized abortions. Nevertheless, popular pressure caused by
the housing shortage and low incomes has prompted the regime to permit doctors to perform abortions more often. East
Germany has also become the first communist country to market contraceptive pills. They are legally available only by
prescription, but physicians have wide latitude to authorize use
of the pills in "social cases." One justification offered in the

SED press for oral contraceptives is that they will reduce the number of abortions.

The Wall cannot stop the decline of the labor force caused by the war and the low postwar birth rate. East Germany now has fewer than 8 million people gainfully employed. The number is not expected to increase appreciably until 1980 or even later. To mitigate the critical labor shortage, the DDR finally arranged in 1966 to employ surplus Polish workers in several East German plants along the Oder-Neisse frontier, as well as to import more restaurant and kitchen hands from Czechoslovakia and Hungary to work at East German resorts during the summer season. The SED took such steps reluctantly, fearing that workers from the "fraternal" communist countries would bring liberal ideas in their lunch pails. West Germany, on the other hand, has eased its labor shortage by employing more than a million "guest workers" from Mediterranean countries. One of East Germany's industrial managers told me he would welcome Polish workers in the 22 precision instrument and optical goods plants under his supervision. But at the huge Schwarze Pumpe lignite complex a director says that "our historical experience is against employing foreigners."

East Germany's shrinking population is at least homogeneous. Some 70,000 Sorbs in the southeastern corner of the country are the only national minority. They are descended from the original Slavonic inhabitants of the area. They have their own communist-run front organization, the Domowina, and a publishing house that prints literature and a daily newspaper in the Sorb language, which is akin to Czech. The Sorbs are preserved as a kind of ethnic oddity to demonstrate the blessings of communist rule.

Religious minorities are not a serious problem either. More than 80 percent of East Germans are nominal Protestants, members of the Evangelical (Lutheran) Church. There are a small Roman Catholic community and about 1,500 Jews, most of them elderly. The Jewish community in the DDR is dying out, not as the result of emigration, which is rarely allowed, but for natural reasons. Synagogues have been rebuilt with state aid in East Berlin, Leipzig, Dresden, and other cities, but when I arrived late for an appointment to visit the Leipzig synagogue the cantor of the Jewish community told me it was impossible.

"Why?" I asked. "Is it closed?"

"No," he said, "it is dark now, and the synagogue has no lights."

The DDR radio now broadcasts Jewish music and regular Sabbath services. Some Jewish cemeteries and community houses have been reopened, and anti-semitic propaganda is officially prohibited in the DDR. But Jews play no role in public life or the professions. The only Jews in high places are Foreign Minister Otto Winzer, Albert Norden, the Politburo's propaganda specialist, and Dr. Gerhart Eisler, head of the State Committee on Broadcasting, all avowed atheists.

The Evangelical Church in Germany has often proved to be a malleable instrument in the hands of whatever regime held power. Some pastors were imprisoned after the communist takeover, but the last one was out by 1964, according to information available in West Berlin. Although freedom of worship is officially recognized in the DDR, young people are under strong pressure to participate in the so-called "youth consecration" to socialism instead of the usual church confirmation. East German churchmen must subscribe to the regime's principal policies, especially in foreign affairs.

Four satellite political parties are allowed to lead a kind of twilight existence in the DDR. The East German branch of the Christian Democratic Union (CDU) was originally affiliated with the party that governs the Federal Republic, but it has long since been brought under strict SED control. In the words of the official DDR travel guide, the party "unites Christians who work actively for peace and progress"—as defined, that is, by non-Christians. The Democratic Peasants' Party of Germany (DBD), perhaps the most hapless of the lot, is supposed to rally collectivized farmers behind the regime. The Liberal Democratic Party of Germany (LDPD) appeals—again in the travel guide's words—to the "predominantly progressive forces among the lower and middle strata of the petty bourgeoisie." Most of its members are former independent artisans who now belong to craft production cooperatives or small businessmen in "partnership" with the regime. For ex-Nazis who have seen the light there is the National Democratic Party of Germany (NDPD), which includes many former Wehrmacht officers and soldiers re-educated in Soviet POW camps.

Although the satellite parties exert no effective influence on policy, their presence in the National Front of Democratic Germany serves as a fig leaf for the SED dictatorship. In departing from the one-party Soviet system, the East German party has in effect duplicated the United Front set up by the communists in China.

Like other communist states, the DDR presents an elaborate façade of parliamentary democracy based on a high-sounding and detailed constitution. The Volkskammer, or "People's Chamber," whose members are elected from a single list of candidates, is supposed to be the "highest organ of state power." It sits in East Berlin. Although the East German regime insists that East Berlin is the capital of the DDR, the Russians still refuse to let East Berliners vote for Volkskammer deputies. The Parliament includes members of the SED and the satellite parties as well as representatives for the four largest mass organizations: the Federation of Free German Trade Unions (FDGB), which claims a membership of almost six and a half million; the Women's Democratic Federation of Germany (DFD); the Free German Youth (FDJ), the East German "Komsomol"; and the so-called German League of Culture (KB), which runs houses of culture in town and countryside. The mass organizations are, of course, transmission belts for making the SED's authority felt in every corner of East German society. At regular intervals the Volkskammer elects members of the State Council, whose chairman, Walter Ulbricht, is Chief of State as well as First Secretary of the SED. After the DDR's first president, Wilhelm Pieck, died in 1960, Ulbricht created the State Council to enhance his own

prestige and bring the government bureaucracy under his personal control, as the SED already was. The State Council is
suitably adorned with the leaders of the satellite parties and
mass organizations. In theory, it functions as a standing committee of the Parliament with power to decide questions of
defense and foreign policy. In fact, its role is largely to ratify
decisions of the Politburo, although the State Council does
have some important legislative functions of its own.

The executive organ of both the Parliament and State
Council is the DDR Council of Ministers, not to be confused
with the cabinet of a Western country. It supervises the work
of government departments, including the newly re-established economic ministries. The Council's chairman is Willi
Stoph, a former mason and Wehrmacht corporal, who rose to
the rank of general in the East German "People's Army" and
became Defense Minister before moving into his present position. During Otto Grotewohl's long illness Stoph served as Acting Chairman of the Council of Ministers, finally succeeding
formally to the office on Grotewohl's death in 1964. Stoph, who
was fifty at the time, is one of the more attractive East German
leaders. His demeanor is modest. He enjoys talking to Western
correspondents at receptions. His reputation as a "liberal" may
be exaggerated, but Stoph gives the impression of being less
doctrinaire than Ulbricht and the other Moscow émigrés. For
several years the Russians took such an inordinate interest in
eliciting Westerners' reactions to Stoph that it was widely assumed they were grooming him to take Ulbricht's place. This
now appears unlikely, if only because Stoph's experience has
been largely in government work rather than in the party apparatus. If the SED follows Soviet form and separates the
government and party leadership when Ulbricht goes, it is
likely that Stoph will remain as Chairman of the Council of
Ministers. (Incidentally, rather than using his cumbersome official title every time, I propose to follow the usual practice and
call him "Premier" or "Prime Minister," although his authority
hardly warrants such a designation.)

The motive force behind the East German regime is the

SED or, more specifically, the Political Bureau (Politburo) of its Central Committee. The party's total membership is estimated at 1,750,000, which is equal to 10 percent of the population of the DDR. At least half the members are opportunists who have joined because the party card is the best passport to preferment in a communist society. How many of the rest are dedicated communists is impossible to say. On the basis of many talks with party members, I believe that ideology now plays a much lesser role than the self-protective instincts of any minority in a predominantly hostile society. Group solidarity is not to be despised, especially when the group controls the means of compulsion. More than 96 percent of the officers and 43 percent of the noncommissioned officers in the 195,000 strong "People's Army" are SED members. The party is equally strong in the Air Force, the Navy, the "People's Police," and the Secret Police (SSD). All these forces combined would of course be no match for the 20 Soviet divisions stationed in East Germany, but that is not their purpose. The SED's quiet struggle for autonomy within the Soviet orbit is being waged by political and economic, not military, means. The East German forces would be equally incapable of meeting any West German or NATO attack without Soviet support. The role of the "People's Army" and the DDR's paramilitary formations is therefore mainly internal. The SED hopes to mold these forces into an instrument for maintaining its own power if and when Russian troops are ever withdrawn.

Regardless of ideological apathy or rank careerism, the East German Communist Party is a tough, cohesive organization, the product of long struggles, most of whose members realize they have no future without the party. The interesting people in the SED are not the languid old-timers, who make up the bulk of the Politburo, but those in the second echelon, which will inherit power once the old guard has passed from the scene. There are a growing number of "young Turks" among the 120 members and 60 candidate members of the SED Central Committee, theoretically the supreme arbiter of policy between party congresses. In fact, the Central Committee's Secretariat and its Politburo make all important decisions. The Secretariat consists of some 20 departments dealing with such questions as industry, agriculture, ideology, propaganda, and security. Each department has a professional staff and a chief who is usually a member or alternate on the Politburo. As First Secretary of the party, Ulbricht directs the Secretariat and supervises the work of all its department heads. He controls the party and state apparatus on a day-by-day basis. He has more inside knowledge on more subjects than any other Politburo member. He can often confront that body with a *fait accompli*. If it should persist in policies he opposes, Ulbricht can effectively sabotage its operation. He is the "boss." I shall have more to say about this extraordinary man in the next chapter, when I shall also discuss his heir apparent, Erich Honecker.

Most other members of the 12-man SED Politburo are non-entities. Hermann Matern, whose snow-white hair makes him look distinguished, spent his exile in Moscow and has long served in the key position of Chairman of the Central Party Control Commission, but he is Ulbricht's age and clearly no candidate for the succession. Alfred Neumann, who signed the Soviet-East German Trade Pact, is a product of the working class, a one-time carpenter, a veteran of the Spanish Civil War, and an ex-inmate of Gestapo prisons. He looks older than his fifty-six years and probably lacks the intellectual ability to progress after his idol, Walter Ulbricht, is out. The most pathetic figure on the Politburo is Friedrich Ebert, seventy-one-year-old former Social Democrat and son of the first president of the Weimar Republic, who wears what one Scandinavian journalist has aptly called "a mask of corpulence and indolence." The Politburo has two practicing ideologists—the comparatively moderate Kurt Hager and the venomously anti-American Albert Norden—whose task would be completely impossible if Bonn did not hand them so many ready-made issues. The other full members of the Politburo are such little-known work horses as Paul Froehlich, the Leipzig party boss, and Paul Verner, who runs the organization in East Berlin.

There is more talent among the seven Candidate members. Erich Apel is gone, but a core of reform-minded younger men remains. It includes: Guenter Mittag, thirty-nine-year-old economist, co-author of the "new economic system," and head of the Central Committee's heavy-industry section; Dr. Werner Jarowinsky, 39, an authority on supply problems, and Central Committee Secretary; and two agriculture specialists, Georg Ewald and Gerhard Grueneberg. The forces of reaction among the candidate membership are led by Hermann Axen, the moon-faced former editor of the central SED organ, *Neues Deutschland*, who was promoted to be Secretary of the Central Committee early in 1966. Axen appears to have been put in charge of the crackdown on artists and intellectuals that began about the same time. Not since Rosa Luxemburg and Karl Liebknecht fought on the Berlin barricades has German communism produced a leader of real stature. Whenever I watched members of the SED's present high command in public, I was struck by how shabby and ill-at-ease they looked, like a group of elderly vagrants being herded to church. As the English journalist John Mander has written, East Germany reminds one of an army whose officers have run away, leaving the NCO's in command.

The younger party leaders dress better, hold themselves erect, and project an air of businesslike efficiency. But they lack flair and what the Germans call "Format." They are little known outside the ranks of the party and government. The new generation still envelops its ideas in Marxist rhetoric and technical jargon to cushion the collision with orthodoxy. As a result, there is little popular reaction to the muted revolution now going on in the party's thinking.

The revolution in thought means a revolution in control of the SED. Whoever controls the SED controls East Germany, subject to the ultimate sanction of Soviet power. That sanction, as I will argue later, is difficult or impossible to invoke under the circumstances that exist in world communism today.

The DDR is, therefore, a major variable in the German equation rather than a minor constant to be added or subtracted after all other elements have been resolved. It has already survived longer than the Weimar Republic or Hitler's "thousand-year" Reich.

The fate of Germany will henceforth be decided not only in Moscow, Washington, London, Paris, and Bonn, but in East Berlin as well.

[2]

The Last
Apparatchik

■

ON APRIL 30, 1945, Adolf Hitler shot himself to death, and his body was burned in the garden of the Reich Chancellory. The same day an American Douglas transport coming from Moscow landed at a military airfield about fifty miles east of Berlin. The plane carried the Red Star of the Soviet Air Force and ten German communists, including one whose papers identified him as "Walter Adolphovich Ulbricht."

Early the next morning, while other members of his group still slept, a staff car took Ulbricht from Soviet headquarters at Bruchmühle into Berlin. It was the first time he had seen the city in twelve years.

Berlin was a vast petrified forest of disemboweled buildings. The streets were choked with rubble and littered with uprooted trees, dead horses, abandoned streetcars, and burned-out tanks. Putrefying corpses and clogged sewers emitted a nauseating stench. The city's underground railway tunnels were caved in and filled with water and slime. Flames still licked at the wreckage, and a heavy pall of smoke hung overhead. Berliners, dazed and starving, were beginning to creep

out of their bomb cellars. Few who saw Ulbricht that morning
could have guessed that a new dictator was in their midst—
one who would hold power longer than Hitler himself. If Ulbricht was moved by his first sight of Berlin in ruins, he gave
no hint of it when he returned to Soviet headquarters that
evening. To his fellow German communists who plied him
with questions about the city, Ulbricht simply replied: "You
will see for yourselves."

The future dictator of East Germany was then fifty-one
years old. He had already spent almost thirty years in the
service of Soviet communism. He had become the international
communist *apparatchik* par excellence—stateless, selfless, and
soulless. He had learned the art of survival and adaptation. In
his new role as Moscow's proconsul in Germany, he would
emerge as a manipulator of men, a master tactician, and one of
the most durable political enigmas of the twentieth century.

In the former red-light district of Leipzig there is a run-
down stucco tenement dwelling in Gottschedstrasse bearing a
plaque that reads:

> Walter Ulbricht, First Secretary of the SED, co-
> founder of the KPD in Leipzig, closest comrade-in-arms
> of Ernst Thaelmann, outstanding leader in the construc-
> tion of socialism and promoter of youth, was born in
> this house on June 30, 1893.

A small pipe projects over the plaque. Sometimes a wilted
flower is stuck in it; a sign in the window says "custom tailor-
ing." The street is usually deserted.

The fact that Walter Ulbricht began life among the prostitutes of Leipzig was the consequence of his parents' poverty
rather than moral turpitude. His father, a small tailor, and his
bedridden mother were both Marxian socialists, although they
clung desperately to the lowest rung of the petty bourgeoisie,
that class that has bred so many German misfortunes in this
century. According to Carola Stern's excellent biography of
Ulbricht, his younger brother emigrated to America, leaving
him to bring their father home from Social Democratic Party

meetings where the elder Ulbricht was inclined to imbibe too freely. Young Walter was studious, unprepossessing, and painfully shy. The shyness remains with him to this day. Contrary to a widely held notion in the West, Ulbricht is by no means unintelligent. As a youth he read voraciously and showed a remarkable gift for assimilating abstract ideas. At thirteen he devoured Darwin's *Origin of Species*. A few years earlier a young seminarian in Caucasian Georgia had read a smuggled copy of the same book and told his schoolmates: "They are deceiving us. There is no God." I have often wondered if Darwin's effect on the tailor's son in Leipzig was as powerful as on that young Georgian, the future despot of the Soviet Union.

Carola Stern records that even in primary school Ulbricht was regarded as one of the "Reds" in class because of his Marxist upbringing. Despite his unorthodox politics, his former schoolmates have trouble remembering him. After eight years of schooling young Walter was obliged to start earning money as a joiner's apprentice. He devoted his evenings and Sundays to meetings of the local Young Workingmen's Educational Society, which organized nature walks in the German tradition and campaigned against "exploitation, alcohol, smoking, card playing, soccer, and pornographic literature," according to a former member. The Victorian bourgeois virtues propagated by the society find expression today in Ulbricht's stodgy clothes, his strait-laced public manner, and his so-called "Ten Commandments of Socialist Morality," which include such exhortations as "You shall live a clean and decent life and care for your family" and "You shall strive to improve your efficiency, be frugal, and ensure socialist work discipline."

As a teen-age youth, Ulbricht followed German working-class tradition and wandered through Italy, Switzerland, and Austria, doing odd jobs as part of his apprentice training. His intellectual horizons remained as narrow as ever. Already in this period his writings have a maddeningly wooden quality.

In 1912 at the age of nineteen he embarked on his true calling—party politics. He joined Germany's Social Democratic Party but seceded three years later with the splinter group that refused to vote war credits for the Kaiser. Ulbricht's military career was inglorious; he was twice arrested for desertion and confined in a stockade. After the armistice the squeaky-voiced young Saxon went around the country trying to convince wounded soldiers that Germany was on the threshold of a Bolshevik-style revolution. They laughed in his face. Ulbricht soon found he was no spellbinder.

In January 1919 he joined the newly founded German Communist Party (KPD) and helped to organize its branch in Leipzig. The following year he married Martha Hauk, a piano-maker's daughter, who was also a party member but appears to have shared little of her husband's enthusiasm for the cause. She bore him a daughter (now married and living in West Germany) before Ulbricht was sent to handle party affairs in Jena. After that she rarely saw him. One day in 1933, when he had already grown a beard to elude the Gestapo, Ulbricht returned to their drab Leipzig flat, gathered up a few things, and vanished. It was the last time Martha Ulbricht saw her husband. The police came later to search the apartment, but they left her alone, and she was allowed to continue working as a seamstress in Leipzig. Ulbricht legally divorced her in 1951 to make way for his second marriage. Martha still lives in the Leipzig apartment and occasionally watches her former husband on television.

In the early years after the First World War the Bolsheviks pinned their own hopes for survival on a communist victory in Germany that would be the signal for world revolution. Rosa Luxemburg, Karl Liebknecht, and other brilliant KPD leaders were slaughtered in the attempt to reproduce the October Revolution in Germany. Defeat spread confusion and despair among the German comrades. Into this situation there stepped Walter Ulbricht, a man who mistrusts brilliance as much as he abhors confusion. By 1922 he had made his first pilgrimage to Moscow. Thereafter his rise was rapid. When the Comintern directed the German party to be split into easily manipulated factory groups, Ulbricht overrode all objections to carry out a reorganization that further weakened the KPD. He was already adept at carrying out orders, but his political judgment was often egregious. As a communist deputy in the Reichstag he continued to vilify the Social Democrats as the "main enemy" until Hitler seized power. In October 1933 he escaped to Paris where he organized a party headquarters in exile and frustrated efforts by the German Social Democrats to establish a united anti-Nazi front among the émigrés.

Ulbricht was summoned to Moscow early in 1938. He found the Soviet capital gripped by terror. The great purge was at its height. Thousands of Soviet and foreign communists, including many Germans who had taken refuge in Moscow, had already been executed or shipped to concentration camps. Wolfgang Leonhard, then a student in the Soviet Union and later a high SED official, has described the feeling of hopelessness that overcame the émigrés:

> Those who went about as quiet as mice got arrested just as much as those who never missed any possible (or impossible) opportunity of enthusiastically quoting the leading articles of *Pravda* at the top of their voices. People who went straight back to their garrets after work, and never stirred out again, still fell victims to the NKVD; so did those who made a principle of noticing nothing unusual and behaving precisely as before. Those who were overcautious and burned half their libraries (including authorized books) were no likelier to escape arrest than those who refused even to make up their stoves for fear of being suspected of having documents they wanted to burn. There was simply no such thing as a formula by which innocent people could make their innocence look convincing.

The émigré German communists shared their sleepless nights in the Comintern's Hotel Lux off Gorky Street. Ulbricht moved in and was soon joined by the wife of a KPD member who had been exiled to a small town on the Volga. Thirteen years later she became Lotte Ulbricht after being formally united in "socialist matrimony" with the ruler of the

DDR. Erich Wendt, her first husband, returned from his Volga exile after the war to become a ranking SED official. He died in 1965.

During those anxious days in the Hotel Lux, Ulbricht was involved in the communist equivalent of the eternal triangle. Rose Michel, a young French communist with whom Ulbricht had been familiar in the 1920's, lived in a garret above the room occupied by Walter and Lotte. The triangle was really an irregular quadrilateral because Ulbricht's lawful wife was still in Leipzig. He proved his tactical finesse by surviving seven years in Moscow without being purged by Stalin, deserted by Lotte, or denounced by Rose. It goes without saying that he also climbed during this time to a commanding position in the German Communist Party.

It is often asserted in the West that Ulbricht profited from the purges by incriminating his rivals in the party or, at least, by doing nothing to save them from the Soviet secret police. Carola Stern has investigated this question as much as is now possible and finds no support for such charges. In fact, she cites cases in which Ulbricht tried (usually unsuccessfully) to intercede for his comrades. On the whole, his behavior seems to have been no better and no worse than that of other foreign communists caught in the web of Stalinist intrigue.

Ulbricht's role in Spain during the Civil War is also controversial. Some former communists have accused him of responsibility for the wholesale liquidation of anti-Stalinist revolutionary fighters. Others who were in Spain during the war say Ulbricht made only a few brief visits to the Republican forces. In any event, his activities in Spain were not on a scale to arouse Stalin's suspicions.

Although he may not have been a purger, Ulbricht publicly praised the terror as "a shining example of the ruthlessness with which the socialist state—regardless of personal prestige or earlier services—liquidates the 'fifth column' before it can go into action."

The Hitler-Stalin pact of August 1939 was an even greater shock to the German communists than to other parties. Many who had wound up in Siberia were handed back to the Gestapo. But Ulbricht reacted with robotlike predictability. He discerned a new "revolutionary development" in the Nazi Party, now supplanted as the "main enemy" by Anglo-French imperialism. Six days before the German attack on Russia, when rumors of an invasion were already circulating in Moscow, he dogmatically informed German communists that "there will be no war." When it came, most KPD émigrés were shipped east; Ulbricht, Pieck, and a few others were allowed to stay in Moscow to guide psychological war against the invaders. Ulbricht broadcast over front-line loudspeakers to German troops at Stalingrad and later tried to win captured German servicemen for the Soviet-sponsored National Committee for a Free Germany. The officers, most of whom came from upper- or middle-class families, regarded the Saxon communist as a contemptible turncoat. They preferred to deal with the Russians directly. Ulbricht soon returned to the more congenial work of organizing communist cadres to administer the future Soviet Zone of Germany.

While the war still raged Stalin had predicted that Russia and the West would each incorporate their occupation zones in Germany into their own political systems. He told his confidants that all Germany would eventually become communist, but in public he proclaimed the limited goal of an "anti-fascist democratic front" in Germany. The KPD Manifesto issued on June 11, 1945, declared: "We are of the opinion that it would be wrong to force the Soviet system on Germany." It called for a "parliamentary, democratic republic."

German communists who had endured the horrors of Nazi concentration camps rather than renounce their faith in the revolution were perplexed by this tepid statement of the party's goals. When one party member asked how the KPD program differed from that of any bourgeois party, Ulbricht is reported to have replied: "Just wait a bit, comrade. You'll find out."

He was true to his word. Potential sources of opposition were quickly snuffed out. Heavy industry was nationalized and

large estates expropriated without compensation. The pretext
of denazification was used to remove anyone likely to ob-
struct the communist takeover. The Social Democrats, who
had quickly become the largest party in the Soviet Zone, were
forced into a merger with the KPD in April 1946 to form the
communist-dominated Socialist Unity Party of Germany
(SED). Bourgeois parties like the Christian Democratic Union
were harnessed to the so-called "bloc of anti-fascist democratic
parties," which later became the rubber-stamp "National Front
of Democratic Germany."

"It must all look democratic," Ulbricht told his lieutenants,
"but we must have everything in our hands."

Communist efforts to apply the same tactics in the Allied
occupation zones were thwarted. The Berlin blockade was
Stalin's last serious bid to drive the Western powers out of
Germany. When it failed he decided to build Soviet-style socialism in one part of Germany just as he had built socialism in
one country during the interwar period. Ulbricht had already
seen the handwriting on the wall.

The Tito-Stalin break in 1948 was the signal for a large-
scale purge of the SED. Party members who had spent their
exile in the West were shelved or expelled. The Association of
Former Concentration Camp Inmates was dissolved. Stiff-
necked old communists who refused to grovel to the Russians
were denounced as Titoists, and the SED was remolded in the
image of the Soviet Communist Party. By the time he became
Secretary-General of the Central Committee in July 1950 Ulbricht was in undisputed command of the East German
party.

That same year, at the age of fifty-seven, Ulbricht took up
tennis. Jauntily outfitted in white shorts and a visored cap, he
took regular lessons and proved an adept pupil. But on the
morning of June 17, 1953, his trainer waited in vain; Ulbricht
had more pressing business. The East German workers had
risen in revolt against the state that professed to be theirs. The
day before, demonstrators had defied the police and marched
through East Berlin demanding Ulbricht's removal and free

elections. The spark that ignited their wrath was Ulbricht's decision, taken over Soviet objections, to increase output norms in state-owned industry by at least ten percent. Discontent had been rising steadily as the result of food shortages, police terror, and the collectivization drive in the countryside. East Germans were fleeing to West Berlin at the rate of more than 25,000 a month. Faced with an imminent economic collapse, Ulbricht had appealed for a large new Soviet credit, but Stalin's successors in the Kremlin had problems of their own. They told him to halt "class warfare" in East Germany and provide his people more consumer goods, as Malenkov was doing in Russia. For the first time in his life, so far as anyone knows, Ulbricht defied the Russians. Instead of easing up, he tightened the screws by raising labor norms. Moscow was furious. Ulbricht's days in power seemed numbered. Then came the seventeenth of June. When the demonstrations became an insurrection, Soviet tanks intervened and crushed it ruthlessly. By nightfall the Red Army was again master of every city in East Germany. The question of concessions to the workers no longer arose.

It is one of the paradoxes of postwar history that the dictator of East Germany was saved by an uprising aimed at overthrowing him. The new Soviet leaders realized they could not safely dispense with Ulbricht's services. At the same time East Germans realized that the policy of "rollback" proclaimed by the new Republican administration in Washington was a hollow campaign slogan. They could expect no help from the West. June 17 also deepened the divisions among East Germans. While the workers hurled stones at Russian tanks, the East German intellectuals who talked so much about freedom stayed in their comfortable apartments and villas. Three years later when the intelligentsia tried to duplicate the "Polish October" in the DDR they got no help from the working class. Ulbricht's brand of divide-and-rule had succeeded.

The aftermath of June 17 and Lavrenti Beria's fall from power in the Soviet Union also enabled Ulbricht to overcome the most serious threat to his position that has ever arisen in the SED. Wilhelm Zaisser, the "General Gomez" of Spanish Civil War fame and then chief of the East German secret police, had joined with Rudolf Herrnstadt, brilliant editor of *Neues Deutschland,* in demanding Ulbricht's removal. They called for concessions to the peasant and middle classes as well as new efforts for German reunification. Before June 17 a majority of the SED Politburo probably sympathized with them. After the abortive revolt Ulbricht moved swiftly to expel Zaisser and Herrnstadt from the leadership and to link them with the fallen Beria. But whereas Beria was executed before the year was out, Ulbricht merely expelled his rivals from the SED and relegated them to obscurity. Zaisser died in 1958. Herrnstadt is reportedly working as an archivist.

The last major challenge to Ulbricht's control of the East German party came in the wake of Khrushchev's secret speech denouncing Stalin in February 1956 and the "Polish October" later that year. SED functionaries whispered that de-Stalinization could not be carried out in the DDR by the most notorious Stalinist left in the Soviet bloc. Opposition within the party coalesced around three men: Karl Schirdewan, Ulbricht's deputy in the Politburo and heir apparent to his position; Fred Oelssner, the party ideologist; and Ernst Wollweber, Zaisser's successor as secret police chief. They were later accused of organizing an "anti-party faction" aimed at overthrowing Ulbricht, relaxing controls, and seeking German unity "at any price." At about the same time Wolfgang Harich and other SED intellectuals began to agitate for a "Polish October" in the arts and sciences.

Ulbricht held on grimly while one Stalinist landmark after another was submerged by the new tide rolling across Eastern Europe. Shortly before the Budapest uprising he reportedly told a Hungarian communist: "Just keep on this way. First you get rid of Rakosi, then you make reforms, and in the end there's collapse." His gloomy prognosis proved to be correct, but again, as on June 17, the violence of the onslaught and the inevitable Soviet reaction saved Ulbricht from political extinction. When pictures of mangled Hungarian secret police

reached East Berlin Ulbricht told the SED Central Committee: "Now you know what's in store for you if you give way
before the enemy." His warning carried all the way to Moscow. Khrushchev realized it was no time for experiments in
East Germany. Ulbricht was given a free hand to keep order in
his own house. He disposed of the intellectuals first, sentencing
Harich to ten years in prison and two of his confederates to
lesser terms. Schirdewan, Oelssner, and others were allowed to
linger in limbo for more than a year before they were publicly
denounced and expelled from the Central Committee and all
other party posts. Schirdewan later recanted his heresy and has
been rewarded with a job in the Potsdam archives. Oelssner
heads an institute of the East Berlin Academy of Sciences.
Wollweber is said to be afflicted with asthma. None of the
culprits has been shot.

Ulbricht's time of troubles in his own party was over by
early 1958. He could now turn to consolidating the state structure of the DDR. The first order of business was to close the
escape route through West Berlin. The upshot was Khrushchev's ultimatum to the Allies in November 1958 to withdraw
their troops from West Berlin in six months or face the consequences of a separate Soviet-East German peace treaty. Ulbricht warned Berliners at that time they would pay dearly for
defying the communist power that surrounded them on all
sides. Neither the Allies nor the Berliners were impressed. The
ultimatum was ignored.

It would be interesting to know whether the idea of building a wall through Berlin came from Ulbricht or from the
Russians. At one of his rare news conferences two months
before it was actually put up, Ulbricht may have tipped his
hand when he told a questioner: "No one has the intention to
build a wall." From the communist standpoint, the Wall was a
brilliant solution to what had seemed an insoluble problem.

The West generally interpreted the Wall and the forcible
collectivization of agriculture early the previous year as a
reversion to undiluted Stalinism in the DDR. This view
seemed to be confirmed by the introduction of compulsory

military service in January 1962, higher work norms in industry, and stricter ideological controls in education. In fact, East
Germany was on the threshold of de-Stalinization. As Carola
Stern has perceptively observed: "In Ulbricht's scheme of
things collectivization and the building of the Wall were the
two most important prerequisites for de-Stalinization." What
has happened in East Germany since the Wall is the main
subject of this book.

Ulbricht's attempt at what might be called "personal de-
Stalinization" is one of the most striking features of this period.
Idyllic family portraits are published of Ulbricht at home with
Lotte and their teen-age adopted daughter, Beate. Accompanied by his wife (who is a Central Committee member), the
septuagenarian dictator now visits every corner of the DDR,
advising factory workers and collective farmers on their problems and trying to build the image of a benign father of the
nation. His foreign travels serve much the same purpose. With
obvious difficulty, Ulbricht tries to unbend and make small talk
with ordinary people. For foreign visitors he exudes statesmanlike moderation and self-assurance. He even risks an occasional
attempt at humor. He likes to be photographed with young
people and to pose as their champion in the councils of the
party. "I would like to say that I was not yet thirty years old,"
he told the Sixth SED Party Congress, "when I was elected to
the KPD Central Committee. A full beard is not absolutely essential for recognition by older people!"

The old German communist Clara Zetkin once said of
Ulbricht: "Look into his eyes and you will see how scheming
and dishonest he is." Although he now affects a jovial manner,
Ulbricht still avoids looking into the eyes of his conversation
partners. The few Western correspondents who have inter-
viewed him find his good humor quickly turns sour under
questioning. Within the SED, Ulbricht's rudeness is proverbial.

However his personal style has changed, the cult of Ulbricht's personality still reeks of Stalinism. His birthdays are
celebrated with fawning tributes in the press and pledges of
higher output in his honor. Delegations of children, factory

workers, and party functionaries troop to his office to offer congratulations. Ulbricht's framed likeness adorns every office, clubhouse, and factory bulletin board in the country. Chemical plants, pig farms, and trawler fleets are named after him. The FDJ theme song, "It's good fighting with Walter Ulbricht at our side," proclaims:

> The workers make us bold and strong;
> They make the party move along;
> With Walter Ulbricht we can't go wrong.

Hundreds of poems are composed in his honor, such as the one by the worker-poet Otto Gotsche:

> The foe has spewed hate and scorn, as of yore,
> And because they hate him, we love him all the more.
> And in the enemy's heart echoes our call:
> Walter Ulbrichts are we all.

Undeceived by what Macbeth called "mouth honor," Walter Ulbricht is escorted wherever he goes by a carload of plainclothesmen of the SSD (Secret Police) and by his chief bodyguard, Franz Gold, a former Nazi who now holds the rank of general in the Security Service. Ulbricht's two-story villa in the "Bonzograd" compound for senior party leaders north of Berlin is protected by a high reinforced-concrete wall patrolled around the clock by a full company of security troops and illuminated by floodlights at night. Special passes are required of anyone seeking admission. According to Carola Stern, the Ulbrichts moved into their ten- or twelve-room villa in 1960 after construction of the new VIP colony had been delayed by the events of June 17, 1953, and again by Khrushchev's de-Stalinization speech in 1956. They had previously occupied a modest one-family house in the Niederschoenhausen district of East Berlin. It too was guarded by police and troops.

Ulbricht's way of life has remained petty bourgeois. He uses no tobacco and permits no smoking in his presence. He drinks little. In their old home Lotte would busy herself in the kitchen preparing sausage, schnitzel, or cold cuts, while the dictator of the DDR received guests in a woolen lounge jacket and camel's-hair slippers. When dinner was ready, Frau Ulbricht would bustle into the dining room in her apron, calling out: "Now quit talking politics and come to dinner."

Ulbricht still begins his day with morning calisthenics, often followed by a walk through the surrounding woods before breakfast. He is driven into town about 9 a.m. and rarely finishes his round of conferences before ten or eleven at night. He has an unbelievable capacity for sustained hard work and is often able to have his way simply by outlasting other participants in a discussion.

Ulbricht's health, traditionally excellent, has now become a congenial subject of conjecture in West Germany and other Western countries. Perhaps because his voice is so high-pitched, rumors that he suffers from cancer of the larynx have circulated for years. They gained new currency when Ulbricht's voice failed at the beginning of a public speech early in 1964. Later that year Khrushchev's son-in-law, Alexei Adzhubei, then editor of the Soviet government newspaper *Izvestia*, visited West Germany and dismissed complaints about Ulbricht with the observation that the old man would not be around much longer. Some of Adzhubei's interlocutors have quoted him as saying Ulbricht has incurable cancer of the larynx. After the SED chief failed to deliver a scheduled New Year's Eve broadcast at the end of 1965, the East German news agency reported he had gone on "recuperative leave." Reports circulated in West Berlin that he had suffered a mild heart attack. Five weeks later Ulbricht was back at his desk, apparently fully recovered and active as ever. Nevertheless his grip on the party seemed to have loosened. As the West Berlin sociologist P. C. Ludz observed: "For the first time in party history a strain of uncertainty could be detected in Ulbricht's speeches." Under pressure from the SED's hard-liners he called East Germany's intellectuals to order, reined in the newly independent economic managers, and wavered after offering to hold public debates with West German Social

Democratic leaders. Whether Ulbricht was actually being blown off course by opposition in his own party or whether, as so often before, he was simply tacking with the wind, was unclear.

Since the fall of Schirdewan and his "anti-party group" in 1958, the mantle of crown prince has appeared to rest on the shoulders of Erich Honecker, an Ulbricht protégé almost twenty years younger but every bit as colorless as his mentor. Now fifty-three, Honecker began life as the son of a communist miner in the Saar. At the age of ten he joined the communist "Young Pioneers" and became a full member of the party eight years later. He was arrested twice by the Gestapo for underground activity and sentenced to ten years in prison. The Red Army freed him in 1945. Honecker was immediately assigned to organize the Free German Youth and later to convert it into an instrument of communist control. In 1957 he returned from two years of "special training" in the Soviet Union to take charge of military and internal security questions for the Central Committee Secretariat. As a full member of the Politburo since July 1958 and Secretary of the Central Committee and the National Defense Council, Honecker supervises the Ministries of Defense, State Security, and Internal Affairs. He is second only to Ulbricht in the number of political offices he holds. Honecker's wife, Margot, whom he married in 1953, is Minister of Popular Education and a Candidate member of the Central Committee. Like her husband she has received training in the Soviet Union. Honecker is said to be of only average intelligence, but he has the cunning of a seasoned *apparatchik,* coupled with an instinct for swimming with the tide. His praise of Ulbricht is frequent and fulsome. It has often been requited. Honecker was the only Politburo member besides Ulbricht to deliver a major report at the party's Sixth Congress in 1963. When "hoarseness" prevented the SED chief from giving a public speech the following year, faithful Erich stepped up to read it. When Ulbricht decided to tighten the reins on the intellectuals and younger industrial managers late in 1965, Honecker was given a leading role in explaining the new measures to the December plenum of the SED Central Committee. During Ulbricht's convalescence early in 1966, Honecker was named to act as party leader.

Honecker is clearly a man in Ulbricht's image—doctrinaire, autocratic, and practically devoid of imagination. He is also clearly the anointed successor, but my feeling is that his reign will be short. The age of the *apparatchik* is drawing to a close in East Germany.

Whatever course his life now takes, it is clear that Ulbricht will not achieve his lifelong goal of bolshevizing all Germany. He has held power longer than Hitler or all the presidents of the Weimar Republic combined, but he will never unite Germany under his rule. In another man this disappointment might have led to bitterness. Ulbricht, on the contrary, has softened slightly in his old age. He is no longer a petrified imitation of Lenin. His mind, still conscripted in the service of an atrophied ideology, now fights less ruthlessly to make its own conscription universal. Perhaps this is because he is the last member of a lost generation in a divided country. Like Kipling's cat, Walter Ulbricht now walks alone, and to him all places are the same.

[3]

The Third State

■

EAST BERLIN has a night life all its own. The best place I found to observe it was from a fifth-floor room on the west side of what remains of the old Adlon Hotel. The Wall was below my balcony, the floodlit Brandenburg Gate to the right, and the dark mound marking the site of the Reich Chancellery and Hitler's bunker just to the left. Beyond the blackness of the Tiergarten, West Berlin's new skyscrapers stand out like beacons against the night sky. The scene is never static. Searchlights on the communist side sweep across the cleared "death strip" and explore patches of darkness among the cinder blocks and barbed wire of the Wall. Like nightclub performers, East German guards are bathed in light for a few moments, then vanish as the beam continues its relentless probing. There is no sound except the hoarse barking of police dogs straining at their leads and an occasional shot fired by a nervous guard somewhere on the Wall.

Atop the Brandenburg Gate a pale blue light shines through the bubble top of an East German lookout post next to the Goddess of Peace. On the other side of the massive doric columns of the Gate, just beyond the Wall, the Street of the Seventeenth of June (formerly Charlottenburg-Chaussee) cuts a swath of light through the inky Tiergarten. The roof garden of the twelve-story Berlin Hilton in West Berlin glows warmly in the distance, and beyond it the lights of the Telefunken skyscraper on Ernst-Reuter-Platz seem to offer refuge in the night.

Far off to one side, the moving sign on Potsdamerplatz flashes news bulletins for the benefit of East Berliners under the heading "The Free Berlin Press Reports." Hitler's ashes are scattered in the no-man's-land separating the two worlds. Grass now covers the low mound over his bunker. A monument to the German communist leader Ernst Thaelmann is supposed to be erected there someday. The only people now permitted in the enclosure are East German guards. By day it looks like any other shaggy, deserted East Berlin park. At night it always seems one shade darker than the rest of the city.

While we lived at the Adlon, I used to stand on our balcony every night observing the surrealist drama unfolding below. When I had had enough, I would go inside and sit down on the threadbare old couch in our sitting room. But I was still in the land of make-believe. As in other hotels, there was a bell to call the chambermaid, but I knew no one had answered that summons for twenty years. I could pick up the telephone on the heavy mahogany-inlay desk and dial a number, but that too was futile, because the old night porter had first to plug me in and he was always asleep at this hour. Our room was one of about seventy salvaged from the wreckage of the old Adlon after Allied bombers struck it repeatedly during the war. The prewar Adlon was immortalized by Vicki Baum in *Grand Hotel,* which was later made into a movie with Greta Garbo. In those days the Adlon was host to princes, diplomats, maharajas, artists, actresses, well-heeled spies, and expensive prostitutes. The spies are now out in the cold, the prostitutes have been collectivized, and all the others have departed, at least from the Adlon. Weeds and shrubs grow in former royal suites that stand open on one side like the cells of a honeycomb. Rusted steel girders protrude in every direction. The main part of what John Gunther called "the greatest hotel in

Europe" is completely demolished. What remains is the servants' quarters, the old kitchen, a handful of guest rooms, a creaking back staircase, and the former deliverymen's entrance now converted into the reception lobby. The Adlon now belongs to the hotel chain run by HO, the state retail organization. There is no elevator and no room service. The dining room set up in one corner of the old kitchen is small and dingy, but the food is good by East German standards. The waiters take a kind of whimsical pride in working amid remembered grandeur. They even try to keep the tablecloths clean. One morning when I came down for breakfast the desk clerk told me the dining room was reserved for a delegation of SED members from Gera, a provincial center in Thuringia. She made a wry face as the visitors trooped by. "Please take your breakfast in the staff quarters," she said to me. "I'm sorry for the inconvenience. You'll be served right away." Some of the old Adlon *esprit de corps* survives.

The regime prefers to quarter foreigners in the boxlike Berolina or in one of East Berlin's other new hotels away from the Wall. My wife and I were put up in the Adlon because we were traveling with our small dog and the East Germans (unlike the West Germans) prohibit dogs in their newer hotels. I suppose they think the Adlon is too far gone to matter. When I mentioned that we were living there, East German officials always clucked disapprovingly. They were puzzled and a bit suspicious when I said we preferred it to the jerry-built modern hotels in East Berlin.

To me the Adlon epitomizes Berlin—a kind of hyphen between two systems, two ages, two worlds. The hotel and the city are both overpopulated by memories. West Berlin has 2,200,900 people, thousands of cars, and the tumult of freedom. East Berlin has 1,100,000 people, few cars, empty streets, and the hush that seems to come with communism. But the two parts of the city share an indivisible past and an unquenchable irreverence. There are formidable differences between East Germans and West Germans and even between West Berliners and West Germans, but Berliners are still one

people. In a sense, the communists' theory of three German
states is correct, except that the third state is not West Berlin
but all Berlin. It is primarily a state of mind.

The Berlin mentality has always baffled Walter Ulbricht
and the East German communists. The city is proletarian but
not communist. At the height of communist prestige in October 1946, the SED got less than one fifth of the votes in greater
Berlin. Ulbricht never made the mistake of allowing East Berliners to vote in another free election. For fifteen years the
SED virtually ignored its part of Berlin like a foster parent
who hates the sight of his deformed child.

I shall never forget the first time I saw Unter den Linden.
It was the summer of 1955, and I was on my way to the Soviet
embassy for a visa to Moscow. I knew of course that Berlin's
most famous street had been grievously damaged, but I was
unprepared for the devastation that surrounded me on all
sides. I emerged from the U-Bahn near Brandenburg Gate and
walked down the middle of Unter den Linden between the
four rows of silver linden trees replanted soon after the war.
Even they seemed more dead than alive. On either side stood
crumbling, dismembered hulks that had once been the pride of
imperial Germany. Their windows were gaping holes, like the
eye sockets in an old skull. Except for the few gaunt East
Berliners on Unter den Linden, the scene reminded me of the
ruins of Jerash or Persepolis. The garish 600-foot façade of the
Soviet embassy on that street of desolation seemed to mock the
Germans and proclaim the final victory of Slav over Teuton in
their age-old struggle for Central Europe.

Not until after the Wall went up August 13, 1961, did the
East German communists feel really confident of keeping their
truncated capital. It was then that they decided to rebuild East
Berlin and to try to narrow the disparity between it and the
Allied sectors. They set out to make Unter den Linden the
most elegant boulevard between the Elbe and the Pacific.
Bulldozers cleared away the rubble. Buildings too badly damaged to be saved were leveled while workmen began toiling
around the clock to restore the rest. They are still at it. But

Unter den Linden can already stand comparison with any street in West Berlin or West Germany. The beautifully rebuilt State Opera House stands opposite the Humboldt University and the former State Library, opened for business soon after the war but only recently restored to their former luster. Now there are modernistic ministry buildings on both sides of Unter den Linden and smart shops selling Paris gowns, sporting goods, and *objets d'art* at prices designed to milk foreigners and discourage ordinary East Germans. A swank "auto salon" offers immediate delivery on Wartburgs and Trabants purchased in hard currency and a four-year wait for any East German even if he is able to put down from seven to ten thousand East marks. Near the Brandenburg Gate where Unter den Linden intersects Wilhelmstrasse (renamed Otto-Grotewohl-Strasse in 1964 after the death of the DDR's first prime minister), a new "embassy quarter" is being erected with more haste that the DDR's prospects for diplomatic recognition outside the communist world would seem to warrant. The United States still has title to the property on the corner of Unter den Linden and Schadowstrasse, where the prewar American embassy stood, but Washington is not likely to assert its rights so long as the Red flag flies from Brandenburg Gate. The site is now occupied by the glass and steel headquarters of the DDR Ministry of Foreign and Inner-German Trade. Brandenburg Gate, closed to traffic since the Wall was built, may now be reopened to augment or replace Checkpoint Charlie (Friedrichstrasse) as a crossing point for non-Germans.

The East Germans are building what they call a "gastronomic complex" on the corner of Unter den Linden and Friedrichstrasse, where Berlin's artists and writers used to gather at the Café Bauer. Directly opposite, there will be an eight-story hotel catering to foreigners. It is not likely to remind anyone of the famous hotels that used to line the boulevard.

Not everything has changed on Unter den Linden. The statues of Prussia's most celebrated soldiers—Scharnhorst, Bluecher, Yorck, and Gneisenau—removed in 1950 are now back on their pedestals suitably rechristened "heroes of the freedom wars." Under their stony gaze, young soldiers of the "People's Army" in traditional Prussian battledress goose-step through the changing of the guard in front of the old Royal Guard House, now known as the "Memorial for the Victims of Fascism and Militarism." The old Prussians would feel at home.

One refuge from both Prussianism and communism is the so-called "Museum Island" in the Spree River within sight of Unter den Linden. The eighteen Ionic columns on the magnificent portico of the Old Museum are now back in place. The National Gallery, the Pergamon Museum, and the Bode Museum were restored and reopened earlier. Their somewhat depleted collections of classical antiquities are well displayed, the attendants are courteous, but East Berlin's museums have a moldy, forgotten air. I always have the feeling that the regime begrudges the money it has to spend on them for prestige reasons.

Unter den Linden ends in the battered, old copper and sandstone Dom, or Cathedral, whose 374-foot cupola used to be known as the "summit of tastelessness." Berliners now have more important things to grumble about. The first time I reconnoitered the Cathedral I found all the ground-level entrances boarded up. A scrawled notice announced that services were held once a week in the basement.

Across the former Lustgarten from the Cathedral the Hohenzollerns once dwelt in terrible Teutonic splendor in the old Schloss or Royal Palace. The 1910 Baedeker calls it "a handsome example of the German Renaissance, highly extolled by contemporary critics." Later critics thought differently, but Berliners remained passionately attached to the Schloss even after it was severely damaged by Allied air attacks. Every Berliner believes the old pile could and should have been restored. Nothing the communists have ever done aroused the people of the city more than the decision to dynamite the Schloss to clear space for Marx-Engels-Platz, East Berlin's Red Square. It must gall the spirits of the Kaisers to know that

a joiner from Leipzig now takes the salute from German le-
gions on ground once hallowed by Hohenzollern feet. The
communists plan to erect monuments to Marx and Engels in
the square. One portal from the old Schloss where early German communists battled police is incongruously preserved as
the entrance to the new gray, beige, and red limestone building that houses the State Council, the DDR's highest govern-
mental body. To make way for the State Council, one of old
Berlin's most picturesque streets, Sperlingsgasse, was bull-
dozed out of existence along with the 300-year-old tavern, the
Raabe-Diele, frequented by Wilhelm Raabe in the middle of
the last century when he was writing his famous chronicle of
the Street of Sparrows. Most such historic fossils in East Berlin
have already fallen victim to communist city planners. One
survivor is a tiny pub called the Historische Weinstube on
Poststrasse across the Spree from the State Council's stone and
glass palace. The first time my wife and I went there we
thought the Weinstube must have gone out of business. The
front door, blackened with age, stood ajar on creaking iron
hinges. One of the picture windows was broken, and the paint
on the others was peeling. The inevitable window boxes looked
as if they had not been tended for years. Undaunted, we
walked up two worn cement steps, pushed the door open, and
entered a narrow hallway lighted by one dim bulb hanging
from the ceiling. We eventually found a brass handle that
opened another blackened door, admitting us to the one-room
tavern. It was crowded, but there was little noise. Young
couples conversed quietly at tables by the wall. An elderly man
who turned out to be the owner welcomed us with that long-
suffering smile one comes to know so well in East Germany.
He handed us a well-thumbed wine card listing Hungarian,
Rumanian, Bulgarian, Russian, and other Eastern bloc vintages
but none from the Rhine or the Moselle. "We have schnitzel
and salad tonight," he announced proudly. We found out later
that the state-run food distribution system often overlooks the
Historische Weinstube, perhaps because it is privately owned.
The staff consists of the owner and his wife. They always seem

uneasy, but the atmosphere in their tiny establishment is *gemütlich,* a rare thing in East Berlin.

Such nooks are not long for the new world the SED is building in East Berlin. There is no quota for *gemütlichkeit* in communist plans. To satisfy their craving for modernity and to over-awe West Berliners, the party oligarchs have ordered the construction of a 1,200-foot television tower in the center of Alexanderplatz, Berlin's once-throbbing commercial hub. This structure, reputedly to be the highest in Europe, will have a roof garden, rotating observation platform, and a restaurant in the sky. Future diners will have an excellent view of West Berlin, which may not always enhance their enjoyment. Alexanderplatz is to be enlarged fivefold and ringed with new buildings for the DDR "People's Chamber" and Council of Ministers as well as what the East Germans call a "super department store." The wave of the future is already evident around Alexanderplatz in the new domed Congress Hall and the thirteen-story House of Scientists and Teachers with its crude socialist-realist murals on the outside walls. This complex is to be connected by broad thoroughfares to Marx-Engles-Platz and Unter den Linden as well as the already aging Karl-Marx-Allee (formerly Stalinallee). This monstrosity in white tile and gingerbread was built in the early postwar years when East Berliners were freezing amid the rubble. The show street was renamed in 1961 when de-Stalinization was renewed in the Soviet Union. It still looks as if it had come straight out of Moscow or Kiev. Many Meissen ceramic tiles used in apartment house façades on the "first socialist street in Germany" have fallen out, leaving ugly gaps. Others are discolored. Food stores on the ground level display jars of vegetables with congealed grease about an inch thick at the top.

A new residential quarter built at the western end of Karl-Marx-Allee in the early 1960's shows better design and execution. East German construction standards are still so low, however, that an American friend of mine refused to believe that the new Berolina Hotel was less than a year old when he stayed there in 1965.

East Berlin used to be a city of rubble. Today it is a city of vacant lots and construction sites. The skyline looks like the profile of a child's jaw before the molars have come in. There is a disturbingly intermittent quality about the city. Every downtown building seems encased in scaffolding, and cement mixers are more common than cars. Of the few cars in East Berlin, most carry Western license plates. As in other East German cities, elaborate schemes have been devised to handle traffic problems that will probably not arise for a decade.

The East German regime's most ambitious construction project is the Wall. It has already cost an estimated 100 million East marks and is constantly being strengthened. It is not one wall but a succession of barbed wire, concrete, and cinder-block barriers augmented by moats, tank traps, and electrified fences. These ramparts run 28.5 miles through the heart of Berlin and more than 71 miles around the so-called "zonal border" between West Berlin and East Germany proper. They are manned by 14,000 East German border troops using a network of 203 watchtowers equipped with searchlights and more than 236 bunkers, pillboxes, and dugouts. The whole system is linked by special telephone connections and some 230 dog patrols. The guards have orders to fire on would-be refugees. Despite the requirement that they patrol in pairs, which are frequently rotated, more than 2,000 border troops have defected since the Wall went up. About a quarter of them escaped to West Berlin; the rest crossed into West Germany. Since the DDR was founded in 1949 a total of about 30,000 members of the East German armed forces—equivalent to two entire divisions—have skipped to the West, giving Ulbricht's state the world's highest military desertion rate. Ordinary East Germans have no better than one chance in three of getting out. Some 400 made it across the Wall in 1965 and almost 2,000 others escaped through the Zonal frontier into West Germany. Since the Wall was built more than 128 East Germans are known to have been killed trying to cross the great divide. Thousands of other cases of fatal shootings of would-be refugees are unknown in the West.

Many escapes involve a high quotient of heroism and self-sacrifice by Germans on both sides. But there is another side to this story, which is often omitted from Western accounts.

The art of "exfiltration," as it is called in West Berlin, has become highly refined and increasingly mercenary. Professional tunnel diggers like Wolfgang Fuchs, operating out of West Berlin usually with the connivance of the authorities, have repeatedly arranged mass escapes under the Wall. Tightrope performers have been enlisted to organize spectacular over-the-Wall breaks. Refugees have even escaped under the Spree or Berlin's lakes in improvised snorkel submarines.

Students at West Berlin's Free University have been recruited to smuggle refugees out in their cars or to deliver forged or stolen passports to East Berliners. Several dozen, including some Americans, have been caught and sentenced to prison terms by the East Germans. One such courier, Robert Mann of Sepulveda, California, admitted after his release from prison: "I was a small wheel in a large organization. The SSD [East German Secret Police] knew a lot more about it than I." An American girl theology student at the Free University and two former U. S. Army corporals were arrested on similar charges by the East Germans late in 1965. Two other American servicemen were sentenced to terms of imprisonment early the following year by a U. S. court-martial in West Berlin for having sold their uniforms to enable three East Germans to pass through the Wall. American officials feared the other side might retaliate by barring Allied servicemen from East Berlin, but the communists made no immediate move.

When the rector of the Free University objected that the school was being used as an arsenal and students were spending most of their time organizing escapes, he was denounced by the West Berlin press and student leaders. One of the most notorious "escape helpers," a 25-year-old medical student, later expelled from the university, told reporters modestly: "I wish no great recognition for my deeds; on the other hand, I don't want anyone to prejudice our work."

So long as the "work" appeared to have purely humanitarian motives, the escape helpers could count on public support. Now, however, ugly rumors have started about exorbitant advance fees being extracted from would-be refugees or their relatives in the West. Tunnel diggers have sold exclusive rights to their stories to West German and foreign news media. Publicity agents have collected fat fees for "advising" escape helpers in their dealings with officialdom and the press.

Even the most carefully prepared escape attempts do not always succeed. When they are thwarted there is often bloodshed. Every East German guard killed in such an affray is given in a martyr's funeral by the regime. The combination of circumstances, coupled with West Berlin's interest in renewing the holiday-pass agreements with the East, means less public and official support for the exfiltration engineers.

Berliners on both sides are gradually learning to live with the Wall, but anyone beholding it for the first time is appalled. "Like looking into an open grave," Edward Heath, the British Conservative Party leader, murmured as he gazed at the expanse of tank traps and barbed wire that makes Potsdamerplatz, once the busiest square in Europe, look like a deserted battlefield. On one side of Bernauerstrasse in the French sector the Wall coincides with the front of high tenement buildings whose windows have been bricked up to prevent people from jumping into West Berlin. The buildings look as if they had been blinded. On the pavement below, small wooden crosses mark the spots where refugees plunged to their deaths in the first days after the Wall went up. The buildings on Bernauerstrasse are now vacant except for East German guards who patrol the roofs.

The Wall at Potsdamerplatz or Bernauerstrasse hardly fits the SED's dream of a "modern state frontier up to the world standard." To make the Wall more "cosmetic" and to render escape more difficult, the East Germans are now replacing the concrete slabs and rusted barbed wire that make up the Wall in most places with a neat wire-mesh fence. Behind the fence a cement-lined ditch ten feet deep and fifteen feet wide is being dug like a moat more than 100 miles around West Berlin. Behind the ditch a cleared strip at least ten feet wide will be ploughed to show footmarks. So-called "whip lamps" will illuminate it at night. Guards will patrol the border along an asphalt road running between the ploughed "death strip" and a chain of permanent observation towers. Ordinary East Germans have been barred since 1963 from a 110-yard-deep "dead zone" on their side of the border. Only trusted party members or elderly pensioners (who are permitted to leave in any case) may reside in the "no-man's-land." Everything that makes the communist side of the border look like a concentration camp is to be removed. Barbed wire is in short supply anyway. The unsightly tank traps, pillboxes, and dugouts will be moved out of sight behind the border road. They will be replaced in part by "scientific" devices, including more electronic listening equipment to detect tunnel diggers. An electric current strong enough to shock but not kill a would-be refugee will pass through portions of a new fence just inside the first series of barriers. More concealed trip wires connected to an alarm signal will be laid along the border. "Modernizing" the Wall will take time and money. Even when it is completed, there will still be escapes, although the nine-a-week average reported since 1961 is not likely to be maintained.

After he saw the Wall, John Steinbeck remarked that only organisms doomed to extinction grow thick protective scales. His metaphor is striking but misleading. Unlike the dinosaur's armor, the Wall is no futile gesture of self-preservation for the East German regime. It has stanched the human hemorrhage that was enfeebling the DDR. It has ended the era described by Christa Wolf in *Divided Sky* when Rita, the fiancée of a young East German engineer who has fled to West Berlin, buys an S-Bahn elevated-railway ticket to the other side in hopes of persuading him to return:

> She stepped up to the ticket window. "Zoological Garden" [a station in West Berlin], she said. A little yellow pasteboard ticket was pushed toward her. "Twenty," said

the woman behind the glass. "And if I return?" Rita asked haltingly. "Then forty," said the woman, took the ticket back and shoved another through the little window. That was the difference between this city and all other cities in the world: for forty pfennigs she held two different ways of life in her hand.

Now only one way of life is open to East Germans. Some prefer death. East Berlin's suicide rate since the Wall was built is one of the highest in the world—twice that of West Berlin. But most East Germans choose life—even under communism. The Wall has forced them to come to terms with themselves and their society. It has stabilized the labor force, reduced absenteeism, and enabled the SED to scrape the Stalinist barnacles off the East German economy. Bonn trumpets that the Wall is an admission of failure but ignores the fact that it has strengthened the East German state and given its rulers new self-confidence. The Wall is the physical expression of the dead end Western policy has reached in Germany. The dream of a mechanical fusion of the two German states by means of free elections is impaled on the barbed wire of the Wall like a lifeless refugee. No policy of strength short of a third world war can resurrect that dream. The Wall is, therefore, one of the pre-eminent political facts of the twentieth century.

The Wall overshadows all else in Berlin, but it has not severed all contact between the two parts of the city, Western propaganda to the contrary. Trade between the two Berlins has expanded since the building of the Wall. West Berlin's exchanges with East Berlin and the rest of the DDR are now running at an annual rate of more than 62 million dollars, equivalent to one tenth of all "interzonal" German trade. West Berlin gets lignite, synthetic oil, sugar, and building materials from the communists. In return, it supplies machinery and capital goods. Feature films produced by West Berlin's declining movie industry are far more popular in East Berlin than the local Defa products. One reason the East can afford imports from West Berlin is that it still operates the S-Bahn in both parts of Berlin and maintains tunnels in East Berlin used by West Berlin's U-Bahn (underground railway). For these services the DDR receives an annual income of several million West marks. When the communists offered to set up visa offices in S-Bahn stations in West Berlin to issue passes for travel across the Wall, the West refused on the ground that the offices would constitute an illegal exercise of "sovereignty." Two years later East German postal officials installed themselves in West Berlin public schools and began handing out holiday passes to West Berliners who had relatives on the other side. One such East German pass office was set up more or less permanently on the Allied side to issue permits for West Berliners to see their relatives on the other side in family emergencies. Why postmen are any less "sovereign" sitting in school gymnasia than officials on S-Bahn platforms is a mystery understood only by German legalists.

The Wall does not interfere with mail service between the Allied and communist sectors. On the contrary, daily deliveries rose to 100,000 letters and 15,000 packages in both directions after the city was partitioned in 1961. Telegraph communication has also continued normal. A West Berliner can even wire flowers to his aunt in the communist sector, because East Berlin's florists belong to the international Fleurop organization. The communists cut normal telephone communication with the Allied sectors on May 27, 1952, but at least three lines still connect the police and fire departments on either side of the Wall. The Allied commandants also have a direct line to the Soviet embassy in East Berlin. Ordinary callers are less fortunate. A West Berliner in the Kreuzberg section who wants to talk to his mother one block away across the Wall must usually wait until his call is routed through Frankfurt-am-Main and Leipzig. The delays are prolonged.

Cooperation on the municipal administrative level is surprisingly good. West Berliners find poetic justice in the fact that about eighty percent of their sewage is still processed on the communist side. The two fire departments exchange information and occasionally join in fighting a blaze near the Wall. Police officers from East and West Berlin used to meet every

day midway across a bridge over the sector boundary to exchange information on common criminals. They now prefer to
communicate by teletype, but direct contacts are still possible
at any of the seven crossing points in the Wall. Two of these
are for use by West Germans going to East Berlin, four for
West Berliners at Christmas and other holiday periods, and
one, Checkpoint Charlie, for Allied military personnel and all
other non-Germans. West Germans and foreigners (except
Allied military men in uniform) enter East Berlin by showing
their passports. West Berliners have so far been barred, except
at holiday times. West-bound traffic through the Wall is
meagre: Soviet military sedans, communist diplomats, a few
reliable SED functionaries, elderly East Germans, and some
critically ill persons with relatives in West Berlin.

Death is a liberator. A Berliner can be buried anywhere in
the city, provided of course that his corpse is accompanied by
valid identification when it crosses the Wall.

Without identification, no one crosses the Wall. A passport
becomes a matter of life and death. On my way back to West
Berlin late one night I cleared the controls at Checkpoint
Charlie, handed my passport to an elderly guard for a final
check, and thoughtlessly started to drive off without it. "Wait a
moment," the old man said quietly. "You can't leave without
your passport. You should know a passport is the most important thing in the world." He smiled wearily, handed back my
passport, and gave the little half salute that uniformed Germans habitually render.

Cultural exchange between the two Berlins tends to be
more stormy than administrative contacts. There have been frequent literary evenings at which authors from both sides read
and discussed their works. The SED has been encouraged to
press its cultural offensive in West Berlin by the recent emer-
gence of neutralist and even pro-communist sentiment in student organizations of the Free University. In February 1966
student demonstrators rotten-egged the Amerika Haus cultural center in West Berlin and tried to tear down the Amer-

ican flag in protest against Washington's Vietnam policy. Mayor Willy Brandt came under attack for failing to control the university; in fact there was little he could do. There has been a sharp decline in the number of East German students enrolled at the Free University since the Wall was built. There has also been an influx of West German students who evade the draft by residing in Allied-occupied West Berlin. Many West Berliners are concerned by what one Free University journal called the city's "cultural provincialism." They agree with Professor Stein, West Berlin's Senator for Science and Art, that "the most dangerous thing is for nothing to happen in the field of East-West exchange." As a consequence, the readings and literary discussions with East German writers are encouraged despite the difficulties of agreeing on participants and subject matter.

By far the most important contacts between the two Berlins since the building of the Wall have been visits by millions of West Berliners to their relatives in the communist sector. The first Christmas Pass Agreement was signed in December 1963. Since then, three more agreements have been concluded to cover holiday-period visits and special passes for West Berliners to cross the Wall in the event of a family emergency. To reach these accords, protracted talks have been conducted at a high level by emissaries of the two sides. In theory, the representative of the West Berlin Senate is simply discussing a "technical" agreement with his opposite number. In fact, the talks, like the pass agreements themselves, are political. The federal government in Bonn and the West Berlin Senate have disagreed repeatedly over how far they should go to meet communist demands. The diehards in Bonn have objected to endorsing an agreement bearing the dread words "government of the German Democratic Republic." They also deplore the permanent presence of East German postal clerks in West Berlin with power to issue Wall passes. Far more important than such legal quibbles, as George Bailey, *The Reporter* correspondent in Germany, has aptly pointed out, is the fact that any pass agreement is a tacit recognition of the Wall and logically rules out official support for activities aimed at breaching or undermining the DDR's "frontier." Bonn wants to continue denouncing the Wall as an outrage against humanity while currying favor with West Berliners by arranging for them to visit their relatives on the other side. It amounts to trying to get something for nothing.

The ultimate arbiters of West Berlin's fate are not in Bonn but in Washington, London, and Paris. The Western Allies have shared neither the federal government's anxieties nor its ambitions in connection with the pass agreements. The Allies generally favor visits across the Wall to help maintain the fiction that Berlin is still under four-power rule. In fact, only two institutions, both in West Berlin, have survived from the days when the Allied Kommandatura ruled the former German capital. At the Air Safety Center, Allied and Soviet controllers are permanently at loggerheads over the use of the three air corridors between Berlin and the West. At the grim Spandau Penitentiary, British, French, American, and Russian troops take turns guarding the last prisoners of the Nuremburg Trials —Rudolf Hess, Albert Speer, and Baldur von Schirach. With only three out of 600 cells occupied, Spandau undoubtedly ranks as the world's most uneconomical prison.

Apart from Spandau and the Air Safety Center, there are as few signs of Soviet presence in West Berlin as there is evidence of Allied presence in East Berlin. The Western powers have rejected Russian requests to set up a Soviet Trade and Cultural Center in West Berlin on grounds of "public safety and order." They recall that the Soviet Intourist travel agency in West Berlin has been bombed twice. Russian artists rarely appear nowadays in West Berlin because Bonn insists they perform both there and in West Germany. Moscow upholds the "three-nation theory" of Germany, although it still sends Soviet Army sedans cruising through West Berlin just as Allied military vehicles circulate in East Berlin under postwar agreements among the victors. The Russians appear to value their access to West Berlin. Some American diplomats who were in Berlin at the time believe that the famous Soviet-American tank confrontation at Checkpoint Charlie in October 1961 could have been avoided if Western officials had reacted to restrictions on Allied access to East Berlin by placing similar curbs on Russian entry into West Berlin rather than making a show of force. The situation today is that Allied military personnel in uniform do not show identification, whereas Western diplomats and all other civilians produce their passports for East German guards.

Berliners were dismayed at America's inaction when the East Germans started building the Wall through their city on August 13, 1961. They were unimpressed by the result of the test of strength at Checkpoint Charlie two months later. And when Peter Fechter, a young East German refugee, was allowed to bleed to death on the Wall under the eyes of American troops, West Berliners staged their first anti-American riot. Whatever misgivings they may feel about Washington's policy, West Berliners have remained the most outspokenly pro-American people in Europe. Emotionally they are already the fifty-first state, an "American colony," as Berliners like to put it. There is a kind of love affair between Berlin and the mighty republic across the Atlantic. I have never seen a city give itself to anyone as West Berlin did when President Kennedy arrived there on June 26, 1963. It was spontaneous combustion. The communists so feared pro-American demonstrations in East Berlin that day that they blocked the view through Brandenburg Gate when the President stopped there. East Berliners retaliated by booing Soviet military cars late that afternoon. The ardor of Berliners' welcome for Mr. Kennedy was exceeded only by their anguish at his death. Late on the evening of November 22, 1963, thousands of West Berlin students staged a spontaneous torchlight parade to express their grief. Candles were lit in token of mourning in almost every West Berlin window and in many on the other side of the Wall. "We felt it more than you Americans," a Berliner remarked afterwards.

There is of course good reason for West Berliners to be

pro-American. Washington's oft-repeated pledge to defend the city, symbolized by the presence of some 6,000 American troops in Berlin, is the only effective deterrent to a communist takeover. The airlift has become a legend, and American economic aid is remembered with gratitude.

Bonn has now taken over the job of shoring up West Berlin's economy, but it is far from inheriting America's place in the hearts of Berliners. The estrangement between East Germans and West Germans has its counterpart in the differences between West Berliners and West Germans. To East Germans and West Berliners, the Federal Republic acts too much like a rich uncle. West Germans, on the other hand, expect more than perfunctory thanks for the aid equivalent to more than half a billion dollars a year that they pump into West Berlin.

The economic gap between West Berlin and West Germany has actually narrowed in recent years. Wages in the city are now on a par with the West German average while taxes are considerably lower. West Berlin has had full employment since 1960. The Wall deprived West Berlin of 60,000 East Berlin workers employed in the Allied sectors, and it frightened some businessmen into leaving the city. But the panic was shortlived. The American garrison was quickly reinforced, and Bonn handed West Berlin a fat bouquet of tax preferences. To attract people and money to West Berlin, Bonn and the city government now offer family bonuses for young couples, housing loans for new arrivals, and lower corporate and personal income taxes. The effect of these measures began to be felt in 1963–4 when West Berlin's population registered a net gain of 25,000, the first increase in six years. The city now even boasts a housing shortage. The problem of attracting young workers and technicians from West Germany is crucial because of the economic burden imposed by the age composition of West Berlin's population. The city must support 268,000 widows. One Berliner out of five is over sixty-five years old, almost twice the ratio in West Germany. The number of deaths exceeds births by about 12,000 a year. More West Berliners go on pension every year than enter the labor force. For political reasons, the West Berlin city government is reluctant to import more laborers from such countries as Turkey, Greece, and Spain.

West Berlin is also handicapped by its isolation 110 miles inside the communist world. It must import practically all its food and raw materials. More than two thirds of its industrial products are sold in West Germany. While there has been no serious interference with Berlin's economic lifelines to the West since 1949, the city's economy remains subject to frequent chills and fevers. West Berlin's growth rate usually lags behind West Germany's, although 1965 was an exception. To mitigate the effects of West Berlin's isolation and to make the city an entrepôt for East-West trade, Mayor Brandt proposed in 1966 that the three Allied sectors be converted into a free trade zone. Bonn, which would have to put up most of the money, was understandably skeptical of the idea.

Despite its problems, West Berlin is far from being the beleaguered island often pictured in Western propaganda. The three Allied sectors account for little more than one half the area of greater Berlin, but they still cover more ground than Pittsburgh, Cincinnati, and San Francisco combined. Less than one third of West Berlin's 188 square miles is classified as built-up; more than one half is devoted to farms, parks, forests, and lakes. Within the city limits are seventy miles of navigable waterways and one of Europe's largest inland ports. West Berlin manufactures every third cigarette and every fourth dress produced in the noncommunist part of Germany. Even without East Berlin, it is the largest city in Germany and the most important industrial center between Moscow and the Ruhr.

West Berlin's gross output of almost 4.5 billion dollars a year exceeds the gross national product of one quarter of the member states of the United Nations, including such European countries as Ireland and Greece. The city is also one of Europe's most flourishing tourist centers.

Lest anyone conclude that East Berlin is a truncated trifle, it should be pointed out that the communist sector numbers more people than the District of Columbia and covers an area fifteen times the size of Manhattan. Berlin is a "whale" of a town.

Compared with the communist sector, West Berlin is a sparkling diamond in the dark void. But compared with other major Western cities, as one writer has observed, it seems more like a cultured pearl. Christopher Isherwood has compared the neon-lit splendor of the Kurfürstendamm around the Kaiser Wilhelm Memorial Church to a "sham diamond in the shabby twilight of the town." Like the rest of West Berlin, the Kurfürstendamm trails off into mediocrity long before you reach the end. The sidewalk cafés quickly give way to used-car lots. Not all West Berliners work in skyscrapers or live in the modernistic Hansa Quarter. The slums of Wedding, Kreuzberg, and Neukölln are as forbidding as many parts of East Berlin. The difference is that there is animation in even the poorest parts of West Berlin. There is none on the other side.

Mayor Brandt's Tourist Department has coined the slogan "Berlin is worth a trip." It is of course worth much more, so much in fact that neither side in the East-West struggle will give up its part of the city, short of war. Berlin is not only a symbol; it is an enormously valuable concentration of human and material resources strategically placed in the middle of Europe. An American correspondent formerly in Germany used to speak of West Berlin as a bird "dying in its gilded cage." Even if this threatened to be true, the city would not be allowed to die economically or in any other way. Too much is at stake in terms of power and prestige. The Russians now insist they want no forcible change in the *status quo* in Berlin. Bonn and the Western Allies are also ready to accept the present situation, provided that there is no interference with their access rights. The SED still talks of incorporating West Berlin in the DDR, but the most it can do under present circumstances is to make life difficult for the West by harassing German traffic on the autobahn or by sending East German helicopters over the Allied sectors. The variable element in this equation is the population of West Berlin. Public opinion polls show West Berliners overwhelmingly in favor of extending the holiday-pass agreements on the present terms. As the prospect of reunification becomes more remote, the new generation in the city may come to believe that the real battleline does not run along the sector boundary in Berlin but between Berlin and Bonn. Aid from the federal government may not always outweigh West Berliners' yearning to end their ghetto existence, even on communist terms. There is no question that West Berliners would ever vote an SED government into power, but as time goes on, they will be increasingly prepared to bargain with the East German regime for trade, contacts, and elbowroom. The old shibboleths about refusing to talk to the bad men in Pankow have worn thin. Berliners agree with their former Protestant bishop, Dr. Otto Dibelius, that nothing is "more frightful and dangerous" than the isolation of East Berliners and other East Germans. The more prosperous West Berlin becomes in its own right, the less it will be inclined to follow Bonn's crabbed line toward the DDR. It is not poverty but prosperity that makes West Berliners chafe at being confined to their enclave, much as East Germany's recent material progress has generated demands for wider horizons in all fields. The Western Allies have never shared Bonn's qualms that the DDR could somehow win recognition by inadvertence on the part of the West. If their responsibility for the city is to continue indefinitely, the Allies will not oppose easing tensions by promoting contacts across the Wall. Each of the occupying powers would welcome an opportunity to reduce its garrison in Berlin. The Russians favored the original Berlin Pass Agreement and would welcome further steps to legitimize the Wall. Other European communist parties that have trouble explaining the Wall to their followers are pressing the East Germans to adopt a more humane policy. For its part, the SED well knows that East Berliners will remain sullen and disgruntled until at least some fissures are opened in the so-called "antifascist defense wall." The body politic called "Berlin" may be severed and sundered, even mangled and mutilated, but it has survived and begun slowly growing back together.

The late Hendryk van Loon told the story of the small bird that came once every year to sharpen its beak on a giant rock; when at last the rock was entirely worn away, he said, one day of eternity would have passed. The Wall will not be torn down; it will be eroded, but much faster than van Loon's rock.

(4)

Millionaire on
Probation

■

THE DISTANCE BETWEEN Bonn and Berlin is
approximately 300 miles and 200 years. Bonn is ambling
through the eighteenth century while Berlin has already been
mutilated by the twentieth century. Bonn is Beethoven and
the Rhine and a government in search of a capital. Berlin is the
Iron Chancellor and the icy Spree and a capital in search of an
empire.

Germans turn to Berlin as Moslems pray to Mecca. No
one bows to Bonn except collegians, civil servants, and others
whose affairs call them there. Bonn is cleaner than Berlin,
more beautiful, and much better preserved, but it is not a
capital.

No one has ever explained how Bonn became the world's
most permanent provisional capital. Some say Adenauer
wanted it there because his family home at Rhöndorf on the
Rhine is within easy commuting distance. Others say Bonn was
chosen because it was politically neutral. Any big West German city would have offered better facilities to the new federal
government in 1949, but there were objections to each.

Frankfurt-am-Main was said to be too commercial. Munich was stained with Nazism. Hamburg was too far north. Accordingly, Bonn was selected for its inoffensiveness.

"Oh, Bonn, yes, I know," a steel-company man in the Ruhr said when I told him I lived in the federal capital. "That's where our people used to go when they retired. I hear it's a nice quiet place."

Bonn is less tranquil since bureaucrats, politicians, diplomats, lobbyists, and newsmen began competing for the town's limited *Lebensraum* and trying to drive to work on its one north-south thoroughfare. The "federal village," as West Germans disparagingly call their capital, now reaches out octopus-like to embrace a dozen other villages on both sides of the Rhine. Bonn is suburbia run riot. The housing shortage is still acute. The Canadian ambassador commutes several times a day between his home in Cologne and his office in Bonn fifteen miles to the south. The Costa Rican ambassador lived in a hotel for a year before he could find permanent lodgings. The French ambassador endures his German exile in a castle so far south of Bonn that he is effectively insulated from all unwanted contact with the capital. The Soviet embassy is almost as remote, perhaps for different reasons. Most diplomats accredited to the federal government live and labor in Bad Godesberg, a once-staid spa and health resort that still refuses to integrate its telephone system into that of Bonn, just to the north.

Bonn itself now counts 150,000 residents. It will soon be completing its second decade as the capital of the richest and most populous nation in Western Europe. But Germans still refuse to admit its existence. They still resist plans to build a parliament house or an office for the federal chancellor or even a road to the Bonn airport, which is not Bonn's anyway but Cologne's. To reach the airport means threading your way for as much as an hour and a half through a dozen Rhineland hamlets and over narrow country lanes. If you fly to Bonn, your airline ticket and the claim tags on your luggage will read "Cologne" because Bonn is uncity. That is why most of the

twenty-odd federal ministries are still housed in former Wehrmacht barracks or in other improvised quarters and why
both houses of the West German parliament still meet in a
converted teachers' training college.

The Christian Democratic Union (CDU) has controlled
the federal government since its founding, but when one considers accommodations, it is no better off than the opposition
Social Democratic Party (SPD) or the small Free Democratic
Party (FDP), junior member of the government coalition.
The CDU and FDP are headquartered in dilapidated man-
sions in the old part of Bonn, while the SPD dwells in an
unsightly temporary "barrack" on the main road to Bad
Godesberg.

The press—German and foreign—is still billeted in rickety
two-story frame barracks called "temporaries" by the U. S.
Army when it put up similar structures at the beginning of the
Second World War. The federal Chancellor toils nearby in the
Palais Schaumburg, an eighteenth-century residence, scoffingly
dubbed the "Bonn White House."

Germans say that the next worse thing to working in Bonn
is visiting there. The hotel shortage should have attracted
Conrad Hilton long ago. Important or well-heeled visitors are
often put up at the mountaintop Petershof on the opposite
bank of the Rhine, where they have a superb view of the
countryside and virtually no contact with the federal capital.

Bonn's problem is that it is unfocused. There is no center,
no middle, no heart, just vast expanses of periphery. It is as if
the capital of the United States had been shifted to McLean,
Virginia, or Charles de Gaulle had moved the seat of the
French government to Colombey-les-deux-Eglises.

Bonn must have the highest rate of official absenteeism of
any capital in the world. It is not government in exile but
government *in absentia*. An outsider might conclude that being
caught in Bonn was a punishable offense for any federal minister or high-ranking civil servant. There have been occasions
when not a single cabinet minister was in the capital. The urge
to be elsewhere becomes a compulsion on weekends, holidays,

or whenever there is an excuse to get out. Bonn's always feeble pulse then drops to zero. Erhard leaves for his vacation retreat on Tegernsee in Bavaria. Vice-Chancellor Erich Mende flies to Berlin. Ordinary members of the Bundestag go home to hear their constituents' complaints, and even the international news agencies padlock their Bonn bureaus, so sure are they that no news will break. In August, when everyone who is anyone takes at least a month's vacation, I used to walk down the middle of the street in the government quarter, listening to the echo of my own footsteps. The atmosphere is delightful if you like solitude.

Besides absenteeism, Bonn can probably boast the highest "gripe" rate of any capital in the world. Nowhere do more people spend more time complaining about less than in the "federal village." Germans incline to be hypochondriacs in any case; in Bonn their natural anxieties reach morbid depths. "Low pressure" is blamed for a variety of ills, including headache, backache, undefined "circulatory disturbances," and a general disinclination to work. When it rains (as it often does), Germans complain that Bonn is too damp. If the summer is dry (which it sometimes is), they find the heat intolerable. In fact, Bonn is exceptionally healthful. The climate is as delightful as the surrounding countryside. Children flourish in Bonn, perhaps because they are unaware of the political and social climate.

The outside world thinks of Bonn only as the seat of the West German government. But the city has other, far more beautiful faces. The old Bonn of crooked lanes and eighteenth-century residences is slowly disappearing, although it still helps to snarl downtown traffic. Bonn, the university community, lives a cloistered life behind ocher-colored walls and hoary elms. The new Bonn—the seat of the government and of those connected with the government—is a city of transients. The federal Chancellor entertaining the party faithful in his new wood and glass official residence feels only slightly more at home than the African diplomat ordering his first meal in halting German. Old Bonners are becoming a rare species.

Old Bonn and new Bonn exert a kind of mutual repulsion on each other. Each goes its own way, and the city suffers.

Intrigue, however spurious, can often redeem a dull capital. Bonn seems fated to traffic only in gossip. Most capitals experience political crises. Bonn endures a seemingly endless succession of "affairs," such as the "Spiegel affair," the "telephone affair" (involving Allied wire tapping in West Germany), and the "Huyn affair," in which Foreign Minister Schroeder was the target of a scheming subordinate. There is a contrived quality about political controversy in Bonn that makes even important disputes seem petty.

Because Bonn has an air of unreality, the outside world also seems unreal when viewed through the Rhine mists that envelop the capital. The repetitious discussions of reunification seem even more academic than they are. East Germany seems far off, and the rest of Eastern Europe might as well be on another planet. Western Europe seems almost equally remote, although Bonn and the Rhineland have historic ties with France and the Low Countries. The American embassy in Mehlem, a subdivision of Bad Godesberg, stands on stilts beside the Rhine, a many-splendored bureaucratic relic of the occupation era. The occupants of the relic live in the so-called "golden ghetto" in nearby Plittersdorf, an originally all-American community with its own club, PX, cinema, baseball diamond, and church. Even the most energetic American officials find it hard to overcome the isolation of ghetto life and the frustrations of a ponderous embassy and to relate themselves meaningfully to German society.

German officials and foreign diplomats are unanimous in complaining that they feel alienated from the rest of Germany when they sit in Bonn. The reason is that most West Germans usually make wide detours around their capital. Intellectuals despise Bonn. Businessmen deplore it except when they come seeking official favors. Government servants dread it, especially when service there means a cut in their allowances. Such feelings are not a simple question of taste or self-interest. They reflect a lack of identification between West Germans and their government. Bonn is the butt for a divided nation's political frustrations. German patriotism still exists, but there is no such thing as federal German patriotism. Bonn, like the Federal Republic government itself, evokes no positive emotional response and conjures up no compelling images. It is a stopgap, and Germans treat it accordingly.

No book on East Germany would be complete without a look at West Germany. What might be called "the Bonn mentality" goes far toward explaining the immobility of the federal government's policy toward the DDR. The explanation is also to be found in the curious alignment of political forces and personalities in Bonn.

The most notable but by no means the most forceful personality in Bonn is Professor Ludwig Erhard, federal Minister of Economics for fourteen years and Chancellor since October 1963. He is an old-fashioned economic liberal, a man of genuine goodwill, and a professor who has never completely reconciled himself to politics. Unlike his autocratic predecessor, Erhard reigns but does not rule over a bickering three-party coalition that makes the Federal Republic look increasingly like the Fourth Republic of France. Erhard despises political infighting but is unable to arrest its spread in his own party. He has a disconcerting habit of letting his principles get swallowed up in compromises that leave all parties dissatisfied. His horizons are broad, but his steps are crabbed. Soon after taking office as Chancellor, Erhard made a series of much publicized visits to Western European capitals with the aim of giving new impetus to the drive for a European political community. At the end of his wanderings the outlook was worse than ever. Less than two years later de Gaulle was threatening to disrupt even the European Economic Community. Erhard's effort to open direct talks with Moscow on the German problem met an equally disastrous rebuff. In domestic policy Erhard has set as a goal what he calls the *formierte Gesellschaft* (structured or harmonious society), a Teutonic equivalent of President Johnson's Great Society program. Forsaking strict *laissez faire,* Erhard now calls for increased expenditures on town planning, health services, education, and natural resource conservation.

Despite his obvious aversion for many aspects of politics, Erhard remains the "election locomotive" of his Christian Democratic Union party. His ever-present cigar and generous proportions evoke feelings of well-being in most German voters. He seems a kind of natural assurance of stability. At sixty-nine his health is not exceptional, but there is no sign that he will step down before the 1969 elections, if then.

The most controversial and probably the most intelligent member of Erhard's cabinet is his foreign minister, Dr. Gerhard Schroeder, a Protestant Düsseldorf lawyer who began political life as a protégé of Konrad Adenauer, whom he served as Interior Minister before becoming Foreign Minister in 1961. He and Adenauer are now bitter enemies, primarily because the former Chancellor suspects Schroeder of sabotaging the Franco-German entente. During my time in Bonn, I had the privilege of getting to know Schroeder well. I saw him in his office and at home and accompanied him on campaign stumping-trips to the Ruhr. I found him thoughtful, articulate, and remarkably frank. One problem is that his conception of foreign policy is too sophisticated for many of his party colleagues to grasp. His clinical approach to political questions hardly conforms to the beer-drinking tradition of German politics. As a result, Schroeder is not popular in his own party. His range of action is severely limited by sniping attacks from his enemies in the government coalition.

Schroeder's contribution to Bonn's foreign policy has been twofold: he has activated the policy of building bridges between the Federal Republic and Eastern Europe (except the DDR), and he has resisted French efforts to make West Germany an obedient Gaullist mouthpiece in NATO and the Common Market. In both phases of his policy, he has been forced to go slow or even mark time by opposition within the governing coalition. For example, Schroeder would like to establish full diplomatic relations with the Eastern European communist states, but he is thwarted by champions of the hard line.

Schroeder is sensitive to the changes now taking place in Eastern Europe but insists they do not affect the DDR. He opposed the first Berlin Pass Agreement in 1963 and has been cool to subsequent agreements. I do not expect the impetus for a change in Bonn's policy toward East Germany to come from the Foreign Ministry so long as Schroeder is its chief. Like Erhard, he is a staunch champion of the American alliance. Schroeder, who was fifty-five when he began his second term as Foreign Minister in 1965, is able and ambitious. His lack of any substantial popular following is his chief handicap domestically.

Schroeder's principal rival is Franz-Josef Strauss, by far the most colorful figure in German politics today. Strauss is brilliant, unscrupulous, and inordinately ambitious. As Bonn's Defense Minister from 1956 until 1962, he sired the Bundeswehr and won the admiration of the Pentagon. In those days Strauss was 150 percent pro-American. Now he is a "European," who often sounds like an old-fashioned German nationalist. He opposes the Multilateral Force (MLF) or any of its variants and advocates German participation in a European nuclear force that could be ordered into action without American approval. Early in 1966 Strauss began suggesting a "partial" withdrawal of American troops from Europe, allegedly to enable the United States to wage the war in Vietnam without a West German "expeditionary force" (which Washington has never requested). He does not propose that Bonn follow President de Gaulle's example and withdraw from the NATO integrated command structure, but Strauss champions a sweeping reform of the alliance and a largely autonomous European defense system based on Franco-German nuclear cooperation. His pleas for "Europeanizing" the German problem have a distinctly Gaullist ring. Strauss opposes, however, most of the French leader's policies toward Eastern Europe, including recognition of the Oder-Neisse line. Strauss rejects proposals for increased contacts with the SED and deprecates Schroeder's efforts to establish a West German presence in Eastern Europe. Strauss has recently begun talking a good deal about budgetary problems in what is interpreted as a bid to return to the cabinet as Finance Minister. Since being forced out as Defense Minister in the wake of the "Spiegel affair," in which he arranged the illegal arrest of the magazine's publisher and editor on charges of betraying state secrets, Strauss has had to content himself with the leadership of the CDU's powerful Bavarian affiliate, the Christian Social Union (CSU). With 49 seats in the Bundestag, the CSU could bring down the Erhard government if it ever chose to withdraw from the coalition. Strauss runs his party much as Boss Crump ran Memphis. Opposition by the FDP and within the CDU kept Strauss out of the cabinet after the 1965 elections.

At fifty-one Strauss has not given up. His immediate goal is the Foreign Ministry or the Finance Ministry. His ultimate goal is the Chancellorship. Strauss is now seeking to rehabilitate his image in German politics, to present a conciliatory and moderate front. But a faint odor of scandal continues to dog his tracks. His most important gifts are clarity of mind and oratorical ability scarcely matched anywhere in Germany today. He speaks with vigor and conviction, whether he is addressing a plenary meeting of the Bundestag or a Saturday night rally in a Munich beer hall.

Although there are no brown-shirt stains in his own past, Strauss has moved steadily to the right in recent years. He opposed the extension of Nazi prosecutions beyond the original 1965 deadline and now frequently takes up cudgels for right-wing groups. He has said that a new Führer could arise if Germany continues to be frustrated in its desire for national unity. Many Germans fear that Strauss himself could be such a leader. His electrifying speeches evoke painful memories. Although he now seeks to play down his reputation for ruthlessness, he has also made clear that he offers a "nationalist" alternative to Erhard and Schroeder. His is the only effective opposition voice in West Germany today. The mass of West Germans would probably turn to Strauss only after more trusted leaders had proved unable to cope with a major national crisis or if they seemed unwilling to pursue a radical approach to reunification when all other doors were closed.

The man to whom the Christian Democratic party bosses are most likely to turn after Erhard is Rainer Barzel, majority leader in the Bundestag, who reminds some people of the younger Lyndon Johnson. Germans call Barzel a "full-blooded politician." A Catholic, born forty-two years ago in the part of East Prussia now in Poland, Barzel is able to appeal to his co-religionists in the Rhineland as well as to the predominantly Protestant expellee groups from the East. He has always been a young man in a hurry. After war service in the navy air wing, he studied law, became West Germany's youngest provincial minister and, later, the youngest federal minister when Adenauer appointed him at the age of thirty-seven to the Ministry of All-German Affairs. Barzel echoed the strident anti-communism then in vogue and even organized a "Save Our Freedom" movement with the professed purpose of identifying "Leftists" among West German public figures. He was dropped from the cabinet in 1963 to make way for the FDP's Erich Mende and promptly took over leadership of the CDU in parliament from the ailing Heinrich von Brentano. Barzel has demonstrated a Johnsonian gift for achieving consensus among rival groups. His own political philosophy can be fitted to suit the exigencies of the moment. In December 1963 when Mayor Willy Brandt's government pressured Bonn into accepting the first Berlin Pass Agreement, Barzel remarked sourly that the "West Berliners get their security from the Americans, their subsidies from Bonn, and their passes from Ulbricht." As Minister of All-German Affairs he was associated with hardline policies, but in recent years he has veered toward the more flexible Erhard-Schroeder policy in foreign affairs.

Adenauer's decision to retire from the chairmanship of the CDU prompted Barzel to canvass openly for the top party post early in 1966. Erhard belatedly recognized the challenge to his position and succeeded in getting himself elected as CDU chairman by a 413-vote majority at the party convention. Barzel was picked as first deputy chairman with only 385 votes, reflecting a "stop-Barzel" movement among some delegates. Nevertheless, his political position and control of the party machinery are now virtually unassailable. As majority leader in parliament and *de facto* head of the party, Barzel is the leading candidate to succeed Erhard in 1969, when the present Chancellor will be seventy-two years old. On his second image-building trip to Washington in June 1966 Barzel suggested that Russia be offered German trade and technology on favorable terms as well as the right to keep troops in a reunited Germany as the price of giving up the DDR. The proposal attracted interest in America but was promptly disavowed by Erhard and the CDU.

Despite his youth, energy, and obvious ability, Barzel is not widely liked outside the party. His vaguely unctuous manner reminds some of Richard Nixon. He seems to arouse the same distaste in many Germans as Nixon does among some Americans.

On January 5, 1966, Konrad Adenauer celebrated his ninetieth birthday, still convinced he was the wisest German of them all. Three months later he relinquished his last important political post as CDU party chairman. He professes to disapprove almost everything Erhard and Schroeder do, but, like an old volcano, his opposition only erupts occasionally. Adenauer still puts in a full day working in his office in a wing of the parliament building. His parchment-like face looks no more weathered than it did a decade ago. His eyes may be a bit mistier, but his mind is still clear, albeit constricted by the rigidities of advanced age. As senior schoolmaster to the world, he feels compelled to offer instruction on all subjects. On a single day I have seen him lecture an American diplomat on the perils of détente, advise German motorists on safe driving, counsel newsmen to be more careful in their reporting, and warn everyone in earshot that the times are perilous. The real symbol of the federal government is not the demilitarized Nazi eagle but the censorious Adenauer fore-finger.

Many of Adenauer's early reflections on Erhard have now proved to be well founded; the former Chancellor has not, however, enhanced his stature by repeatedly violating his pledge of loyalty to his successor. Periods of quiescence have been followed by outbursts of crabbed Adenauerian criticism. The CDU parliamentary group has admonished Adenauer on several occasions, but he understandably no longer takes mortal reproaches very seriously. After all, he can remember Bismarck and the day on which the refurbished Cologne Cathedral was first opened.

To the extent that his opposition has a basis in principle, Adenauer is concerned about the steady deterioration of Franco-German relations and de Gaulle's overtures to Moscow. The effect of Adenauer's criticism of Erhard has been the opposite of what he intended. De Gaulle has treated his German allies with disdain, threatened to wreck the Common Market, undermined NATO, and made common cause with Russia against West German participation in Allied nuclear strategy. It is now clear that the only entente de Gaulle had in mind when he signed the French-German treaty with Adenauer in January 1963 was one under his own direction. As events have repeatedly belied Adenauer's policy recommendations, his influence in the CDU and with the German public has dwindled. He will remain a captious critic of his successor's government, but Adenauer no longer plays a decisive role.

At the end of his odyssey Adenauer looms large, in part because most West German politicians are such pygmies. Talented young Germans generally shun politics, although new blood is desperately needed. Few Bundestag back-benchers on either side of the house have "profile," as the Germans say. The debates are notoriously dull, and parliamentary committees in West Germany wield little real power. One man who wants to invigorate the Bundestag is its president, Eugen Gerstenmaier, a prominent Protestant member of the CDU who has a record of wartime opposition to the Nazis. Even if he succeeds in this endeavor, he is not likely to challenge Erhard or Barzel for the Chancellorship. Gerstenmaier supposedly aspires to the Presidency, a largely ceremonial position under Bonn's Basic Law, or constitution. The incumbent President, Heinrich Luebke, is a Catholic, a former CDU Minister of Agriculture, and an outspoken partisan of a so-called "Grand Coalition," including the CDU and the SPD. His views on reshaping the government have naturally brought Luebke into conflict with Erhard, who vowed again after his election as CDU party chairman not to accept such an arrangement. Although the President would like to exert an influence on all phases of policy, his role is circumscribed by the largely honorific nature of his position.

The junior partner in the present coalition is the Free Democratic Party (FDP), which embraces a wide variety of mavericks of all political hues. The party chief, Erich Mende, is a dashing former Wehrmacht officer, a holder of the Iron Cross, an engaging conversationalist, and the government's main advocate of talks, even negotiations, with the DDR. As Vice Chancellor and Minister of All-German Affairs since October 1963, Mende has realized more fully than most of his cabinet colleagues the erosive effects of time and the Wall on what he calls "all-German consciousness." He points out that Austria wants no part of union with Germany today, although as recently as 1919 the Austrian Parliament voted unanimously for *Anschluss* with the Reich. Mende fears that East Germans may experience a similar estrangement from the Federal Republic unless contacts are promoted across the Wall. His efforts to translate his ideas into action have been frustrated by his party's weakness at the polls and fears of alienating the refugee groups. In the FDP, Mende's authority is openly flouted. While he has talked vaguely of direct approaches to Moscow, members of Mende's party have gone so far as to suggest the neutralization of Germany or a deal with the SED to restrict emigration from East Germany in return for removal of the Wall. Mende realizes the need for revamping Bonn's propaganda to East Germany, but he has done little to make the Ministry of All-German Affairs more effective in this respect.

In the 1965 elections the FDP played the right-wing nationalist card and lost. It polled less than ten percent of the vote (a drop of more than three percent since 1961) and again failed to win a single constituency in the direct voting. But the FDP's 49 voting deputies in the Fifth Bundestag again give it the balance of power between the CDU-CSU and the opposition Social Democrats. After protracted bargaining, the FDP won four cabinet seats. The CDU has thirteen (including Erhard), and the CSU has five. Mende and his colleagues are not likely to exert any more influence in the second Erhard government than they did in the first, despite their overrepresentation in the cabinet. If the majority of German voters ever opt for right-wing nationalism, they will probably choose Strauss, not Mende or the FDP.

The oldest party in Germany is the SPD, which has not tasted the sweets of national power since before the time of Hitler. The Social Democrats have increased their share of the vote in the last two national elections, but they are still below forty percent. In 1965 the SPD campaigned again on the Godesberg program, which renounces nationalization as a basic policy and appeals to Catholic and middle-income voters, traditionally suspicious of the party's Marxist origins. In its zeal for votes, the SPD has jettisoned the last vestiges of Marxism. In 1965 the party offered an echo, not an alternative, in both domestic and foreign policy. Its domestic policy is unchanged, but the SPD has begun pursuing a more "independent" foreign policy, demanding that Germany renounce any role in nuclear weaponry and offer to compromise its territorial claims on Poland.

The SPD faces a crisis of leadership. When the Wall went up in Berlin in 1961, Mayor Willy Brandt grew to heroic proportions in its shadow. Now Berlin is comparatively quiet, and Brandt's stature has shriveled. His ideal of political perfection died with President Kennedy. Brandt wept uncontrollably when he learned of the assassination in Dallas. Since then, he seems to have lost much of his earlier flair.

Like many other German politicians, Brandt realizes that Bonn's policy on reunification and relations with East Germany has reached a dead end. In the summer of 1963 one of his closest advisers, Egon Bahr, who is also the Mayor's press spokesman, made a speech suggesting that Bonn could promote basic changes in East Germany by reaching limited agreements with the SED regime. Bahr's call for "change through rapprochement" riled the waters of German politics like an exploding torpedo. Intellectuals tended to sympathize with the move. But the loudest voices were negative, and Brandt backtracked hastily.

Later that year Brandt addressed a letter to the East German regime that eventually resulted in West Berliners being allowed to spend Christmas with their relatives in East Berlin for the first time since the Wall was built. When the SED challenged his party to an open debate early in 1966, Brandt promptly accepted and persuaded Erhard to go along with the idea.

Cast in the role of West Germany's leading spokesman in the confrontation with the communists, Brandt was able to win re-election as party chairman at the SPD congress in Dortmund later that year despite his 1965 election defeat. Forsaking equivocation on foreign policy, he urged an immediate start on drafting a German peace treaty, diplomatic relations with Eastern Europe, and outright denunciation of the 1938 Munich agreement as steps toward healing the breach with Czechoslovakia.

Despite his strong showing at Dortmund, Brandt faces a growing challenge to his leadership of the SPD. The main contenders are Fritz Erler, the party's floor leader in the Bundestag and its ranking intellectual, and the young Hamburg senator, Helmut Schmidt, who specializes in defense matters. Erler is an adept debater, but he lacks mass appeal. Schmidt is still largely an unknown quantity. The man who runs the SPD is Vice-Chairman Herbert Wehner, a former communist with an old *apparatchik's* knowledge of party organization and administration. His morose and sullen personality, not to mention his background, rules him out of the competition for the position of SPD candidate for Chancellor.

Hungry for office and burdened with a generation's accumulation of deserving party wheel horses, the SPD is unable to offer a genuine alternative to CDU rule. The party's tactic has been to attack Erhard personally and to exploit differences within the little coalition in hopes of paving the way for a "Grand Coalition."

Without internal unity or effective external opposition, the CDU-CSU-FDP coalition lives in limbo. Erhard aptly expressed its predicament on New Year's Day, 1966: "I cannot allow the impression to grow among the public that the coalition has already collapsed and ought to be replaced." The government does not act; it reacts. Faced with a marked slowdown in West Germany's economic boom, Erhard called for belt-tightening on all sides after he had won the 1965 election. The main cause of concern was the swing from a foreign payments surplus of 250 million dollars in 1964 to a deficit of 1.5 billion dollars the following year. Prosperous West Germans are gorging themselves on imports and overpricing their exports on the world market. Tankers once built in Hamburg or Kiel are now commissioned in Osaka or Yokohama. Japan undersells German cameras and even exports toys to the Federal Republic. At the same time, foreigners shopping for West German securities or plant sites have poured money into the already overheated economy, aggravating the labor shortage and generating new inflationary pressure.

As soon as the ballots were counted in 1965, Erhard called for drastic budget cutbacks amounting to nearly 2 billion dollars. Defense outlays were pared by some 375 million dollars. Reaction in the country was unenthusiastic. Rudolf Augstein, the sharp-tongued publisher of *Der Spiegel,* echoed the thoughts of many Germans when he wrote:

What he [Erhard] has done to balance the budget is

vintage Adenauer; the screws are applied a little here and a little there, so that scanty and belated honor is done to basic law. But no self-willed approach is apparent, which could stay the growth of inordinate demands and strip custom of its hard crust of complacency. . . . In any case he does not even have a program, only a lot of principles which he had long since abused even while he, pure of heart, still enunciated them.

As the Federal Republic approached the end of its second decade of statehood, it hesitated to take new initiatives in foreign or domestic policy. Bonn was concerned about the disintegration of NATO but waited for Washington to offer remedies. The question of a German role in nuclear strategy marked time after Erhard found himself the lone champion of the American proposal for an inter-Allied missile fleet with mixed crews. Officials in Bonn hinted that they were willing to renounce claims to the Oder-Neisse territories, but the public position continued to be that Germany's 1937 boundaries were valid until a final peace settlement.

Bonn's much publicized "peace note," sent to 110 governments in March 1966, offered to sign nonaggression pacts with all Eastern European states (except the DDR) and to cooperate in progressively reducing nuclear weapons in Europe. The note reiterated the claim that "Germany continues to exist within its frontiers of December 31, 1937," and avoided repudiating outright the 1938 Munich agreement by which Hitler annexed the Sudetenland. Official Soviet and Polish reaction was predictably contemptuous. Commenting on Erhard's boast that he had taken a bold new initiative, the independent *Frankfurter Rundschau* remarked: "Ice-cold irons can, to be sure, be taken in hand with confidence, but they can no longer be forged. . . . Our offers of a price are made only after our currency has become worthless." Erhard's approach to East Germany was even more gingerly. He rejected what he called "measures likely to deteriorate the conditions for reunification in freedom," meaning formal talks with the DDR.

Whereas Adenauer had stipulated that further steps toward East-West détente be accompanied by progress toward German unity, Erhard took the more moderate stand that nothing should be done to "aggravate" the country's division. The Chancellor called it "a policy without exaltation and without self-delusion." Germans were inclined to add "without imagination."

Erhard's first meeting as chief of government with President Johnson in June 1964 was awkward and even tense. The President lectured the Chancellor on the need for more flexibility in German policy toward Eastern Europe. Later meetings have been more congenial, and the two leaders are said to have developed easy personal relations.

American exhortations to show more imagination cannot make up for the fact that Erhard is not master in his own house. So far as Eastern Europe is concerned, he is hamstrung by diehards in his own party who constantly invoke the Hallstein Doctrine, devised in 1955 by the former State Secretary in the West German Foreign Ministry after Adenauer had agreed to establish diplomatic relations with the Soviet Union. The aim of the doctrine was to protect Bonn's claim to be the sole legitimate representative of the German people. As originally interpreted, it forbade the Federal Republic to maintain diplomatic relations with any state (except Russia) that recognized the DDR. The hard-line opposition in the CDU-CSU still upholds this version of the doctrine. However, Foreign Minister Schroeder and the other advocates of a "flexible" Eastern European policy now argue that the doctrine applies only to states that recognize the DDR after having already established diplomatic relations with the Federal government.

The only countries with which Bonn has actually broken diplomatic relations under the doctrine are Yugoslavia and Cuba. Trade continues with both countries. West German tourists throng Yugoslavia's Adriatic coast, thousands of Yugoslavs work in the Federal Republic, and Bonn continues to indemnify Belgrade for Nazi depredations. The DDR, incidentally, has never paid a *pfennig* of compensation to Yugoslavia or to any other country victimized by German aggression.

Erhard has rightly said: "The policy of a big country cannot be shaped without political self-confidence." The protracted debate over the Hallstein Doctrine reflects Bonn's lack of self-confidence. The Federal Republic is a big country that often behaves like a small one. Its conscience is so tightly corseted in legalism that the communists can convince their subjects that Bonn has no conscience. When large issues are at stake, the federal government quibbles and niggles until even its friends grow impatient. Its hesitations overshadow West Germany's basic generosity. That cultivated citizen of the world, Albion Ross, who knew Germany before the war as a student and later as a correspondent for *The New York Times,* used to say that the West Germans have now acquired the narrow-gauge mentality of Swiss hotelkeepers. This judgment is unfair to most Germans, but it sometimes applies to their government. Time and political frustration may yet, of course, re-create the broad-gauge Teutonic thinker that the world has learned to dread. But for the moment the bane of Bonn is not ambition or sinister intrigues but a kind of bloated self-righteousness. The federal government is like a millionaire on probation, afflicted with a lurid past, an affluent present, and an uncertain future. Burdened by his heavy baggage of riches and anxiety, he stumbles along the low road to salvation.

[5]

Pragmatism in
Purgatory

■

MAUERSTRASSE used to be one of Berlin's busiest shopping streets. Today it is bisected by the Wall, a dead end between two worlds. On the communist side the old brownstones look shabby and deserted. Your footsteps echo on the pavement as you walk west on Mauerstrasse (ironically, it means Wall Street) toward the Wall with the green "death strip" before Checkpoint Charlie on the left.

The look of death about Mauerstrasse is deceptive. Behind the grimy façade of Number 83/84 sits one of the liveliest apostles of the new economic order in East Germany today. He is Helmut Wiedmer, a hard-headed manager-technocrat in his early forties who could easily hold a comparable job in Hamburg or Düsseldorf or on the other, more famous, Wall Street. Wiedmer is production manager for an association of 22 state-owned East German plants manufacturing computers, photographic equipment, optical goods, and industrial regulating systems. He and his fellow managers in some 80 other nationalized industrial trusts (known as VVB's by their German initials) are charged with converting East Germany into one of the world's most advanced industrial states.

That they have a long way to go is evident from the moment you enter Wiedmer's headquarters. Two creaky flights of stairs lead to a cluttered anteroom occupied by several secretaries. Wiedmer's office is a dark, narrow room with a conference table covered in green felt at right angles to his desk.

"Sixty percent of my salary depends on whether I make a profit or not," he said, as he poured me a glass of East German brandy one morning. "Twenty percent depends on the exceeding of productivity norms in our plants."

Wiedmer is an engineer by training. His manner is relaxed and forthright. As he explained his role in East Germany's new economic system, I could hear a knell sounding somewhere in the distance for the old breed of German communists: gaunt, embittered survivors of Hitler and Stalin, who for almost two decades had guarded the country's economic bastions against all enemies except bankruptcy and their own incompetence. Recently, they have counterattacked in a partially successful effort to restore centralized control over the economy, but in the long run they are headed for the "dustbin of history," to use a phrase they would understand.

"There's a kind of natural selection going on here," Wiedmer said with a wry smile, "the old dogmatic bureaucrats being replaced by younger, technically qualified men. We still have many incompetents and time-servers, but they're gradually being weeded out."

He handed me two of his calling cards—one in German, the other in English. "I need both kinds," he said. "I make three or four trips abroad a year—Poland, Moscow, West Germany, Canada, Japan, to name a few places. I even looked into your country from Vancouver. That's another advantage of the new setup. Now we can travel abroad and learn from everyone."

Like his counterparts in other VVB's, Wiedmer enjoys powers and privileges exceeding anything a communist state has ever granted its industrial managers. Within limits set by the national economic plan, he can hire and fire, shift labor from one plant to another, borrow money (at interest), allocate investment capital from earnings, distribute profits to himself and to other members of the concern, and deal directly with foreign and domestic customers—all without passing through a single ministerial anteroom. VVB directors must, however, submit their production plans to one of the nine newly re-established industrial ministries in East Berlin, which also exercise ultimate financial control. The East German economy is still centrally planned. But, as Wiedmer says, "If your plants make profits, you don't see the planning people for long stretches. They don't come around here very often, I can assure you."

Profits depend on prices, among other things. This is where the rub may come. Wiedmer showed me several thick volumes he had compiled comparing the prices and quality of his VVB's output with those of similar foreign products. "We rate each of our products and the best foreign-made goods on a mathematical scale. We have to because we export as much as forty percent of our output, and almost half our exports go to such capitalist countries as Japan, West Germany, Sweden, Finland, Belgium, and France. So we have to be competitive."

To the East Germans, everything is capitalist outside the communist world. As Wiedmer talked, I wondered how the communists would ever gauge the real efficiency of their economy if the capitalist world made nothing comparable. I was reminded of a plaintive remark by an East German planning official to a West German journalist: "Without the London commodity exchange we couldn't work. But who will keep us posted on world market prices when socialism has finally triumphed in the whole world?" To paraphrase Voltaire, if the capitalist world didn't already exist, the communists would seemingly have to invent it.

For East Germany, in the world but not quite of it, the search for what the SED now calls the "world standard" in industrial output is no easy task. All communist states face the same problem. Their planners and factory managers have traditionally thought in what is now disparagingly referred to as "tonnage ideology"—a preoccupation with the volume of physical production without regard to quality, cost, or saleability. Communist prices have been administered prices, sometimes used to limit consumption of scarce goods, but rarely reflecting true supply-and-demand relationships. As a result, prices in communist economies have become as rigid and unrealistic as Stalinism itself.

Trade among communist countries is conducted under barter and clearing agreements in which the relative political power of the partners is often more important than the value of the goods they have to exchange. Trade with the capitalist world, traditionally regarded as a necessary evil on the road to autarky, has also been carried on without regard to economic criteria. Communist regimes are often ready to subsidize their exports, even to dump them on capitalist markets, in order to earn needed foreign exchange.

For almost two decades after the Second World War artificial internal and external prices masked economic stagnation in the Soviet bloc. Statistics of rising physical output created the illusion of prosperity amid actual poverty. At the same time, the rate of return on investments in industry began a lengthy decline. Two East Berlin economists, Professor Friedrich Behrens and Dr. Arne Benary, were denounced as "revisionists" in 1956 for pointing out these facts and for suggesting radical reforms that found official favor six years later. In the Soviet Union the same reforms are associated with the name of Dr. Yevsei G. Liberman, a once-obscure professor of economics at Kharkov University, who promises to rank among the fathers of modern Marxist economics.

As befits Germans, the SED has garnished its new economic policy with such pseudoscientific terms as "the closed system of economic levers" and "coordinating interlocking production branches." The "economic levers" boil down to the profit motive and other financial incentives.

Like other industrial managers in East Germany, Helmut Wiedmer understands profits. He wants to earn more. He could if he could get the labor or machinery he needs. "We employ 40,000 workers in our 22 plants," he told me, "but we need 5,000 more right away. With our present work force we can run only a shift and a half per day. Next year we'll be in even worse shape because of retirements and the low postwar birth rate, which means fewer new workers entering the labor force." By 1970, in fact, East Germany's labor force will have declined by almost a quarter million to about 7,400,000. It will be 1980 before the downtrend is reversed.

Under such circumstances productivity becomes a life-and-death matter. The SED now recognizes that the keys to productivity are profits and investments, not exhortation. What distinguishes the new economic system from previous reforms is the pivotal position occupied by the industrial managers. Subject to the ultimate control of the Council of Ministers and the State Planning Commission, they can now plough back pooled profits from their enterprises or distribute them as bonuses to their work force. They can run some of their plants at full strength while others shut down for retooling. They can go to a special industry branch of the Central Bank and borrow money for expansion at two to twelve percent interest depending on their inventory and the size of the loan. Under the new system, banks are supposed to act like banks instead of niggardly cashiers. They are to go out and look for potential borrowers.

The eighty-odd VVB's turn out some seventy percent of East Germany's industrial production and account for all major industries. They also control smaller plants, including private, cooperative, and "mixed" concerns, in the same "product group." The VVB's do not stop at the end of the production line. They are responsible for marketing and service, including consumer research, and will progressively take over the pricing of their own products. The touchstone of their success is planned profit, something comparatively new in communist economics.

The old system strangled initiative. The new one is supposed to stimulate it. Regardless of the ultimate outcome, the new economic system is one of the most revolutionary experiments in the communist world since de-Stalinization. In a sense, it is the economic counterpart of the political de-Stalinization begun by Khrushchev in 1956. Changes in economic practice are only beginning to catch up with the revolution in communist economic thought. The pace is halting and painful. But in East Germany, a country notorious for the alienation of its people from their regime, the new economic system has sparked hope, even optimism, for the first time since June 17, 1953. Returning from a tour of East Germany in 1964, Graefin Doenhoff, the astute political editor of *Die Zeit* of Hamburg, wrote:

> We soon realized that everyone—writers, scientists, white-collar employees, workers, those who are for and those who are against the regime—all look spellbound to the new economic policy. Some hope for more liberalism or, rather, less dogmatism from it; others hope their regime will thereby become more efficient and hence more popular.

Helmut Wiedmer shares these aspirations. As an executive of a VVB, he must constantly fight government red tape and ideologically motivated interference. As an SED member, he hopes the DDR may one day become a really going concern. "Every time I go over there," he said with a nod to the West, "they ask me to stay. Sure, I could be making 100,000 marks a year as a technical director at Siemens, but here I'm a young man with a highly responsible job, and I feel a challenge."

"Do you find your party work bothersome?" I asked.

"No, not nowadays," he answered without hesitation. "There's been a big improvement in recent years. Now they devote more attention to economic questions and less to the origin of man and other philosophical problems. The main thing is to get rid of the old dogmatists and to bring up younger men."

Wiedmer's income after taxes is 25,000 East marks, modest by Western standards but high for East Germany. "You have to pay for performance," he confided with an air of self-satisfaction. He drives two cars, one his own, the other furnished by the VVB. He and his wife, who works as a secretary, occupy a three-room apartment in the Pankow district of East Berlin. His hobby is cameras. Like other members of the new East German élite, he has climbed high enough to see the peaks ahead. Ideology does not cloud his pragmatic vision of personal profit and preferment.

Wiedmer and his like are not the only East Germans to benefit from the new economic system. Beginning in April 1966, working time was cut from 48 to 45 or 44 hours a week. Most East German workers now get every other Saturday off in addition to the regular Sunday holiday. More goods have appeared in stores, although prices are still high and quality low by Western standards. According to the regime's statistics, the DDR's industrial production rose by seven percent in 1965, a growth rate comparable to West Germany's.

The statistics of economic success do not reflect the continuing frustrations of daily life in East Germany. Only those who have lived or traveled widely in communist countries can appreciate the corrosive vexations of living in scarcity economies.

East Germany enjoys the highest living standard of any communist state. Yet the moment an East German sits down to breakfast, he feels the pinch. There is no cream, no grapefruit, no pineapple, no oranges (except perhaps at Christmas), and no bananas. East Germans have not tasted many kinds of fresh fruit for a generation. Real coffee costs from $8.00 to $10.00 a pound, tea is $5.50 a pound, and cocoa more than $3.60 a pound. Milk, on the other hand, sells for about 9 cents a bottle. Butter, still the basis of most German cooking but rationed at half a pound per person every ten days, is of poor quality and costs sixty cents a half pound. Eggs are often unobtainable.

Having bolted a meager breakfast of ersatz coffee and bread, the average East German dons a flimsy knee-length rayon raincoat that costs him $37.50 ($7.50 for the same coat in West Berlin) and goes out to wait for a creaking, clattering streetcar that belongs in a museum. An industrial worker in East Germany earns from $120 to $150 a month. At this rate he puts in 20 hours on the job to buy a pair of shoes, but if his feet are large, there may be none to fit him, because factory managers can economize on leather by manufacturing only smaller sizes. I have never understood why women face the opposite problem. The DDR women's ready-to-wear industry caters to medium and large-size customers. To go shopping with a petite wife is, according to *Neues Deutschland*, "asking too much of even the nerves of a robust husband." High prices add to the nervous strain. A woman's wool knit suit of what would be considered medium quality in any Western department store retails for almost $100 in the big state-owned department store on East Berlin's Alexanderplatz. A very inferior pleated wool skirt in the same store costs $13.90. These prices explain why unsaleable dry-goods inventories worth $187,500,000 accumulated in East German warehouses one year. There are other warehouses crammed with useless typewriters, unwanted toys, and accordions equally offensive to eye and ear. East Germany is short of everything except shoddy, overpriced merchandise. It is enough to cause the death of any salesman.

Marvels of ingenuity and endurance are necessary to find commonplace items of daily life in East Germany. Nails are unavailable except in the required size. All doors are at odds with their hinges. Cheap plastic faucets, the only kind to be had, leak constantly, leaving brown stains in washbasins and bathtubs. A homeowner with a little extra cash cannot repair his gutter or put on new siding because materials are lacking. Anyone able to afford a meal at one of the DDR's "Class I" restaurants must queue for a table and then cool his heels before the waiter brings a menu. An evening at the cinema is inexpensive but is suffused with so much political propaganda that the number of East German movie-goers has been dropping by 20 million a year since 1960. Twenty-eight theaters have closed in East Berlin alone, and there is not a single downtown cinema in today's "socialist" Dresden.

Television is the East German's window to the West, virtually the only one left. Tuning in Western programs, which can be received clearly in East Berlin and throughout much of the DDR, is no longer forbidden, although discussing them or inviting others to watch is prohibited. A small set with a 43-centimeter picture tube costs $400, and larger models go up to $850. But East Germans are willing to husband their last marks to enjoy the release that television offers. Consequently, there is an antenna on almost every roof in the country, and no one bothers to conceal the fact that he watches Western programs. The ratio of television sets to population is as high in the DDR as it is in West Germany, although real wages are 30 to 40 percent lower.

The average East German eats more grain and potatoes than a West German eats, but much less of the more expensive foods. More than half of the East German housewife's budget goes for food, compared to one third in West Germany. Except in East Berlin and in Leipzig at fair time, a trip to an East German market is usually an exasperating experience. Meat rationing has been formally abolished, but butchers still maintain lists of authorized customers. My wife found the main meat market in Weimar clean and tidy, with a government listing of prices for everything from filet steaks to veal cutlets, but the shop was devoid of meat except for a few sausages hanging from one wall and a slice of pig's leg selling for $1.15 a pound. East Germans hunger not; neither do they eat very well.

In 1876 a German engineer developed the first commercial internal-combustion engine, but his secret seems to have been lost in the DDR. Cars are a rarity. The East German autobahns are so little used, in contrast to the overburdened West German highways, that there is not even a grease trail on the inside lane. When West Berliners drove into the communist sector of the city in December 1963 during the first Christmas pass agreement, the "People's Police" looked on in bewilderment at the worst traffic jam in East Berlin's history. When I traveled in the DDR I usually drove a rented Volkswagen

1200, one of the smallest cars made in West Germany. It was always an object of intense curiosity, attracting crowds of on-lookers who would stand about for hours examining every detail of the vehicle.

At the western end of Unter den Linden almost in the shadow of Brandenburg Gate there is a modernistic showroom displaying East German automobiles. No prices are listed, even in the slick-paper colored brochures advertising the products of the "people's-owned" car plants. This is under-standable. A tiny two-door Trabant 601, with a two-cylinder motor and plastic body, costs 7,850 marks—almost $2,000—without extras. An East German worker would have to put aside his entire salary for almost two years to buy a Trabant, which is smaller, less efficient, and far more expensive than a Volkswagen. The station wagon version of this car sells for 9,300 marks. East Germany's so-called "luxury limousine" is the Wartburg 1000, a little four-door sedan with a noisy three-cylinder engine that costs 16,800 marks. The coupé model of the same car retails for 17,200 marks. Delivery time for all East German cars is four years from the date of order, except for those who pay in convertible foreign exchange. For them, the price is halved and delivery is immediate. There is even a "People's-Owned Gift Service, Inc." in East Berlin, with branches in Switzerland, Denmark, and other Western coun-tries, that will gladly arrange prompt delivery of a new Wart-burg or Trabant to any East German whose capitalist friends or relatives are willing to lay down hard cash for a gift car. East Germany still produces fewer than 100,000 passenger cars a year, less than the number of Volkswagens made in a month. By 1970 the "perspective plan" calls for only 150,000 cars a year.

East Berlin's most popular newspaper is the little *Neue Zeit,* not because its news differs from *Neues Deutschland* or any other DDR paper, but because its classified columns serve as a clearing house for the country-wide grey market in old cars and spare parts. Only the most inveterate automobile buff in Europe or America could identify all the hoary models put up for sale or exchange in the *Neue Zeit*. A prewar Adler Junior, for example, is offered for 2,230 marks; a 1939 Ford-Eifel is valued at 2,600 marks; an Eifel Kabriolet fetches 3,500 marks; a wartime Mercedes is advertised at 4,000 marks. These, it should be pointed out, are officially approved valuations. In most cases, the actual purchase price is even higher. A recent issue of *Neue Zeit* carried the following proposition:

> Weekend property, 600 sq. meters, forest near Mecklenburg lakes, and Trabant, 500 cu. cm., in good condition, to exchange for Trabant 601. Communications to (2) R V 4069, *Neue Zeit*, Berin W 8.

Another car-owner advertised for a prewar Opel as a source of spare parts and said that he would accept one damaged in an accident. Provincial craft cooperatives often put in urgent pleas for such things as a front axle or a new truck motor. On the autobahns East German cars often look like Rube Goldberg composites of various different models. I remember seeing one wheezing car of many parts that sported the Mercedes star on its radiator. East Germans wealthy enough to buy two Trabants or Wartburgs are well advised to do so. They can "cannibalize" one to provide spare parts for the other. It should be added that, whatever car they drive, they must pay at least 1.40 marks for a liter of gasoline that soon corrodes the cylinder heads of the engine.

The new economic system is an attempt to overcome such privations and to make East German products competitive on the world market. The young SED economists understand the country's economic promise will never be fulfilled unless East Germans can enjoy more of the things they want. The old debate over producers' goods versus consumers' goods is now recognized as irrelevant. The producers' goods will not be forthcoming in the requisite quantity or quality unless enough food and consumption goods are on the market to stimulate East Germans to work harder. Such facts were apparent to many in the SED long before Liberman published his now famous article on the profit motive in *Pravda* in September

1962. The reforms the East Germans have now carried out, albeit somewhat diluted by the decisions of the SED Central Committee meeting in December 1965, go beyond anything the Russians or other Eastern European communists have done. For the first time the DDR regime has something to be proud of. As a young East German professor told me: "We're in the forefront of the socialist bloc. Our new economic system incorporates some of Liberman's ideas, but it's ahead of the Russians." While the Liberman debate was still raging in the Soviet Union, the SED acted with surprising boldness. The "Guidelines on the New System of Economic Planning and Directing the Economy" were adopted in July 1963, only ten months after Liberman's *Pravda* article. They amounted to an officially sponsored revolution in the East German economy.

Central planners were ordered to restrict themselves to a few key index figures and to stop interfering in day-to-day industrial operations. State subsidies to industry were cut or canceled. VVB managers were empowered to conclude legally binding contracts with suppliers and customers and told to find profitable markets for their products. The DDR's sluggish foreign trade organizations are gradually being transformed into sales agencies for the VVB's. In domestic trade, associations of state-owned department stores already place orders directly with manufacturers, specifying quality, assortment, and price. Installment buying has been introduced for television sets, refrigerators, and other consumer durables, with repayments over two years at six percent.

In line with its new emphasis on cost accounting, the regime is revaluing the entire industrial plant of the DDR before fixing new depreciation rates. This is the first time that anyone in East Germany will have a reasonably accurate idea of what the country's capital stock is worth. Interest will henceforth be charged on capital, including finished inventories, in hopes of penalizing plants for turning out unsaleable goods. Cost accounting is to replace traditional communist bookkeeping. It is as if the British Empire had been ruled for a hundred years without the aid of a map, and finally got one.

Equally important is the reform of East German prices, the first comprehensive overhaul since 1953. The aim is to have prices cover costs and to eliminate many state subsidies. Coal, for example, is now priced for the first time according to grade instead of gross weight. Basic raw material prices were raised about twenty percent in the first stage of the reform. Tin was more than quadrupled, copper almost doubled, and lead upped fivefold. Reductions in the ubiquitous turnover tax are supposed to enable the government to hold the line on consumer prices, but signs of black-marketeering are already evident.

Price reform requires an astounding mobilization of bureaucracy. Three hundred and fifty working groups composed of economists, technicians, and officials labored for months in 1964 to produce almost 300,000 new prices in the first stage of the process. Ulbricht promises that "flexible" industrial prices based on changing market conditions will be introduced after the completion of the price reform in 1966. He has not explained how the new system will work or how inflationary pressures will be contained.

In the heyday of "tonnage ideology," factories shunned synthetics and other light materials and produced the heaviest, most cumbersome goods possible because their performance was usually rated on volume, not marketability. The new economic system has yet to overcome East Germany's chronic shortages. Some form of rationing or allocation of goods will be needed for a long time to come. Moreover, the fundamental problem of price-fixing remains unsolved.

According to East German economists, profits under their system are not the aim of all economic activity, as in capitalism, but "the objective standard of the utility of social labor." This rationalization does not alter the fact that the rekindled profit motive may force prices higher and magnify the conflict between industrial managers and central planners. Ulbricht will side with the planners in a showdown. But if the new economic system does produce a modicum of prosperity, there is little doubt that the sluice gates would eventually be opened wide to more initiative by the architects of better times—the industrial managers. Nothing succeeds like success, and no regime in the world yearns more than the SED for a taste of success. Despite the setback sustained in December 1965, there can be no permanent turning back from the goals that are now gospel throughout the European communist world. Recentralization is a symptom of fear among the SED old guard, but, as Radio Free Europe's well-informed East German analyst, Dorothy Miller, has remarked, "The logic of the new economic model and the pressure of rational operating procedures will call this recentralization move into question." In fact, the move to restore the old command economy is stillborn. Younger SED leaders now realize that there is no hope of achieving the planned two-thirds boosts in industrial production and productivity, to say nothing of foreign-trade targets, by 1970 without giving everyone from plant directors to charwomen a meaningful stake in making the East German economy a going concern. The younger men know that the Kremlin will no longer bail the DDR out of its economic difficulties. On the contrary, the East Germans must now repay with interest what they borrowed from the Russians in the postwar years; they must also meet the stringent delivery quotas set by the new five-year trade pact with Moscow. A reasonably unfettered economy is the DDR's only hope of meeting these demands.

The new shibboleth in the DDR is not centralized planning but autonomous management at the plant level. Management, in fact, has become an obsession with many East Germans. A flood of new books with such titles as *How to Invest Money in the Most Profitable Way* and *To Manage—but How?* is pouring off the DDR's presses. Everyone from cabinet ministers to lathe operators has been told to attend seminars at which the mysteries of the new economic system are explained. A management training institute, the first of its kind in East Germany, is now in operation. Ulbricht now extols the virtues of capitalist management and boasts that the VVB's apply some capitalist techniques. The SED demands "measures to replace those cadres who, in the long run, can no longer be equal to their future tasks for reasons of health and age and of insufficient qualifications." According to a resolution adopted by the party early in 1965, such members "are to be prepared in time for an activity acceptable to them and corresponding to their abilities." This sounds like a prescription for oblivion. Today's industrial managers must, in Ulbricht's words, be "distinguished by a readiness to accept responsibility, by creativeness and boldness, but also by businesslike objectivity, sober reckoning, and iron work discipline." As Carola Stern has observed, such men previously ranked as candidates for East German prisons.

The search for new blood has produced a corps of industrial executives who must be among the youngest in the world. Wolfgang Lungershausen, director-general of the office machinery VVB, is thirty-eight. The average age of directors at the huge Schwarze Pumpe lignite-processing complex is thirty-four. Some managers, such as Gerhard Zimmermann, who made his reputation as director of the DDR's thriving shipbuilding industry, and thirty-seven-year-old Rudi Georgi, who headed the sheet-iron and metal wares industry, were promoted to the newly re-established economic ministries in December 1965. These two men, like other recent additions to the DDR's economic cabinet, are fervent disciples of a system of monetary incentives based on world market conditions, including conditions in the capitalist world. Although they now occupy ministerial chairs, their attitude is radically different from that of the dogmatic old party functionaries who used to "boss" the economy from the East Berlin ministries. The new ministers are not likely to disturb profitable operations under the system that they helped to create when they were working as managers.

Moreover, the newcomers have found colleagues of their own generation and outlook already entrenched in important positions in the East German administration. Dr. Guenter Mittag, in charge of heavy industry and construction for the Politburo and a close collaborator of the late Erich Apel, is thirty-nine. Dr. Werner Jarowinsky, a Central Committee secretary and First Deputy Minister of Trade and Supply, is thirty-nine. His superior, Guenther Sieber, was a full minister at the age of thirty-five. The new Chairman of the Planning Commission, Gerhard Schuerer (who was Apel's deputy), and the Minister of Foreign and Intra-German Trade, Horst Soelle, are comparative oldsters at forty-five and forty-one, respectively, although neither of them joined the party until after the war. Summing up the situation, an East German professor told me: "Ulbricht is an old man, but he is surrounded by a younger brain trust."

The young brain trusters are all loyal SED members, although some of them are latecomers to the party. They are committed to upholding the party's control of the East German state. Their reformism involves no challenge to the SED's monopoly of political power in the DDR. For their services, the party rewards them handsomely. There is no upper limit on executive salaries in the DDR, which means that the VVB directorships are coveted more than ministerial posts with their fixed perquisites. Hundreds of thousands of key men in East German industry, including plant managers and engineers, have individual contracts with the state assuring them higher pay and better working conditions.

The new breed is the antithesis of the SED old guard. They have never been hounded by the Gestapo and the NKVD. None of them has lived as a despised expatriate in a Moscow hotel room, shuddering at every footfall in the corridor. They may have venerated Stalin from afar, but they were never obliged to make cringing obeisance at the dictator's feet. They feel no sense of guilt for German history. They do not regard being German as being unclean. They are curious about the West, not afraid of it. For them, economics, not politics, is in command. Their economics comes closer to econometrics than to the petrified Stalinist doctrine. The new-generation East German managers and economists share the view expressed in *Neues Deutschland* by one of their contemporaries:

> No one in the world is in possession of generally valid truths. . . . Even the knowledge of relative truth requires

hard work and the collective wisdom of a large number of qualified and experienced Marxist-Leninists. . . . Working on the method of economic management never comes to an end. New conditions constantly arise which must be mastered by new, more perfect methods. In the realm of methodology there does not exist any absolute truth either, in the sense of an eternally valid insight.

How Stalin must writhe in his little grave under the Kremlin wall when he hears such blasphemy!

The new breed is pragmatic. They have shed the old German social democratic belief in the ultimate perfectibility of man. They need no Marxian exegesis to justify the profit motive. Socialist morality does not deter them from using "topless" models (albeit with only their backs showing) on advertising brochures for East German cameras. The new managers, unlike the old guard, can laugh at themselves and at Marxism. They can enjoy an anti-regime joke as much as a parish priest relishes a racy story. But they are a serious lot, hard-working and intense. They mistrust pomp and propaganda. Their aim is to reform the economy, not transform society. But where communism reigns, society and economy are coterminous. One embraces the other. In their unspectacular way, subject to setbacks and reversals, the DDR's young technical intelligentsia have set out to build a new society under the ragged banner of Marxism-Leninism.

(6)

Uncertain Harvest

∎

THE COUNTRYSIDE between the Elbe and the Oder is a museum of prewar Germany. The people are dead or gone or collectivized, but the land is unchanged. Through the winter mist the East German villages look as if they were disintegrating in a formaldehyde solution. The only spot of color comes from the red and white propaganda banners hanging on the larger buildings. The letters HO (standing for Handelsorganisation, the giant state-run retail combine) were painted on store fronts after the war, but they are now almost as faded as the names of the former owners. The bumpy cobbled streets are empty and echoing. The little brick cottages look as if they were shriveling under their peaked roofs. When night falls, an East German village dies. The gas streetlamps surrender to the enveloping darkness. The countryfolk retreat as if they hoped to sever their last contacts with the empty world outside. Most houses show no light after the sun goes down. At 5:30 on a winter afternoon the atmosphere in an East German village is already sepulchral. One or two windows emit a feeble glow like the light inside museum models. The rest is blackness. A knock at a front door brings no answer. The villagers have retired, or prefer to give that impression. It is always earlier than you think in the East German countryside.

Collectivization has written an elegy in blood and tears for this melancholy land. Behind the crumbling façade of the past, the traditional relation between man and the land has been ruthlessly transformed. The revolution began with the arrival of the Red Army in 1945. All estates larger than 250 acres, as well as land owned by former Nazis or Junkers, were confiscated without compensation and parceled out in tiny strips to landless peasants, agricultural laborers, refugees from the Eastern territories, or otherwise unemployable KPD veterans. The former owners were imprisoned or exiled to the windswept island of Rügen in the Baltic. The resulting chaos in the countryside aggravated food shortages in the Soviet Zone but enabled the communists to make a credible case for the collectivization of agriculture. The first machine-tractor stations (MTS's), staffed by politically reliable urban cadres, were set up in November 1946 in centrally located villages and given a monopoly of available farm machinery. They were exact replicas of the Soviet machine-tractor stations later abolished by Khrushchev. The East German MTS's naturally gave preferential treatment to the cooperative farms then being organized and withheld their services from private farmers. In 1952 the Second SED Party Congress openly proclaimed the objective of collectivizing East German agriculture. The death of Stalin and the June 17 uprising the following year forced the regime to slow down its drive to transform rural areas. Some farmers were even allowed to leave the agricultural production cooperatives (known as LPG's by their German initials). Collectivization marked time while private farmers profited from East Germany's chronic food shortage. Even the SED's announcement in 1958 that it intended to complete the "socialist transformation" of the countryside by 1965 caused little alarm, primarily because cooperatives then in operation were so obvi-. ously unprofitable.

The winter of 1959-60 brought misery to Russia and Eastern Europe. The harvest was short. Long queues formed in front of food stores. On February 2 Khrushchev summoned satellite leaders to Moscow and demanded that something be done to overcome the crisis. As far as I know, he did not insist that East Germany complete its lagging collectivization, but Ulbricht took the opportunity to launch an all-out drive against the private farmers who still owned more than half of the DDR's arable land. The campaign began quietly. In true Stalinist fashion, Ulbricht mobilized a small group of party fanatics and instructed them to carry out collectivization throughout the country with lightning speed. The ambitious First Secretary of Rostock district, Karl Mewis, led the assault. Teams of agitators, FDJ activists, and police descended on the villages. They knocked at every door 'and used every combination of cajolery, pressure, and blackmail to persuade farmers to join a collective. Holdouts were threatened with prosecution for alleged black-marketeering and warned that they would get no more seed or fertilizer. When such methods failed, spotlights were turned on the homes of recalcitrant farmers, and they were denounced over loudspeakers. They were summoned to appear before local meetings of the faithful and subjected to public obloquy.

"In many villages the whole thing was over in twenty-four hours," a young East German told me. "Many farmers slaughtered their livestock and fled. Others went insane. In one village, five committed suicide."

Terror brought results. On March 5, 1960, less than a month after the drive began, Mewis announced the liquidation of the last private farm in Rostock district. On April 16 the district of Karl-Marx-Stadt (Chemnitz) became the last to complete collectivization. What the regime calls the "greatest revolutionary transformation in the history of German farmers" had been carried out in just ten weeks.

The result was catastrophic. The exodus of farmers to West Berlin swelled to a torrent. Young men who did not want to leave their homes forever migrated to East German cities or even joined the newly formed "People's Army" or the police. To its surprise, the SED discovered that about 150,000 farmers had disappeared from the land. Among those who remained, there was an alarming upsurge of alcoholism. Old peasants sat by their tile stoves cursing the communists or tended their tiny private plots while the collectivized fields lay fallow and equipment rusted in the rain.

The socialist transformation of the countryside produced new food shortages in the cities and obliged the regime to reimpose rationing, first lifted in mid-1958. Potatoes, the staple item of the diet, became so scarce that even such a favored customer as the "People's Army" was ordered to make stringent economies. By 1962 the SED was in the humiliating position of having to swap 1,000 Wartburg passenger cars for 40,000 privately grown Polish potatoes, losing heavily in the bargain.

Worse humiliations were to come. As agricultural output fell, state subsidies to the floundering LPG's rose. Depending on the work they do, collective farmers are reimbursed in so-called "workday units" whose minimum value is set by law at 7 East marks. Many LPG's have never been able to pay more than 1.70 East marks per workday unit from their own income, so the state must subsidize them and the rest of East German agriculture to the amount of 10 billion marks a year. Moreover, the SED soon discovered that the victorious conclusion of the "class struggle" in the countryside was more apparent than real. While crops rotted in the collectivized fields, LPG members and their wives toiled from dawn to dark in their half-hectare (1.25 acre) private plots. Instead of the two cows they were entitled to own, many families kept five. Instead of raising fodder for domestic livestock on their own plots or buying it from the cooperative, the farmers devised ingenious ways for diverting grain grown on the collective fields to their own use. Cucumbers, onions, and other delicacies grown on private plots and sold on the open market brought incomes up to 18,000 marks a year for some LPG members while the state continued to pour money into the cooperatives.

To curb such abuses, the party has imposed more "exact controls" and demanded increased "socialist consciousness" among the rural population. It now insists that LPG's pay their members and finance a larger proportion of their investment from their own resources. Prosperous collectives must now plough back 70 percent of their "over-plan profits" instead of paying them as wages to the farmers. The regime has stepped up pressure for the "socialization" of all livestock-raising and for the transition from the so-called Type I LPG, in which only the arable land is collectivized, to Type III LPG's, in which all land (except half-hectare private plots), livestock, and other property are held in common. The Type II LPG is an intermediate stage in which farm machinery and draft animals as well as arable land are collectively owned. Fewer than half of East Germany's collectives are Type III LPG's, but they control two thirds of the cooperatively owned land. The SED program calls for the "gradual" transformation of all cooperatives into Type III LPG's, generally thought to mean by 1980.

To overcome farmers' resistance, the regime allows Type III LPG's to buy machinery and fertilizer on favorable terms while less "advanced" cooperatives must take potluck. Despite such advantages, output per acre and per animal on the most "advanced" cooperatives is consistently lower than that on LPG's of Types I and II. Gerhard Grueneberg, Politburo Candidate Member and one of the architects of the 1960 collectivization, has admitted that the least socialized cooperatives average yields of 1,000 liters of milk per hectare, whereas the completely collectivized LPG's obtain only 734 liters per hectare. (In West Germany the average yield is 1,400 liters of milk per hectare.) The disparities are even greater between privately and collectively owned livestock. Grueneberg reports that privately owned cows in Mecklenburg produce 3,900 liters of milk a year while collectively owned cows in the same region produce only 2,500 to 2,600 liters.

Paradoxically, the SED's prescription for raising the output of milk and other agricultural products is more, not less, collectivization.

No one has found a difference in udder development be-

tween private cows and collectivized cows. The difference is in
the fodder they eat and in the care they get. When East German farmers were herded into collectives in 1960, one induce-
ment offered was an eight-hour workday with Sundays off.
They were to have the status of factory hands with the same
paid annual vacations and retirement pensions as other state
employees. In their resentment against being expropriated,
many LPG members adhere to the letter of the law, walking
off the job when their eight hours are up. Even when they are
supposed to be working, they often kill the better part of the
day in "production conferences" that produce nothing but talk.
The *Leipziger Volkszeitung* reported the daily schedule at one
typical LPG:

> Morning, seven o'clock, "staff discussion" with the
> "Chief Section Leaders." Ten o'clock, "Chief Section
> Leaders'" conference in the machine-tractor section.
> Meanwhile, a little something gets organized—but not
> everything—and at one o'clock they meet again in the
> cozy circle. . . . Sound advice from the top, but lower
> down what comes out is nothing.

One of East Germany's most ardent champions of collectivization told me: "In many LPG's the people come in the
morning to ask what they should do. They stand around waiting a long time. Then they get the word and trudge off to the
fields. By the time they've done any work, the morning is
gone."

The SED has finally realized that the eight-hour day is
not practical on a farm and has authorized LPG chairmen to
adjust work schedules accordingly.

Disorganization and lack of motivation are by no means
the only causes of low output in the LPG's. An East German
friend once remarked to me that the regime could never decol-
lectivize because "the farmers simply aren't there any more."
Young people have led the exodus from the land, leaving deserted villages in their wake. I shall never forget stopping to
ask directions at an LPG outside Rostock early one Sunday

morning. After knocking vainly at three or four houses, I found an elderly peasant wandering aimlessly around a barnyard, his breath reeking of schnapps. He was the only sign of life at the LPG that morning.

The average age of East Germany's collective farmers is fifty-six. On the fully collectivized Type III farms, one person in fourteen is under twenty-five. On other collectives, the proportion is nearly one in thirty. To combat superannuation, the SED now promises collective farmers slightly increased retirement pensions if they "win and train necessary successors for their work." To attract young people back to the land, Ulbricht has decreed that collective farmers should lead a "cheerful and cultural life." Youth has ignored his appeal, and life on the land continues its cheerless course.

Half of all LPG members are women. Practically all of them are required to labor in the collectivized fields. The labor famine is so severe that college students, schoolchildren, and even soldiers are regularly mobilized to help bring in the harvest. Losses remain high. In the fall of 1965 about one fifth of the East German potato crop was never harvested.

In January 1963 Ulbricht told the SED Congress: "The decrease of the number of people working in agriculture, because of old age, which can already be estimated, will demand an increase of production for everyone working in agriculture by about eighty percent for slaughtering of animals, by about ninety percent for milk, and by about sixty-five percent for sugar beets."

These olympian gains in productivity, supposed to be achieved by 1970, are completely illusory. East German livestock gets barely three quarters as much fodder as West German animals, and their output is disproportionately lower. Prewar crop yields in what is now the DDR were equal to or a little above production per acre in West Germany. Since the war they have been consistently lower, especially on the LPG's. A study by the Bonn government for the period 1956–61 shows that East German farmers produced 77 percent as much grain, 70 percent as many potatoes, and 66 percent as many sugar beets per acre as West German farmers. East German yields have improved since 1961 with the consolidation of many new LPG's. In December 1965 Ulbricht boasted that the DDR had achieved a grain yield of 29.2 quintals per hectare (42.5 bushels per acre), exceeding the West German average for the first time. But he made no comparison for yields of other crops.

In terms of tractors owned by the collectives, the East German farmer is almost as highly mechanized as his American counterpart, although far behind the West German farmer. Figures on horse-power supposedly available tell only part of the story. Ulbricht has publicly admitted that East German tractors require a general overhaul after only 1,500 to 2,000 hours of service, whereas even Soviet and Rumanian models go about 4,000 hours before they need general repairs. In 1964 he reported that, out of 80,000 tractors in use in the DDR, 24,000 had broken down and had to be replaced.

The LPG's have also been chronically short of fertilizer, although official figures show that consumption compares favorably with the West German average. Part of the problem may be that fertilizer intended for the collective fields is diverted to the farmers' private plots. To overcome the fertilizer shortage, one SED Central Committee member suggested that all arable land in East Germany be covered with a fifty-centimeter-thick layer of human excrement. This novel idea was dropped after it was found that even in the production of excreta the DDR could not keep up with demand. More practical steps were taken in 1965 when the regime increased imports of commercial fertilizer and fodder from West Germany by DM 160 million. The harvest that fall was the best since the 1960 collectivization.

One reason the SED finally attacked this problem is that its Soviet mentors are now fertilizer-conscious. In the past, however, imitation of the Kremlin's zigzags in agriculture has often proved to be disastrous for the East Germans. The Khrushchevian craze for corn became official SED policy in the latter 1950's, although most of East Germany is unsuited to

corn-growing. There probably would be no private plots in the
DDR today if Khrushchev's successors had not acted to pre-
serve them in the Soviet Union. Ignoring his own record of
slavish adherence to the Soviet pattern in agriculture as in all
other fields, Ulbricht boasted after Khrushchev's overthrow in
1964: "Of all the suggestions that Comrade Khrushchev has
made, for example, about agriculture, we have not imple-
mented a single one. . . . What we have carried out and what
we are bound by are the decisions of the SED Party Congress
and the Farmers' Congress."

In a speech to East German farmers in February 1966 the
SED chieftain was even more scornful of the example set by
the DDR's socialist partners: "We did not copy the many mis-
takes made in other countries because we followed our own
conditions of development." What the SED had done was to
compound the Soviet party's blunders in agriculture.

The effort to make farming fit ideology has made East
German agriculture prohibitively expensive and woefully in-
efficient. Ulbricht admitted in 1963 that one out of every three
LPS's was operating at a loss. Even more unprofitable are the
state farms (VEG's), all of whose land and machinery belongs
in theory as well as in fact to the government.

The SED has now begun to apply to agriculture some of
the cost-accounting principles that led to the new economic
system in industry. For the first time the regime knows what
enormous losses it has been sustaining in the countryside. For
the first time also the party no longer fears "counterrevolution"
among the farmers. As a result, men experienced in agriculture
are replacing party hacks as LPG chairmen with decision-
making authority akin to that now accorded factory managers.
Ulbricht professes to have hopped on the bandwagon in agriculture as in industry: "What happens locally, which sequence
of crops will be selected, which fruit will be cultivated, and
which technologies will be employed—all this will have to be
determined on the spot by the LPG's together with the county
production managements."

Higher premiums based on quality as well as quantity of

production are now distributed by each LPG directly to its
own members instead of being manipulated by local authorities. LPG's are encouraged to conclude "cooperative contracts"
with one another and with equipment and fertilizer suppliers
to ensure timely deliveries and continuous operations. The
farmers can go to court if the terms of the contract are not
met. The SED considers cooperative agreements in agriculture
one of its distinctive ideological contributions to Marxism-
Leninism. Such agreements, it hopes, will take the place of
more painful methods in achieving a gradual transition to total
collectivization, still the ultimate goal of the party's agricultural policy.

Ideology notwithstanding, the collective farm system has
been stabilized. More adequate food supplies are reaching the
cities. On the LPG's, as elsewhere in East Germany, there is a
process of accommodation to the regime. Older farmers stop
fighting the system and return, albeit unwillingly, to till the
fields. The few young people on the land even take a sullen
pride in having mastered seemingly impossible difficulties.

The "New Life" Type III LPG near the medieval city of
Meissen in Saxony is hardly typical, but it reflects what has
been achieved by some collective farms in the last decade. The
"New Life" began in 1953 on three hundred hectares formerly
divided among six private-estate owners who are said to have
fled the DDR before a collective was set up on their land. The
LPG still deposits a nominal monthly rent for the land to a
blocked East-mark account which the owners theoretically
could draw on if they returned to the DDR. That is unlikely.

The yard outside the farm chairman's office was a quag-
mire when I drove in to visit the "New Life." The chairman, a
bull-necked man in a red woolen sportshirt, greeted me heart-
ily and proceeded to pour glasses of schnapps for himself, his
chief bookkeeper, the village schoolteacher, and me as he re-
lated the farm's history:

"The beginning was difficult. We had to slaughter seventy
percent of our livestock right away because we had nothing to
feed them. The fields were in terrible shape."

"Yes," the schoolteacher, who sported an SED button in his lapel, broke in, "we've seen hard times here. I've been here since 1946. I've seen the worst."

"Since 1960," the chairman continued, "the 'New Life' has been a self-supporting enterprise. It has repaid all but 60,000 marks of the 650,000 marks it borrowed from the state at two percent interest to buy equipment and construction materials."

With considerable pride he announced that the average income per member is 10,000 to 11,000 marks, twice the average income for East German collective farmers. It comes from a variety of sources, including workday units, output premiums, payment in kind, and income from each member's private plot.

"We now have 132 members," the chief bookkeeper reported, "and about thirty private cars. Practically everyone has a motorcycle."

His words were punctuated by the clatter of an East German Trabant in the yard outside. The owner, who was having trouble getting his vehicle out of the mud, had paid 8,000 East marks after waiting more than four years.

"Lots of our members have the money to buy a car," the chairman said, "but they still have to wait years. You need patience."

East German communists like to tell stories about collective farmers driving to work in the fields in their Wartburgs or Trabants, but most LPG members are lucky to have even a motor bicycle.

The "New Life" is exceptional in another way. The average age of its members is thirty-eight, compared with the DDR average of fifty-six. The farm now embraces 720 acres and plans to specialize as a seed producer. Its income is high enough to keep younger members from migrating to Leipzig or Dresden. The "New Life" is also able to translate the SED's promises of sickness benefits and two-week annual vacations into reality. All married members own their homes, which they may pass on to an heir. Hardly the norm in the DDR. I visited several farmers' residences and found them as neat, airless, and overstuffed as any bourgeois German *stube*. Each had a television set and at least one radio.

Escorted by the chairman, the bookkeeper, and the schoolteacher, I stalked over the farm's rutted roads until we spied a group of women removing soil cover from potatoes. "Don't talk to her," the bookkeeper said laughingly, pointing to a burly woman with a hoe. "She's down on men since her husband left her." The woman told me she had to support her six-year-old boy from her earnings on the farm. "Where's your husband?" I asked. "Oh, he went off to another LPG," she said offhandedly. "I'll never see him again."

We walked past the drab little farm store to the hen house, which had no heating and the foulest air I have ever breathed. A young girl who looked no older than fifteen was in charge. Her chicks looked scrawny.

"Our field work is eighty percent mechanized," the chairman told me as we groped our way out of the hen house, "but our livestock operations are still backward." As he spoke, we could see a solitary tractor driver in the distance dusting insecticide on an alfalfa field.

"The state guarantees to take everything we produce," the bookkeeper broke in. "We're obliged to sell about half our grain output to them."

"What price do you get?" I asked.

"Not much. Eighteen marks per centner. It's a kind of agricultural tax." Then, brightening, he went on: "But we don't sell the state any more grain than we have to. We can make more by putting our grain into livestock. We could produce much more if we could get the fertilizer we need."

I had heard the same complaint from other East German farmers.

"Of course, things are a lot better here in Saxony," the chairman said, "than up north in Mecklenburg. That's poor country. They have only eight people per hectare there; we have twenty-three here. More than a hundred villages in Mecklenburg have no paved roads, and it wasn't until 1956 that the last village up there got electricity."

As I started to take my leave, the bookkeeper recited what was obviously a set speech for Western visitors: "We are pleased to have answered all your questions and shown you how we live and work. We hope you will return soon. But we also hope you tell the truth about our agriculture and the socialist achievements of our republic. We have sometimes had unfortunate experiences."

The chairman and the schoolteacher shifted awkwardly during the little homily. When it was over, they said good-bye almost apologetically.

From what I have seen of the East German countryside, I expect it will be many years before the SED's ideology takes root there.

One of those who labors to marry ideology and agriculture in East Germany is Professor Rudolf Schick, sometimes referred to in the SED press as the "Fodder Master of the Republic." As director of the plant-breeding institute at Gross-Lüsewitz near Rostock, this ambitious agro-politician enjoys such unusual perquisites as a Mercedes 220 for his personal use.

Schick received me early one Sunday morning in the converted manor house on the former estate where his institute is located. The old mansion is now dark and seedy. The door to what had been the drawing room was locked, and Schick had considerable trouble finding the key.

"Many tears have been shed and lots of misery caused by our collectivization" he said as we sat down, "but thirty years from now no one will remember the tears or the sorrow. We're investing huge sums in education, and soon we'll be seeing the return on our investment: people with a ten-year education, even specialist certificates, who will make much more adaptable farmers than we have today. You can't do much with the people over sixty."

Schick, who is a former Nazi, is now in his early sixties.

I asked if East Germany might eventually retreat from collectivized farming as Poland and Yugoslavia have.

"No," the professor retorted. "There's no chance we'll follow the Poles or Yugoslavs. The Poles liquidated their collectives and set up large state farms, hoping to induce people to join. That didn't work. They also hoped to export agricultural products to the West, but now they import farm products. As for the Yugoslavs, they bought out small holders and used their land to set up big state farms. They did this so that no peasant could say the state had seized his cow or his land. I consider this system as painful as collectivization."

Schick insists the small farmer is doomed under any system. "The problem," he says testily, "is whether farming is to be industrialized by the monied interests buying out the little cultivator, as is happening in West Germany today, or whether it is going to be by collectivization."

Schick professes to be unconcerned about East Germany's low yields since farming was collectivized.

"By 1970 we expect to increase agricultural production by twenty-five percent," he said. "We had a setback from 1959 to 1961 due to bad weather and the results of collectivization, but the reversal here was less than it was in any other socialist country. Since 1962 our agriculture has been on the upswing." He neglected to mention that since 1963 East Germany had dipped into its scanty foreign-exchange reserves to import more than twenty million dollars' worth of American wheat to make up the deficit in domestic output and in deliveries from the Soviet Union.

"My friends ask me why I didn't settle in West Germany," Schick continued. "I tell them there's more than enough work here for a single lifetime." As he talked, he guided his Mercedes over the soggy roads of the institute farm. The "work" he had in mind, it soon became clear, was the conversion of East German farms into agricultural factories.

"I'm impatient," he confided. "I want to go ahead faster. But our politicians tell me we must go slow. I tell them: 'I can say what's technically possible. You tell me when it should happen.'

"It's the same everywhere," Schick went on. "Every country is experiencing a flight from the land into the cities. I

1 The day communism was implanted in Germany. A Soviet soldier proclaims the fall of Berlin on May 2, 1945, by hoisting the Red flag atop the gutted Reichstag building.

Eastphoto

2 (a)   13-story House of Scientists and Teachers dominates East Berlin's Alexanderplatz, once the commercial hub of the city.   At right the domed Congress Hall and new apartment blocks.

(b)   Two heavily armed East German border guards atop the Wall.

Wide World Photos

3 (a)   Sidewalk bookseller on East Berlin's Karl-Marx-Allee (formerly Stalin-Allee) advertises state lottery tickets.

(b)   The Adlon Hotel in East Berlin. Guestrooms are former servants' quarters. Burned-out wing at right is all that remains of hotel's main section.

4 Brandenburg Gate, topped by the Victory Goddess's horse-drawn chariot, lies in communist territory behind a big loop in the Wall. The Adlon Hotel (upper left) overlooks West Berlin's Tiergarten (upper right).

5 The end of the line in Bernauerstrasse for a West Berlin street-car. The Wall bisects the street, then makes a right-angle turn to coincide with the bricked-up fronts of East Berlin tenement dwellings whose only occupants are communist border guards. When the Wall first went up, many East Berliners jumped to freedom —or death—from these buildings.

6 Checkpoint Charlie, where Allied troops and other non-Germans go through the Wall at Friedrichstrasse. Queue at right is waiting to check through East German passport and customs shed before entering East Berlin. White line at extreme lower left marks boundary between communist and Allied sectors.

7   Ulbricht in Red Army uniform during the Battle of
Stalingrad, where he broadcast propaganda to German
troops at the front and helped indoctrinate prisoners of
war captured by the Russians.

Eastphoto

8 (a)   Celebrating the fifteenth anniversary of the DDR in East Berlin on October 6, 1964, are (left to right) Premier Jozef Lenart of Czechoslovakia; East German Premier Willi Stoph; Russia's Leonid Brezhnev; Walter Ulbricht; Prof. Erich Correns, president of the DDR National Front Council; and Edward Ochab, Polish chief of state. Eight days later Brezhnev ousted Khrushchev as head of the Soviet Communist party.

(b)   Khrushchev and Foreign Minister Andrei Gromyko (right) with Ulbricht in East Berlin.

Black

9 (a)   Erich Honecker, Ulbricht's deputy in the Politbüro, responsible for security and defense matters.

(b)   Erich Apel, chairman of the DDR Planning Commission, who committed suicide on December 3, 1965, in East Berlin.

10   Leipzig at fair time. The newly completed
Stadt Leipzig Hotel is at right.

11 A typical East German barnyard. This one
belongs to a collective farm at Kleinkienitz.

Wide World Photos

12 (a)   Dresden one year after the Anglo-American raid. A path has been cleared through the rubble, but the city hall (background) and every other major building in the heart of the city remain skeletal wrecks.

(b)   Dresden today is a hodgepodge of tasteless new buildings and distasteful old ones.

YOU ARE LEAVING
THE AMERICAN SECTOR

ВЫ ВЫЕЗЖАЕТЕ ИЗ
АМЕРИКАНСКОГО СЕКТОРА

VOUS SORTEZ
DU SECTEUR AMÉRICAIN

SIE VERLASSEN DEN AMERIKANISCHEN SEKTOR

Achtung!
Hier beginnt die
Sowjetzone

German Information Center

13 The border between West Berlin and East Germany. At left an East German watchtower overlooking the barbed-wire barriers.

14 A friendly exchange between two long-time antagonists. Konrad Adenauer (left) with Professor Ludwig Erhard, his successor as chancellor of West Germany.

15 Former West German Defense Minister Franz-Josef Strauss (left) in confidential conversation with Rainer Barzel, Christian Democratic floor leader in the Bonn Bundestag.

16 West Berlin's Kurfürstendamm, with East Berlin visible in the distance. At left the Kaiser Wilhelm Memorial Church, left as a relic of war. Skyscraper in center is part of West Berlin's new Europa Center.

don't hold with all that nonsense about the farmer's mystic attachment to his land. I look on agricultural problems from a strictly objective viewpoint. The main problem is to make production conditions in agriculture like those in industry and to bring rural living standards up to the city level."

Schick has discarded the cumbersome brigade system used on East German collectives and organized the institute's 460 workers into small production teams which specialize in potato raising, grain farming, or livestock management.

"We have been trying to get more production from our farmers by exhortations," he said contemptuously. "It won't work. We need material incentives. Under the present setup, the members of a big brigade each get five marks if they bring in the harvest on time. If it's one day late, they get four, and so on. These so-called 'target premiums' are too small really to interest anyone, and in any case that's not the way to put agriculture on a profitable footing. Even worse are the special premiums used by many badly run LPG's to ward off some catastrophe. The chairman of such a farm will tell a farmer: 'If you go out and bring that crop in tonight, I'll give you five marks.'"

In what seems to be the pattern of the future for Soviet bloc agriculture, Schick's specialized teams earn attractive premiums based on the annual output of land or livestock under their control. They enjoy what amount to share-cropping rights. Schick's system is remarkably similar to experiments now being carried on in Hungary and the Soviet Union. The Hungarians have introduced their own brand of share-cropping and strengthened the autonomy of collective farms. In Russia small teams of collective farmers are allocated land and machinery for a period of years and made responsible for decisions on cropping as well as for record-keeping and the distribution of earnings among team members. This is Libermanism in agiculture. Its potential impact on the collective farm system promises to be even more revolutionary than the reforms in industry. The final result, as one Soviet agronomist has said, would be to make the peasant again "master of the land."

Private ownership of the means of production in agriculture would be readmitted under the guise of reorganizing the structure of collective farm labor. Schick and other champions of collectivization would passionately deny any such possibility, but their grasp of realities on the land has proved to be defective more than once. In any event, they are under pressure to evolve some system by which the Soviet bloc can begin to feed itself. Ideological shibboleths are now expendable.

All communist states waged what amounted to a civil war against their own peasantry to impose collectivization. The fruits of victory have been bitter. While they continue to proclaim the final triumph of socialism in the countryside, the oligarchs in Moscow, East Berlin, and other communist capitals are faced with the imperious need to feed their peoples by appealing to the acquisitive instincts of that most intractable traditionalist—the peasant farmer.

[7]

Prometheus and
Worthless Life

■

WEIMAR STANDS at the confluence of the German
past. The spirits of Goethe and Ilse Koch meet on the
Ettersberg where Buchenwald still overlooks the royal ghost
town that gave its name to the first German republic. If
he returned today, Goethe would find that his old haunts in
Weimar have become official shrines of the "workers' and
peasants' power" that claims him as a precursor. Ilse Koch
would find her infamous lampshades preserved with equal care
by a regime that strives to identify its enemies with the iniquities of Hitler's concentration camp system. Classical humanism
and Nazi barbarism are both turned to account by the oligarchs of the DDR.

The rest of Weimar and the surrounding area are fading
away like an old lithograph. No bulldozers are mobilized to
flatten the town's ocher-colored eighteenth-century court residences or rococo town houses. They are simply sinking into the
moist Thuringian earth. Weimar is a city of peeling façades,
sagging slate roofs, musty shops, and cobbled alleys where a
car is a rarity after sundown. There is no show street akin to

East Berlin's Karl-Marx-Allee and no new boxlike "residential complexes." It is the only place I ever saw in East Germany where the old order is being allowed to die with dignity.

Weimar's historic Elephant Hotel, well known to readers of Thomas Mann, now offers moldy sheets, baroque bathrooms, and a dining room that smells of cooking oil. Communist slogans and the bearded profile of Karl Marx greet visitors at the entrance. The night my wife and I arrived two violinists were playing a squeaky version of "Old Man River" between the double row of marble columns installed by the Nazis in the main lounge. A handful of patrons sat in clumsy overstuffed chairs, staring blankly into space. It looked like a Roman basilica taken over by Visigoths. Opposite us, three German girls concentrated on their wineglasses while a young Russian soldier and a friend in civilian clothes tried to engage them in conversation. A middle-aged man with an SED button in his lapel watched skeptically from another table. When the young men ordered an unwanted round of beers, the girls excused themselves and left.

The next morning we visited the former town house of Weimar's most famous resident. "J. W. Goethe," as the communists call him (dropping the "von" from his name to make it sound less aristocratic), is revered in the DDR as a classical realist, social progressive, and promoter of road-building. In his poem "Prometheus" the state-sponsored National Research and Memorial Center for Classical German Literature finds evidence that Goethe was an atheist. Facsimile editions of the original manuscript of the poem are handed out to visitors. By dint of diligent research, the Center has also discovered that Goethe "defended the aggrieved bourgeoisie against the nobility's usurpations" and concerned himself with "marital problems in the feudal period under the impact of capitalist ideology." Despite the ideological lacquer applied to his works in the DDR, the German Goethe Society still brings together scholars from both Germanies to discuss such topics as Goethe's lyric poems or his conception of Shakespeare.

The century-old German Shakespeare Society, whose

headquarters was also in Weimar, has been less fortunate. A wrangle over the election of officers split the society in 1963. The following year rival commemorations of the four-hundredth anniversary of Shakespeare's birth were held both in Weimar and in Bochum, West Germany. We attended a performance during the Weimar festival and felt there were more than just election disagreements behind the split. It was a production of *Richard III* performed at Weimar's National Theater where the constituent assembly that fashioned the Weimar Republic met in 1919. The theater was almost half empty, and after sitting through a seemingly interminable performance I could understand why. It was based on a new translation intended to spell out the Marxist interpretation of Shakespeare. During the evening crude murals with faces of exaggerated hideousness were mounted puzzlelike at the rear of the stage, apparently to depict the corruption of English society under Richard. The performance was saved by a gifted actor named Wolfgang Dehler, then only twenty-seven years old, who played the title role in a threadbare mohair cloak trimmed with mothy foxtails. He carried a shield that I judged was made of cardboard. The audience was generally apathetic except during intermissions when it stormed the refreshment stand like a hungry rat pack.

The next morning I invited Dehler to our hotel. We sat drinking what the East Germans call "mocca" for several hours while the heavy-set young actor discoursed volubly on the problems of the stage in the DDR. "Our theater has been hampered by too much political interference from above," he said. "Our artists were discouraged by narrow-minded conceptions imposed on them. Our situation is very difficult, but things are getting better. The other day I talked here to our Deputy Minister of Culture. And I didn't do any bowing and scraping."

Dehler belongs to no party. His wife is from Bavaria. He used to see American films in West Berlin before the Wall was built and thinks East Germans have many "mistaken notions" about Hollywood. It was clear he had studied the role of Richard carefully. "I wanted to do it differently," he admitted, "but our director insisted that I should portray Richard as a man who never shrinks from the most diabolical crime." Dehler and others like him in East Germany do not reject the Marxist interpretation of literature, but they want to make it believable.

"The old-fashioned socialist-realist play where they bring a machine onto the stage when they talk about workers is out," he said with evident relief. "People aren't so stupid any more."

The East German regime promotes the sale of subscription tickets in an effort to assure audiences for propaganda plays as well as for the more popular classics. But the turnout is often discouraging. "In East Berlin I opened in a Bulgarian play before eighty people," Dehler recalls. "I wanted to refund their money, but the management said the show must go on." Dehler professes to be optimistic about the future, but as he got up to leave, he said: "Whether you share our aims or not—and I don't expect you to share them all—you must admit we don't have it easy."

I walked out with him to the big square in front of the hotel. It was Saturday morning, and old women in kerchiefs and frayed black coats were milling around the Neptune Fountain where the public market was set up. It consisted of about half a dozen sawhorse tables, bare except for small piles of dandelion greens, some magenta-gray beets, a collection of medium-sized red onions, a few turnips, and some worm-eaten green apples about the size of golfballs. Most of the shoppers were gathered around a table where a hawker was extolling the virtues of a bottled foot-massage preparation and wafer-thin rubber inner-soles that looked as if they had been nibbled by mice. Business was brisk. The salesman frequently replenished his stock from a car parked behind his table. It was the only vehicle in the whole market place.

In the afternoon we drove up the Ettersberg to Buchenwald. Big groups of Russian soldiers in shiny boots and fresh haircuts spilled out over the road on their way into Weimar.

By the time we reached Buchenwald, the sun had disappeared behind massive black clouds. A middle-aged woman wearing an SED button and a blue guide's uniform welcomed us with a smile and shook hands briskly before taking her place behind a large relief map of the former concentration camp. Smiling again, she motioned us to be seated. Then, as if on cue, her face lengthened, and her voice dropped an octave as she droned through the odious history of Buchenwald. In eight years almost a quarter of a million prisoners passed through the camp's main gate under the sardonic inscription "to each his own." About one in four was shot, starved, frozen, or tortured to death. Buchenwald lacked the gas chambers of such officially designated extermination camps as Auschwitz and Bergen-Belsen, but for a mere "labor camp" it seems to have done its share in destroying what Hitler called "worthless life." In this bucolic setting of rolling hills and thick forests of fir, Goethe composed some of his most famous poems under an oak which has now disappeared. He said the view made him feel "free and large."

Our guide took us to one corner of a courtyard outside the camp crematorium. A few withered floral wreaths marked the spot where the German communist leader Ernst Thaelmann is said to have been executed in August 1944 after surviving eleven years in Nazi concentration camps. The SED has named a street after him in every East German town and scattered Thaelmann statues throughout the country. "Comrade Thaelmann's two murderers now live in West Germany," our guide announced brightly. She proceeded to rattle off their names and street addresses.

Part of the camp has been converted into a museum dedicated to proving that the inmates had already staged a successful uprising before General Patton's troops reached Buchenwald and that most former camp functionaries are now living openly in West Germany. "Buchenwald was a modern slave market," our guide said without apparent emotion. "Here German monopoly capital made huge profits supplying Hitler's war machine." The names of firms now prominent in the Fed-

eral Republic that used inmate labor during the war are displayed in the museum beside pictures of prisoners pulling
heavy road rollers or being flogged by the SS. Each room also
contains its quota of propaganda slogans and pictures of communist inmates credited with organizing resistance against the
Nazis. There is nothing to show that the American Army ever
set foot in Buchenwald.

Having had her fill of horrors, my wife excused herself
and took a seat in the lobby, leaving me with the guide who
finally wound up her harangue by saying: "In our republic we
now have everything we need for a happy future." Once out of
the museum, we drove down the inmate-built road called
"Blood Street" to the 165-foot bell tower designed as
a memorial to the victims of Buchenwald. Before it stands
Fritz Cremer's wrought-iron sculpture depicting the inmates'
uprising. I was tempted to ask our guide if there was also a
memorial to the 10,000 prisoners reputed to have perished at
Buchenwald after it was reopened as a communist concentration camp on August 12, 1945. But I knew that she would deny
everything. In any event, Buchenwald is no longer a place of
confinement, although Goethe would still hardly find it a place
where he could feel "free and large."

The old Nazi concentration camps in East Germany are
more than museums or memorials. They are the temples of
German communism where the SED tries to manufacture a
national mystique out of the struggle of a latter-day com-
munion of saints against Nazi oppression. "Our work here is
primarily political," the director of the memorial at the former
women's concentration camp at Ravensbrück had told me.
"We must always do political work among our people because
we didn't make a revolution ourselves." The rulers of the DDR
seem to find a perverse satisfaction in perpetuating the
memory of iniquities committed by fellow Germans. "In
twelve years a people can be plunged into barbarism," says the
official East German guide to Buchenwald, "but it cannot be
lifted out so quickly. . . . Don't be trusting too soon and too
universally. Only in one third of Germany have the murderers

been suppressed." There is a suggestion that even in the DDR the murderers would soon be back in business if German communists were really Germans. To imply that they are a breed apart carries an invitation to Germanophobes anywhere in the world to embrace the DDR as the most non-German German state they will ever find. But in much SED propaganda about the concentration camps there is also an unspoken pride in the Teutonic potential for destruction.

By the time we returned to Weimar, the streets were dark and deserted. We parked our Volkswagen in the market square and made our way to a little basement tavern near the Elephant Hotel. Most of the tables were occupied by African students and their blond German girlfriends. We finally found two places at a table where a German couple and their three children were finishing a meager supper of sausage and bread. "There's not much choice," the mother of the family said as she handed us a menu. "All our good meat goes to the Russians." As we ordered sausage and beer, three tired-looking musicians in one corner struck up a jazz number. What passed for a dance floor was quickly filled with young Africans and their girls. By law, sixty percent of music played by East German dance bands must be of "socialist" origin, but that night the West wind prevailed. Weimar's smart set twisted with abandon. On our way back to the hotel we passed a group of German teen-agers singing raucously as they lurched across the market square. The young men wore their hair "Beatle" style and sported peg trousers. The day before, the Weimar paper reported that a group of local "Beatniks" had been sentenced to jail for "uttering threats against African students and Soviet citizens." The Russians were, of course, soldiers. The Africans are resented because they have pocket money provided by the DDR and can afford to take girls to places no ordinary East German can afford. A policeman standing by the hotel entrance eyed the young rowdies as they passed but did nothing.

The violinists were performing doggedly in the Elephant lounge when we returned. A few better-heeled Weimar residents and visitors sat drinking Armenian cognac or Russian champagne. The pungent odor of cooking oil came from the open door to the kitchen. I picked up a copy of the local newspaper, a four-page tabloid, with a banner headline proclaiming: "Cooperation Brings Successes." It turned out to be the report of a district committee meeting of one of the DDR's satellite political parties. The back page was more interesting. One story called for more dance halls in Weimar and included a one-column picture of a dancing couple with the caption: "Weimar youth wants to be able to dance on weekday afternoons as well as weekends." At the bottom of the page were half a dozen matrimonial ads. One read:

> Lady, charming and chic, warm-hearted, practical housewife, intelligent (diploma), very slender, attractive, propertied, divorced, seeks a very dear companion in marriage, refined, serious, from 55 to 60 years old, educator, doctor, or veterinarian preferred. Replies to W 1718 TNN Weimar.

My first impulse was to write a letter telling that charming lady that she was two hundred years too late, that the days of Goethe and his beloved Frau von Stein were over. Then I remembered that Weimar lives in the past.

[8]

Requiem on
the Elbe

∎

AT 10 P.M. EVERY FEBRUARY 13 the bells of
Dresden's surviving churches toll in unison for half an hour.
Even the youngest boy in the Kreuzkirche choir knows it is a
solemn requiem for the city itself, for the great baroque
metropolis that marked the artistic frontier of Western Europe.
When it was destroyed, Asia advanced to the Elbe.

February 13, 1945, was a mild, sunny day in Dresden.
Germany had been at war five and a half years, and Russian
troops were only eighty miles to the east, but the city was
practically unscathed. It had experienced only a few nuisance
raids. Dresdeners were confident that Anglo-American bombers would never seriously attack their world-famous treasure
house of art. They boasted that the city was "the safest air-raid
shelter in Germany." In fact, it was a death trap, because
military and civil officials responsible for the city's defense
shared the population's sanguine faith in Dresden's inviolabil-
ity. The few shelters available were hopelessly inadequate
even for residents, let alone the thousands of refugees who had
poured into Dresden from areas overrun by the Red Army.

Ration-free soup was distributed that morning on Prager-strasse, Dresden's fashionable shopping street. In the evening there was a gala performance at the opera and a full house at the circus. Then at 9:35 p.m. the air-raid sirens sounded. Thirty-eight minutes later the first four-motored Lancaster bombers of the Royal Air Force were over Dresden. The English author David Irving reports that the attack would have had to be canceled if the clouds had not parted at that moment.

Two hundred and forty-four Lancasters dropped incendiaries and high-explosive bombs in the first attack. They started fires in every part of the city and knocked out the warning system. A strong wind fanned the flames. When the "all clear" sounded after twenty-four minutes, many Dresdeners emerged from their cellars hoping to save their homes or salvage their belongings. Fire fighters struggled to bring the blaze under control. Their efforts were wasted. Shortly after 1 a.m., February 14, a second wave of RAF bombers attacked the city. This time there was no warning. Dresden was engulfed in a seething ocean of flame that submerged everything in its path. As suffocating smoke curled into the basements, many people rushed out wildly onto the flaming pavement. Dresden became one vast cremation ground. Pilots reported the holocaust was visible for 150 miles. When dawn finally broke through the darkened sky, the survivors crept out to view the still-burning wreckage of their city. As one of them said, "We felt we were at the bottom of a deserted crater, or on some distant planet." Another round was still to come. At noon 1,350 American Flying Fortresses and Liberators arrived to complete the annihilation of Dresden. They found a three-mile-high column of smoke towering over the city and few signs of life below.

No one really knows how many people perished in Dresden on February 13–14. The city's normal population of about 640,000 had been swollen by an uncontrolled influx of refugees. There were too few able-bodied survivors to count or bury the dead. Fearing epidemics of typhus and other diseases, the authorities ordered that bodies be burned in pyres all over town and the ashes dumped in common graves.

For a decade after the war the Russian and East German communists made propaganda capital out of the Anglo-American "terror attack," which they insisted had cost some 150,000 lives, more than twice the number killed at Hiroshima. The figure proved embarrassing, however, when the Chinese communists began citing it as evidence to support their contention that nuclear weapons are not necessarily more destructive than "conventional" ones. The Russians and East Germans promptly scaled down their Dresden casualty estimate to 35,000 or 40,000, which most Western authorities regard as about 100,000 below the actual toll.

The physical destruction is a matter of record. The attack devastated an area of forty square kilometers and completely destroyed 75,000 dwellings, 114 public buildings, 40 hospitals, and 35 schools. The Zwinger Museum and almost every other historical landmark in the heart of the old city were left in ruins.

The East Germans say they removed 16 million cubic meters of rubble. Ironically, Dresden's railway marshaling yards, one of the prime targets of the raid, were damaged only slightly. It took the Germans only three days to restore a double-track line in and out of the city. Nor did the destruction of the inner city advance its capture by one hour. The Red Army finally entered Dresden on May 8, the day Germany surrendered.

In his excellent study *The Destruction of Dresden* David Irving attributes the original suggestion for an all-out attack on Dresden to Winston Churchill. He says the British prime minister hoped to bring word of a telling Allied aerial blow in the rear of German forces on the Eastern front when he met Stalin at Yalta in February 1945. Bad weather delayed the attack until after the Yalta Conference, but the British and American air staffs pressed ahead with their plans. Irving finds no evidence for the widely held notion that the Russians demanded a terror raid on Dresden.

So long as there is a Western world, the destruction of Dresden will arouse fierce passions and deep misgivings. My own feelings are mixed. The decision to bomb Dresden was taken near the end of the most destructive war in history by men who had seen the better part of Europe laid waste by German arms. The Allies were not the first to resort to terror bombing, as the fate of Coventry attests. On the other hand, the raid on Dresden destroyed one of the world's finest cities without shortening the war one day. Gerhart Hauptmann, who survived the attack at the age of eighty-two, drew what seems to be the only possible lesson from the tragedy: "Whoever has forgotten how to weep will learn it anew from the destruction of Dresden." War transcends normal moral criteria, and so does the fate of Dresden. It can be neither condemned nor condoned. It is beyond good and evil.

Dresden today is like a ravaged forest beginning to reseed itself. The dominant motif is emptiness. People who knew the city before the attack say everything now seems closer together. There are a few examples of early postwar Stalinist gingerbread architecture, a growing number of new "residential complexes," and acres of rubble and ghostly façades. In the heart of the old city equestrian figures in stone rear above little boys roller-skating amid weed-covered ruins. Martin Luther is back on his pedestal in front of the Frauenkirche, but the eighteenth-century church, whose sandstone cupola used to dominate the Dresden skyline, is now reduced to two spires and a heap of rubble.

Dresden was razed during one fateful night; Cologne was systematically leveled over a period of years. The end result was about the same. "Why then," asks Rudolf Walter Leonhardt of the weekly *Die Zeit* of Hamburg, "is Cologne today again Cologne whereas Dresden is no longer Dresden?" The apparent answer is that when the new Cologne was built at least something of the spirit of the old city was resurrected. Dresden may one day be entirely rebuilt; it will never be resurrected.

The East Germans are justly proud of the Zwinger Museum. It is the first place to which they take a visitor to Dresden. But even there, where the old Dresden has been most faithfully restored, the old voluptuous grace is gone. Tourist delegations from Czechoslovakia, Poland, and Russia now take snapshots beside the courtyard fountains or glance shyly at the nudes cavorting by the Nymphenbad. Everyone seems a bit ill-at-ease. In the picture gallery they stand before the Sistine Madonna while a guide explains that the great masters of the Renaissance painted only religious or aristocratic subjects because the ruling classes of that day opposed socialist realism. The SED line on art is dispensed in all Eastern European languages to the throngs of sober visitors. The Zwinger in summer is the nearest thing that communism has to the Louvre at the height of the tourist season.

"We have more than two million visitors a year," Dr. Christian Emmrich, the assistant director of the Zwinger, told me as we pushed our way through the crowded galleries. "We have 3,200 pictures in the Zwinger complex today. The Nazis tried to ship them west. The Sistine Madonna was found in a freight car on a tunnel siding. We're still missing about 500 paintings that disappeared during the war. We paid 100,000 marks to get one back when it came to light in London several years ago, although we shouldn't have had to pay anything since it was our property."

The East German regime has repeatedly thanked the Russians for restoring the Zwinger picture collection in the Soviet Union after 1945. "In recognition of the DDR's consistent peace policy," as Moscow put it, the pictures were returned in 1955. Emmrich told me the Russians wanted to "wait and see how things shaped up here" before sending them back. "They didn't charge us for the restoration," he added. "We gave our highest medals to some of their people, and that was it."

Even before the paintings were returned, the Dresden administration had begun rebuilding the shattered Zwinger from photographs. Copies of the original blueprints, used during the prewar restoration, were lost in 1945 and did not reappear until four years later. A part of the picture gallery was reopened on June 3, 1956, and the whole thing was "given to the public," as the East Germans like to say, on October 30, 1960, the four-hundredth anniversary of the Dresden art collections.

On summer evenings the Kreuzkirche choir or Dresden State Opera ballet performs in the Zwinger courtyard to the accompaniment of the fountains and the Nymphenbad waterfall. The copper roofs of the Wall Pavillion and the Kronentor (Crown Gate), as well as the sculptured figures of gods and children, are bathed in soft light. If the occasion is less formal, a jazz band from Prague may invade the courtyard and play music for the twist.

Even "Letkiss" is now permitted in the DDR. To the melodies of *Hello, Dolly!* or *My Fair Lady* Dresdeners undulate across an improvised dance floor with as much skill and exuberance as their contemporaries at Manhattan's Peppermint Lounge. The angularities of the workers' and peasants' state are momentarily forgotten.

There is probably more of the atmosphere of old Dresden in the Kreuzkirche than anywhere else in the city. The Allied raid gutted the old church, destroying most of the stucco ornamentation that began to clutter the interior after 1900. The Kreuzkirche has been restored in its original simplicity and moved to the southeast corner of the Altmarkt (Old Market). One spring evening I went there to record the famous Boys' Choir during vespers. No one in the overflow congregation took notice of me, but after the service an usher asked if I would explain my purpose to the pastor. I found him waiting for me in the sacristy, a middle-aged man with bright, intent eyes.

"They allowed you to enter this country with a tape recorder?" he asked in amazement. Without waiting for me to reply, he continued: "Our churches are very strictly controlled by the state. We aren't allowed to do anything that might look like propaganda for the church without official permission."

I played back part of what I had recorded.

"The quality is amazing," the pastor remarked to an assistant. "That's what you can do with good Western equipment."

At the pastor's request, I returned the next day to get permission to use my tape from Professor Rudolf Mauersberger, who directed the Kreuzkirche Boys' Choir for almost thirty-five years before his retirement in 1965. I found the seventy-seven-year-old church patriarch in a tiny cubicle that served as his office just inside one entrance to the Kreuzkirche. The stone floor was bare. A partition of raw planks and clouded glass separated his office from the entryway. Mauersberger received me warmly. He was eager to hear the tape playback and thanked me for having made it. He said that if the government would let the tape out of the country, he had no objection to its being broadcast. As a matter of fact, the government did let the tape out, and it was aired over NBC.

My most memorable experience in Dresden was the first night I ever saw the city. My wife and I arrived late by car from Weimar and had considerable trouble finding our way through the jumble of urban second-growth to the Astoria Hotel where the DDR Travel Bureau had reserved a room for us. Our wanderings had only begun. The hotel management adamantly refuse to admit our Tibetan terrier, Igloo, who was traveling with us. Rather than leave him all night in our little Volkswagen, we set off to find a hotel more kindly disposed to dogs. We drove for hours through deserted streets, past open fields where the old Dresden had stood and past monotonously uniform apartment houses where the new Dresden was rising. Simply to find another hotel was a major problem, much less gain admission.

For a city of half a million souls, Dresden must be more poorly equipped with hotel space than any other comparable town in the world. In 1965 it had a grand total of 2.7 hotel beds per 1,000 inhabitants. Out of 1,200,000 overnight bookings requested in 1961, the city was able to provide fewer than half.

Unmindful of the odds, my wife and I continued our nocturnal pilgrimage until we found a helpful concierge at what remains of the once-elegant Excelsior Hotel off Pragerstrasse, formerly Dresden's Fifth Avenue. Everything is gone now except for one wing of the hotel. The Excelsior was full, but the concierge gave us the name of a famous old hotel on the opposite side of the Elbe. We drove off through the blackness, across one of the three bridges that again span the river, and up a hill to the charming old Weisser Hirsch (White Stag) residential suburb. With directions from a young man who asked us for a lift, we eventually pulled up before a group of drunken youths who were trying to find their way through a revolving door, the entrance to the celebrated Park Hotel Weisser Hirsch. The lobby reeked of East Germany—that distinctive combination of lysol, cooking grease, and cheap cigarettes, with lysol in the lead. The plaintive strains of a Czech dance band issued from the adjoining dining room. The woodwork was black with age and neglect. A few faded travel posters hung from the walls. The lights were so feeble that most of the lobby was enveloped in cavernous darkness.

"Is this the Park Hotel Weisser Hirsch?" I asked.

The attractive woman at the desk smiled with that wan amusement one sees so often in East Germany.

"Yes," she said, "this is it." Then, after a pause, she added: "We're not supposed to take visitors from capitalist countries, but since it's so late, we'll make an exception in your case." One reason for barring capitalist visitors, I later found out, is the presence of a large Soviet military hospital across the street from the hotel.

On the night we arrived, the Park Hotel's dining room, once a fashionable ballroom, was crowded and smoky. A few couples shuffled around a tiny dance floor. Most of the patrons sat staring moodily into glasses of Russian champagne or Hungarian wine. The tablecloths, as almost everywhere in the DDR, were spotted and soiled. Just to the right of the entrance some stale coldcuts were displayed under a glass counter.

Through the open door to the kitchen came the clatter of dishes and the familiar odor of cooking fat.

Because we were unusual guests, my wife and I, and Igloo, were put up in Haus Emma, an old stuccoed villa used as an annex by the Park Hotel. Haus Emma overlooks the Russian army hospital on one side and a beautiful wooded park on the other. It was an ideal place for us. Porters are rare in East German hotels, so a night watchman at Haus Emma helped us bring in our luggage. Like so many other East Germans, he was fascinated by my tape recorder. After examining it minutely, he produced a much thumbed old Grundig radio catalogue with such pride that I overcame my weariness long enough to admire it. He had little hope of ever acquiring any of the transistor receivers pictured in the catalogue, but simply contemplating them seemed to give him satisfaction,

The next morning I had a long talk with the lady at the reception desk, who turned out to be a lyric poet as well as assistant manager of the hotel. She had known the Park Hotel Weisser Hirsch in better days.

"When I was appointed to this job after the war," she told me with a quizzical smile, "friends in New York cabled congratulations. Of course, they didn't know what this place had become.

"We get lots of Russian delegations now," she went on. "For them this country is the Golden West. But they eat together, come in and go out together, and rarely talk with any of the hotel staff. It's hard to make contact with them."

It was May Day, and the hotel was crowded with delegations from the DDR's "fraternal" socialist allies. Like every other East German city, Dresden was bedecked with red and white banners bearing such slogans as "Long live the first of May—day of struggle for the international working class." Red, black, and gold DDR flags, with the hammer and compass, hung from every building and lamppost. Even the antique streetcars carried flags and slogans as they creaked along. School children and factory workers had rehearsed for weeks to march in the traditional May Day parade. The East German press and radio had urged the populace to turn out en masse.

"When does the parade begin?" I asked a chambermaid when I came back to our room.

"I don't know."

"But aren't you going?" I insisted.

"No, we don't have to go any more."

My wife and I drove across the river and parked near the reviewing stand set up on a vacant lot along Dresden's main street where a "Socialist House of Culture" is supposed to rise. The parade had already begun, and the stand was filled with SED bigwigs. But along the parade route the crowd was anemicly thin or nonexistent. Looking for a vantage point, we climbed upstairs in one of the Stalinesque apartment houses along Ernst-Thaelmann-Strasse (Dresden's Karl-Marx-Allee). I rang a doorbell and asked the man who answered if we might watch the parade from his balcony. "No, I'm sorry," he said, "we already have the French here." He was referring to the Strasbourg city band that had been invited by the Dresden authorities to attend the May Day festivities.

"But I'm from the American radio," I said. "I'd like to record some of the parade from a point where I can see what's happening."

"Oh, from the American radio," the man answered. "That's very good."

We were ushered in at once. The apartment was small but comfortable. From the small entry hall we passed through a bedroom onto the balcony where the Strasbourg musicians in blue uniforms and band insignia were standing in little groups, obviously bored, puffing Gauloises. It was too crowded to sit down or even stand. Noticing our predicament, a German woman on the next balcony invited us over. She was blond and wore black stretchpants, a pink pullover, a fuzzy beige hat, and white cork wedges. Hardly stylish by Western standards, her clothes indicated that she had far more money than most East Germans. She offered us each a small glass of vermouth and brought out an oilcloth umbrella when it started to rain.

Below us, the day of struggle of the international working class was being celebrated by a truckload of cooks in white chefs' hats who carried a sign proclaiming: "We undertake to help raise labor productivity by careful care of the 18,000 students at the Dresden Technical University." They were followed by five young men bearing a huge red banner saying: "The capitalist monopoly of education has been eliminated."

Actors and stagehands from Dresden's theaters were next. Their float consisted of two large pictures of dramatic performances with a sign reading: "For a socialist picture of man in the heads and hearts of our audiences." Over the loudspeaker the official cheerleader shouted "Hurrah" three times. There was no response. As a group of typewriter-factory workers straggled by, he announced that they had pledged to increase their output "in honor of the first of May."

"Don't photograph the gaps," a man on the next balcony said with a laugh, mistaking my tape recorder for a camera. "There are plenty of them."

I found the gaps more congenial than the nongaps: bored, gray men in cheap nylon raincoats shuffling listlessly past the reviewing stand without wasting a glance on the SED provincial bosses.

"We greet the Chairman of the State Council of the German Democratic Republic and the First Secretary of the Socialist Unity Party of Germany, Comrade Walter Ulbricht!" the cheerleader shouted as two men marched by with the leader's portrait. "Hurrah, hurrah, hurrah!" Silence.

A red-painted beer wagon rolled by with a sign exhorting all to "raise high the banner of Marxism-Leninism." It was followed by about eighty German police dogs, each led by a man in uniform. They made more noise than I had heard all day.

Next to the dogs, the most animated participants in the parade were a group of Arab students carrying their own cheerleader on their shoulders. "Long live the fight of Arab peoples for freedom, democracy, and peace," they shouted in unison. They were followed by a lone Chinese who held Peking's flame-colored banner aloft and said nothing.

The next morning I called on Dresden's most distinguished living citizen, the nuclear physicist Baron Manfred von Ardenne, director of the Manfred von Ardenne Research Institute, member of the DDR "People's Chamber," national prize-winner and inventor of the electron-beam multiple-chamber furnace. Von Ardenne spent ten years in Russia after the war, reportedly working on the atomic bomb. He now occupies a luxurious villa overlooking the Elbe from the Weisser Hirsch quarter of Dresden. A uniformed maid (the only one I ever saw in the DDR) answered the door and showed me into a carpeted drawing room with a magnificent view of the river. In one corner was a grand piano. The latest Zenith shortwave transistor stood on a side table. The empire-period furnishings blended tastefully with the wall hangings.

"The fact that you see me here today means that thousands of other Americans will die," von Ardenne announced dramatically as we shook hands. In his mid-fifties, of medium height, von Ardenne exudes vigor and self-assurance. His ruddy complexion contrasts with the pallor of most East Germans. He wore a hand-tailored suit of imported worsted.

"I should be in Toronto today," he explained, "giving a very important paper on my findings in cancer treatment before the international conference on electron science. But the Allied Travel Board in West Berlin refused to let me go. This means that thousands of cancer sufferers in the United States and elsewhere will die because the advances I would have made known in Toronto will not be known so soon."

Whatever his other faults, the "people's-owned baron," as ordinary East Germans have scoffingly dubbed him, does not suffer from undue modesty. There was little need for me to ask questions. A collection of his scientific papers and a copy of the invitation to attend the Toronto conference were neatly arranged on a marble table in the center of the room.

Von Ardenne is one of the DDR's new elite. The regime rates his work and prestige so highly that he is allowed to express unorthodox views. When the editors of *Die Zeit* of Hamburg complained to him about East Germany's rigged elections, he admitted that the SED could not yet win a genuine majority but predicted that would come. He compared East Germany today with Russia in 1930 when the communists did not dare allow a free vote. "But today," he insisted, "the Soviet government would certainly get an overwhelming majority."

When I asked about the economy, he was highly critical. "Of course, we shouldn't try to manufacture everything," he said. "We should specialize in certain lines where we are good, in the electron-beam multiple-chamber furnace, for example. We already make better steel than Sweden does. But we must now remove twice as much earth to mine a ton of brown coal as we did seven years ago when coal prices were fixed. So we have had to reform the prices of coal and other industrial raw materials. Our planned economy will remain, but under the new system we'll concentrate on fundamentals."

The subject of the Wall came up, as it does in almost every conversation in East Germany. "We had to do it," von Ardenne said briskly. "It's always the same when a state depresses the standard of living in order to industrialize quickly. People prefer the bright lights. But we have other things in mind."

On my way out, I asked von Ardenne if he had children. "Yes, a boy and a girl," he said. I reached in my coat pocket for a bar of the West German chocolate I always used to take as a small gift when I went to East German homes. "Here," I said, handing it to him, "I'm sure you don't need it, but please give this to your children anyway." He looked startled, took the chocolate, and then automatically inclined his head as Germans do when they are thanking anyone. A moment later, I was back in the gray everyday reality of the German Democratic Republic.

While I talked to von Ardenne, my wife set out in search of her midmorning cup of coffee. In West Germany there is a cafe or snack bar on almost every block. In the DDR a stranger could die of hunger before he finds a place to eat. After wandering the tree-lined streets of Weisser Hirsch for almost an hour, my wife finally came on a little confectioner's shop crowded with women drinking black coffee (even cream made from whipped margarine costs half a mark a serving) without pastry. For a German woman, this is like making an American eat a bunless frankfurter. There was pastry in the shop, but it was too expensive and unappetizing to tempt anyone.

After my wife had ordered a cup of mocca (1.50 East marks), she was joined by two elderly Dresden ladies. It is not unusual in East German restaurants to sit with strangers. After scrutinizing my wife intently, one of the ladies asked: "We're wondering what nationality you are." Their faces brightened when they heard the answer. They began plying her with questions. They became even more interested when they heard that we lived in Bonn. One woman said: "I'm over seventy and get a pension, but it's not enough. I have to work in a book bindery. It's not my business. I don't own it. I used to own a hat shop. That was lovely. I sold hats to Americans."

Her companion interrupted: "It was so nice when the Americans and English were here."

As they rose to leave, one of the women said: "I'm going to a movie, but if I'd known I would meet you, I never would have made plans to go. This is wonderful for me." Then, clasping my wife's hand tightly, she said: "Please give my heartfelt greetings to Frankfurt-am-Main." She pronounced the words "am-Main" with special emphasis.

Before the war, Dresden attracted artists from all over the world. Dresdeners liked to call it the "German Florence." Goethe nicknamed it "Europe's balcony." Today, the real artists are gone or in enforced retirement. While I was in Dresden I went to see one of the most talented artists, who must be nameless because he smuggles his paintings and woodcuts to West Germany. He is not allowed to exhibit in the DDR. His work does not conform to the official interpretation of "socialist realism."

"We feel we're living in a ghetto," he told me as we sipped

weak coffee in his attic studio. "My last exhibition was in 1961. The party objected. They tried to kick me out of the artists' union. That failed, but I have no chance to exhibit, and it's hard to make ends meet." He discounted chances for an artistic thaw in East Germany.

"We're not isolated here in the sense of being ignorant of what goes on outside," he said. "We know what's up in West German art, and we don't particularly like it. I dislike experiments for experiments' sake. They do a lot of that over there. I sometimes have the feeling that, artistically, anything goes in West Germany and that the search is for something new at any price."

I asked him what he thought of "socialist Dresden."

"Isn't it a horror?" He sighed. "It's criminal what they've done to this city. It was so beautiful."

On my way back to the hotel, I noticed bushes and even trees protruding from the windows of bombed-out villas in the once-exclusive residential quarter of Johannstadt-Striesen. On Ernst-Thaelmann-Strasse a new Hungarian restaurant was filling up with early diners. In the Altmarkt I glanced up at the rococo cupolas and towers atop massive Stalinist apartment buildings with expensive shops on the ground floor. Fortunately for Dresden, the communists did not begin rebuilding the city until 1953, when the heyday of Soviet neo-classical architecture was past. Apartment houses put up in the early postwar period were not only grotesque-looking; the floor supports were so weak that upper-story tenants could not have large pianos. The newer dwellings are in the functional "unity style," monotonous but more attractive than the barrackslike relics of Stalin's era.

I turned down Pragerstrasse, where they handed out ration-free soup the morning before Dresden died. There are open fields on both sides. I watched a tall gantry crane lifting five-ton concrete blocks into place for the foundation of a new apartment house. Prefabricated sections with toilets and wash-basins already attached waited incongruously to be hoisted into position. By 1970 Pragerstrasse is supposed to become a flourishing "socialist" thoroughfare with skyscraper hotels, a twelve-story apartment house, a large modern cinema, a "super" department store, a tower restaurant, and an elevated garage for the hoped-for traffic of tomorrow. It will be the counterpart of the new Unter den Linden and Alexanderplatz in East Berlin. East Germans call such plans "music of the future."

At the end of Pragerstrasse I turned right, passing the blackened hulk of the main railroad station on my way to the river. On one side there loomed the hollow shell of the old residential palace of the Saxon kings. The Semper Opera House on Theaterplatz was boarded up and forbidding. Across the Elbe I could see another skeletal structure. Before starting over the bridge, I stopped to gaze at the sculptured saints who stand, imperious and melancholy, on the balustrades of the Catholic Hofkirche. For almost two hundred years they have kept vigil over the city. Being stone, they cannot learn to weep.

[9]

Fever in the Bloc

■

"CONDITIONS ARE very different, of course, in a highly industrialized country like the DDR and in a huge, underdeveloped country like the Soviet Union. There it takes a long time for changes to seep down from the top."

The director of Leipzig University's Institute of Marxism-Leninism paused and frowned. It was noon, but little sunlight came through his office windows that winter day in 1964. I peered at him closely to be sure I was not imagining things. Never before had I heard an SED member, let alone one of the party's senior academicians, speak so disparagingly of the Soviet "friends."

"Since the end of 1956," he continued, "we've been getting special information from the Russians on important developments. But they didn't give us enough right after Khrushchev was removed. We couldn't answer questions put to us by our students and others. People here were particularly concerned to know if the campaign against the cult of personality was going to be abandoned."

Nikita Khrushchev was then less than two months in his political grave. And it had already come to this! I realized at that moment that a fundamental change of far-reaching importance was taking place in the minds of the younger East Ger-

man comrades. Cringing servility had been replaced by self-
assertion. The SED would henceforth address the Soviet
Communist Party as an equal, at least in ideological matters.
Fawning on everything Soviet as the most "progressive" and
"advanced" of its kind in the world was out; in its stead had
come a more congenial belief in Teutonic superiority. There
had been signs of more independent thinking in the SED for
some time, but Khrushchev's fall was the turning point. Grievances accumulated during two decades of Soviet imperialism
began to find expression in East German party meetings and
even on public platforms. As one SED member in Rostock told
me, "We no longer take Russia as the model for everything.
We may not say so in public, but you can be sure we say it at
closed meetings."

An example will illustrate the changed relationship between the East German and Soviet parties. In 1960 after one of
his periodic pilgrimages to Moscow, Ulbricht forcibly collectivized East German agriculture in slavish imitation of the Soviet kolkhoz system, which he declared was the only one able
to ensure higher yields. Five years later the SED took a different view of Soviet agriculture. It no longer sought to conceal
the fact that East German yields have always been higher than
those in the Soviet Union. Peter Florin, who handles relations
with the other communist parties for the SED Central Committee, voiced thinly veiled contempt for Soviet kolkhozes in a
public speech late in 1965 to the Soviet-DDR Friendship Society:

> The Soviet Union has not reached world standards in
> all sectors, for example, in agriculture. Our Soviet friends
> have to overcome a series of difficulties in agriculture. . . .
> How can we show our friendship in the realm of agri-
> culture? We have decided to increase our agricultural
> production even faster. We are doing this also in order
> to be able to reduce agricultural imports from the Soviet
> Union. At the same time, we would like to impart to our
> Soviet friends our experiences in agriculture in order to
> enable them with the help of these experiences—together

with their own—to solve their problems more rapidly. . . .
At present the Soviet people are trying to improve the
management of their entire economy. In this context they
are interested in the experiences of the DDR. . . . The
German comrades have worked out many new solu-
tions for complex problems in managing the economy. . . .

Short shrift for the Motherland of Socialism! The East German regime has no intention of reverting to private farm ownership, but it clearly no longer regards Soviet agriculture as the
model. "Of course, our collective farms are far from Russian
kolkhozes," a Leipzig professor assured me. "Our villagers
have running water, television, even cars."

Reverence for Russian models has diminished or disappeared in other fields as well. Despite some setbacks, the development of the DDR's new economic system has been consistently ahead of the Soviet Union. The SED has decided to
introduce flexible industrial prices throughout the economy by
the end of 1966 without waiting for Moscow to set the pace.
Even in art and literature, where the East German comrades
are behind the Soviet party, there is no longer the cult of
everything that comes out of Moscow. On the contrary, Ulbricht has forbidden the publication in German of Solzhenitsyn's prison-camp novel *One Day in the Life of Ivan Denisovich* and even withdrew copies of the book in Russian from
East German bookstores. *Neues Deutschland* upbraided Yev-
tushenko more violently than his Soviet detractors have ever
done. Soviet army units, including one complete division, were
placed under East German command for the first time during
the "October Storm" maneuvers by Warsaw Pact forces in the
fall of 1965. East German forces also played a more prominent
part in these exercises than they have done in any previous war
games staged by the Warsaw Pact states. The DDR's "People's
Army" is no longer content to be a mere appendage to the
Soviet armed forces.

The SED's long-repressed differences with the Soviet comrades have come increasingly to the fore as the post-Khrushchev

Kremlin leadership finds itself yet more deeply embroiled with China, the war in Vietnam, and Russia's own economic difficulties. In one sense, the fall of Khrushchev marked the beginning of the rise of the SED. No single hand seized the scepter in Moscow. Lacking anyone of Khrushchev's stature, the Soviet communists are unable to bring the Eastern European parties to heel. Isolated triumphs, such as the imposition of the long-term trade agreement that prompted Dr. Erich Apel to commit suicide, do not change the basic trend toward more autonomy for the SED and other Eastern European parties. The trade pact, in particular, may prove a pyrrhic victory for Moscow.

The Kremlin's already-waning authority in the communist world has been inherited by a colorless collective leadership whose members are all junior to Ulbricht in length of service to the common cause. It is indicative that the SED was the first Eastern European communist party to comment on Khrushchev's overthrow. A special communique issued by the Politburo on October 18, 1964, praised Khrushchev's merits, expressed "profound emotion" at his removal, implicitly questioned the official Soviet explanation, and pointedly reminded the new Russian leaders of their obligation "honorably" to fulfill the provisions of the DDR-Soviet Friendship Treaty signed in Moscow four months before. It was not for love of Khrushchev that the SED indulged in this surprising display of independence. In fact, the fallen Soviet leader had repeatedly angered and humiliated the East German regime, most recently by sending his son-in-law Alexei Adzhubei, then editor of *Izvestia,* on a junket to West Germany to prepare the way for a visit to Bonn by Khrushchev himself. Adzhubei even had the ill grace to assure the "revanchists" in the Federal Republic that Ulbricht was a lame-duck despot suffering from incurable cancer of the larynx. After its editor returned to Moscow, *Izvestia* spoke nostalgically of the "spirit of Rapallo," conjuring up visions of a Soviet-West German reconciliation among the SED faithful. The SED press reacted by censoring accounts of Adzhubei's trip.

As Ulbricht later told the SED Central Committee: "We did not lose our heads . . . during the hostile campaign launched on the occasion of Adzhubei's visit to West Germany and remained calm despite the slanders which arose at that time." Ulbricht is used to capitalist slanders; he was alluding to slanders from his own side, specifically from Adzhubei himself.

The SED has ample reason, in fact, to remember Khrushchev unkindly. But Ulbricht chose to project himself in the role of a senior communist statesman by recalling the fallen leader's services to Marxism-Leninism and by taking a coolly detached view of the differences in the Kremlin. In his cable to Leonid Brezhnev, congratulating him on becoming First Secretary of the Soviet Communist Party, Ulbricht pointedly recalled the understandings they had reached a week earlier when Brezhnev was in Berlin for the DDR's fifteenth anniversary. In a similar congratulatory message to Kosygin, Willi Stoph reminded him of Moscow's obligations under the DDR-Soviet Friendship Treaty concluded the previous June. The SED leaders wanted to make clear they expected the new Soviet leadership to fulfill its commitments to East Germany.

In the months that followed Khrushchev's overthrow the pinpricks from East Berlin grew sharper. Ulbricht boasted that the SED had not carried out "a single one" of Khrushchev's agricultural proposals. With evident satisfaction, *Neues Deutschland* declared: "In the DDR we have not adopted those forms and metods of managing according to the production principle which were applied in the Soviet Union until the decisions of the [post-Khrushchev] November CPSU plenum." It is a fact that the SED never split itself from top to bottom into agricultural and industrial branches, as Khrushchev had done with the Soviet party. Therefore, the East German party announced that there would be no structural reorganization following Khrushchev's departure. However, in December 1965 the SED did abolish the National Economic Council and re-established industrial ministries along Soviet lines.

The liquidation of the cult of Khrushchev's personality in the DDR proceeded almost as casually after October 1964 as Ulbricht's brand of de-Stalinization had in earlier years. Khrushchev's pictures were removed before too long, but collections of his speeches remained in East German bookstores long after they had disappeared in Moscow. On the other hand, the SED showed distaste for the Soviet device of denouncing Khrushchev's errors without naming their perpetrator. The East German press bluntly named Khrushchev in its first commentaries on the reasons for his dismissal. The upshot was that the SED looked more self-assured than its big brother in Moscow. Four months after Khrushchev was ousted, Erich Honecker told a self-congratulatory session of the SED Central Committee: "Even our enemies . . . have had to admit that the SED and Ulbricht have emerged from the aforementioned events [Khrushchev's removal] not weakened but strengthened."

While Khrushchev held sway, the SED had often outdone the Soviet party in reviling the Chinese "dogmatists." With the advent of a new collective leadership in the Kremlin, however, Ulbricht began preaching reconciliation to the disputants in the communist world, as if he had never taken sides in the first place. This was of course the line followed for almost a year by Khrushchev's successors, but Ulbricht went to special pains to appear to be standing above the fray. Although he reluctantly resumed attacks on the Chinese late in 1965, it was clear that his services in communism's great schism were no longer to be had for the asking. When communist leaders, including Chou En-lai, gathered in Moscow in November 1964, as Ulbricht told the story later, "We deemed it necessary in our talks with representatives of the fraternal parties to intercede in favor of a normalization of relations." He boasted that the SED had actually stopped polemics against Peking a fortnight before Khrushchev fell, perhaps because Ulbricht had advance word of the change. Like other communist leaders, Ulbricht is exploiting the Sino-Soviet conflict to give himself more room to maneuver.

Ruling one of the most vulnerable states in the communist

world, the SED has reason to deplore internecine feuds among "fraternal" parties. But the longer Moscow and Peking contend for supremacy, the higher the price either side will have to pay for the East German comrades' support.

As part of his tactic of communist statesmanship, Ulbricht has shown unexpected sympathy for the radically reformist ideas of the late Palmiro Togliatti. Soon after the Italian communist leader's testament had been published in *Neues Deutschland,* I asked a prominent SED ideologist if he thought Togliatti's ideas could be applied in East Germany.

"I would put it the other way around," he replied agilely. "What did Togliatti adopt from our practice? For example, in relations between church and state, we never carried on overtly atheistic propaganda as the Soviet Union and some other socialist countries did. Here we've always had a multiparty system; not the one-party system Togliatti criticized. We made the transition from the dictatorship of the proletariat to socialist democracy in fifteen years, whereas it took the Russians some forty years. In fact, we have been able to take over very little from Soviet experience in building socialism."

These statements are half-truths at best. The East German churches were under severe pressure from the regime during the first postwar decade. Not until 1964 did the last East German pastor emerge from prison. Even today the churches are under rigid political control. The DDR's multiparty system matters little, since the SED makes all important decisions. "Socialist democracy" implies an end to class warfare, but the pressure on individual dissenters in the DDR is undiminished.

If the specious arguments by which the SED tries to identify itself with Togliatti are disregarded, it is plain that the East German party is trying to use his testament as another yardstick to measure its superiority to the Soviet communists. The German comrades have waited a long time for their chance. They have known little but humiliation at the hands of the Kremlin since the KPD was founded at the end of the First World War. In those days, the Comintern goaded the fledgling German party to pursue a suicidal policy of revolutionary vio-

lence. Lenin postulated a communist victory in Germany as
the precondition for successful revolution everywhere. As
Carola Stern has pointed out, defeat fostered a guilt complex
among the German communists, which Moscow sought to
exacerbate for its own purposes. When Hitler came to power
in 1933, the KPD was the largest Comintern section after the
Soviet party itself, but its 300,000 members proved powerless
to stop the Nazis. The degradation of German communism had
reached a new low.

When the Red Army entered Germany in 1945, men
brutalized by years of continuous fighting raped and robbed
without distinguishing between pro-communist and anti-
communist Germans. The German party was obliged to assist
in the systematic plunder called "reparations." West German
authorities estimate that the Russians extracted about 70 billion marks from their occupation zone in the decade following
the war. Through reparations alone, each man, woman, and
child in East Germany was saddled with a debt equivalent to
6,712 marks compared with a per capita burden of 35 marks in
the Western occupation zones. Confiscated German plants
were dismantled and shipped to Russia or turned into Soviet
trust companies to ensure a steady flow of reparations from
current production. When the Soviet companies were dissolved, their assets were sold back to the East German regime
at inflated prices. Ulbricht said nothing about Soviet exploitation of East Germany until February 1964, when he told the
SED Central Committee that Stalin's "theories and especially
his practice" had hindered the DDR's economic development
and made it impossible to introduce the new economic system
until after the Wall went up.

What Ulbricht has called "the greatest long-term agreement," signed by Soviet and East German negotiators after
Erich Apel's suicide on December 3, 1965, ensures that Moscow can continue exploiting the DDR economy at least until
1970. Some of Ulbricht's lieutenants have been more candid
than their chief about the trade pact. The DDR's Foreign
Trade Minister told reporters at the 1966 spring Leipzig fair

that "mutual advantage" must be taken into account in evaluating Soviet-East German trade relations. Another Trade Ministry official told Philip Shabecoff of *The New York Times:* "The terms are considered correct. . . . Besides, nobody among the capitalist nations has offered us any better terms." The new element in this situation is that SED members now openly express their resentment at Soviet exploitation.

The refusal of Kremlin leaders to make good on their threats to sign a separate peace treaty with the DDR probably rankles as deeply with the SED as the Russians' economic extortion. Such a treaty would have given the East Germans control over Allied access to West Berlin. It would have been the first step toward realizing the SED's dream of squeezing the Western powers out of Berlin and imposing communist rule on the whole city. Unwilling to risk a collision between the East Germans and the Allies, the Kremlin has steadfastly refused to renew Khrushchev's ultimatum to sign a separate treaty.

Three days before he settled for building a wall through Berlin, Ulbricht was still demanding a peace treaty: "To put off a peace treaty would almost certainly lead the German people to slip into a new war catastrophe. . . . It is the national duty of the German working class to conclude the peace treaty today, not tomorrow or the day after. . . . That must happen now. It is high time!"

That was on August 10, 1961. Ulbricht is still waiting for a treaty. He is not likely to see one in his lifetime. Even the most ductile mind in the SED must have trouble reconciling Soviet promises with Soviet performance in this department. The much publicized Treaty of Friendship, Mutual Assistance, and Cooperation signed on June 12, 1964, by Khrushchev and Ulbricht in Moscow is no substitute for a separate peace treaty. It speaks only of "a German peace treaty," ignoring the idea of a separate covenant with the DDR. Ulbricht now insists he never wanted a Soviet-DDR peace treaty, but SED memories are not so short. The 1964 Friendship Treaty defines West Berlin as "an independent political entity," without reference to Khrushchev's plan for making it a "free, demilitarized city" or to the SED's oft-repeated claim that West Berlin "lies on the territory of the DDR."

Although Moscow professes to uphold the East German party's contention that Germany consists of three states—the DDR, West Germany, and the "illegal enclave" of West Berlin —it has done little to dissuade its Eastern European allies from signing trade agreements with Bonn that include West Berlin as well as West Germany. The SED has repeatedly charged that such agreements undermine the DDR's security by strengthening Bonn's claim to speak for West Berlin. When the West German Bundestag announced that it would hold a special plenary session in the new Kongresskalle in West Berlin in April 1965 (despite Allied reservations), the SED called on Moscow to take strong measures. The Russians reacted with a perfunctory protest note to the three Western Allies. At SED meetings throughout the DDR there were angry charges of "another Soviet sellout." Under intense East German pressure, Khrushchev's successors finally agreed to impose a partial blockade of Allied military traffic on the Berlin autobahn and to send jets to buzz West Berlin while the Bundestag was in session there. The SED had already ordered a slowdown of West German and West Berlin vehicles on the autobahn. During the Bundestag session, East German military helicopters overflew West Berlin for the first time, ignoring the four-power Air Safety Center. The flights were repeated in the next few days in a gesture clearly aimed to show that the SED could wage its own war of nerves against West Berlin.

Two months before the Bundestag session in West Berlin, I covered Kosygin's first visit to East Berlin as Premier of the Soviet Union. Snow blanketed the ground, but the weather was mild compared with the frigid official reception given the Russian leader. No banners proclaimed the strength of Soviet-DDR friendship; no pictures of the visitor adorned East Berlin's thoroughfares; and no crowds were brought out to acclaim his arrival. In fact, Kosygin arrived almost surreptitiously. He was whisked from place to place in East Berlin with a minimum of security and no fanfare. His dour countenance seemed to reflect his reaction to what seemed a calculated snub by his hosts. In May that year Kosygin returned to East Berlin for celebrations of the twentieth anniversary of Germany's "liberation" by the Red Army. This time he was accorded the protocol courtesies, including a motorcade into the city, but the East German press played down his visit. It was clear that the SED had no intention of prostrating itself before the latest Chairman of the Soviet Council of Ministers. It may have wanted to remind him, as René Bayer later wrote in *Die Zeit*, that "in all questions except those affecting the East bloc's military security, Ulbricht has more power in East Germany than Kosygin has in Russia." The SED is now bent on ostentatious display of its equality in the communist camp.

Moscow's embarrassments in Asia have distracted Soviet attention from Europe, enabling the East German party to pursue its own interests more openly. Like all other Warsaw Pact members except Hungary and Bulgaria, the DDR has felt free to ignore Moscow's example in offering to send volunteers to Vietnam. Since the ambitious Otto Winzer succeeded the late Dr. Lothar Bolz as Foreign Minister in 1965, there has been a notable quickening of the DDR's diplomatic activity, including the DDR's first formal bid for admission to the United Nations, presented by Poland in March 1966. The application came to naught but it reflected the East German regime's stepped-up drive for international recognition.

Despite the changing character of relations between Moscow and East Berlin, the SED is still in no position to defy the Russians on a crucial issue. The DDR is a rump state obliged to import more than 95 percent of its raw materials and more than one third of its grain needs. Russia supplies 94 percent of East Germany's oil needs and almost the entire grain deficit (except when the Soviet harvest fails) as well as the bulk of other imported primary products. The DDR has little hope of ever becoming self-sufficient in food and no hope of developing an adequate raw-material base of its own. East Germany accounts for 23 percent of Soviet foreign trade, but the Soviet Union accounts for more than half of East Germany's external commerce. The five-year trade agreement signed in December 1965 ties the DDR more closely than ever to the Kremlin's coattails. By 1970 the East Germans must sharply increase their deliveries of chemicals, precision instruments, vehicles, and industrial plant and equipment to pay for much larger imports of Soviet rolled steel, aluminum, lead, copper, zinc, and capital goods as well as a continued inflow of Russian crude oil, iron ore, and grain. Even exploration for offshore oil along East Germany's Baltic coast is being conducted jointly with Soviet engineers. The DDR is particularly vulnerable to Soviet economic pressure because, unlike Rumania, it has no highly saleable export commodity with which it can earn foreign exchange in the West.

If East Germany is vulnerable economically, it is defenseless militarily. The strength of Russian forces in the country was reduced slightly in 1964–5, but some twenty divisions—more than a quarter of a million men—are still deployed throughout the DDR. There are Russian encampments outside every important East German city. Their presence is always denoted by small signs in English, French, and German announcing that the area is closed to photographers and to members of the Allied military missions who are still allowed to operate out of Potsdam. Even without the telltale signs, the Soviet camps are immediately recognizable by their unpainted, tumble-down picket fences and the paper or cardboard used to plug barracks windows. Every installation is encircled by wooden watchtowers, barbed wire, and searchlights, reminiscent of a concentration camp. But the inmates of these dreary hutments are surprisingly well turned out these days. Russian soldiers wear clean, well-pressed uniforms and shiny boots. For them, East Germany is an economic wonderland. Most Russian soldiers I have seen in the DDR have been polite and well behaved, although I have watched several drink themselves into a stupor to forget the loneliness and isolation of garrison life in a foreign land. Few of them speak German, and fewer still have pocket money for more than an occasional beer. Although there is much talk about "fraternal relations," Russians and East Germans have practically no social contacts. An East German museum director who shares the former Nazi concentration camp at Ravensbrück with a Russian garrison has never set foot in the commandant's office or in any other part of the area used by the "friends," as SED members are supposed to refer to the Russians. An SED member in Rostock told me that he has no contact with Russians except on the anniversary of the Bolshevik Revolution when he goes with a delegation to present a bouquet of flowers to the local Soviet consul.

Russian troops in Poland cannot move outside their bases without the Polish government's permission. In the DDR such movements are merely the subject of "consultations" between the Soviet and DDR authorities. The Russians also seem to have effective control over the deployment of East German ground and air units. They are usually kept well back from the East-West German border. U. S. Air Force planes that have strayed over DDR airspace invariably meet Soviet, not East German, fighters.

If all political power grew out of the barrel of a gun, as Mao Tse-tung contends, the Russians would be all-powerful in East Germany. The ultimate sanction of force is theirs. But ultimate sanctions are not useful in every situation, as the United States found out when it sought to rely on the doctrine of "massive retaliation." In East Germany, as elsewhere, the political pendulum swings through a wide arc before it is stopped by the barrel of a gun. If the character of change in East Germany today were violent, it would certainly meet a violent Soviet response. But the muted revolution going on between the Elbe and the Oder cannot be suppressed by tanks, as the June 17 uprising was. An evolutionary transformation is taking place within the SED, Moscow's chosen instrument for ruling the DDR. German communism is becoming cautiously German. The Russians cannot halt this change by bombarding SED headquarters or even by sending troops to seize the trouble-makers. Any such Soviet reaction would kill the SED as well as the dissidents. It would also smash the carefully nurtured image of the Soviet party as the first among equals in a fraternity of Marxist-Leninists. The Kremlin would pay this exorbitant price if the SED were about to surrender the DDR to the decision of the East Geman electorate, but the East German comrades have no such suicidal tendencies. Even the most nationalist-minded member of the party is not fighting to liquidate the "workers' and peasants' power" that gives the SED a permanent lease on the government of the DDR. East German communists are becoming more German, but they remain communists. So long as the DDR evolves within the framework of the Soviet system, Soviet military power cannot be readily applied to determine the character of change. Rumania, a country bordering directly on the Soviet Union and completely surrounded by communist states, is a striking example of how a self-willed communist regime can defy the Kremlin and get away with it.

"After all," Ulbricht once told the SED, "we are not alone." In fact, he and the rest of the SED's old guard are increasingly isolated. The DDR is now buffeted by strong winds blowing from other Eastern European countries and from Russia itself. As a Radio Free Europe study puts it, "The dull gray blanket has become the patchwork quilt." Echoing Ulbricht's suspicions, Politburo Candidate Member Horst Sindermann lashed out in February 1964 against "theories of spring" being propounded by revisionist Czech intellectuals. He declared: "We are filled with extreme mistrust of people who come up with a 'new' Marxism. . . . Our party is hardened in battle. . . . Such a party will not allow rotten eggs to be placed in its basket." Sindermann's diatribe could just as well have been directed at Nikita Khrushchev, the man who opened the door to the revisionist plague by trying to de-Stalinize the Soviet empire.

A year after the SED had denounced "rotten eggs," it found them still littering its basket. The East German intellectuals unabashedly continued to import fresh ideas from neighboring communist states. At the same time, the "fraternal" regimes in Prague, Warsaw, and other Eastern European capitals ignored SED warnings about the dangers of flirting with Bonn.

Poland was the first communist state in Eastern Europe to break the taboo on signing a trade agreement with Bonn which also included West Berlin. A West German trade mission opened in Warsaw in March 1963. On a visit to Poland later that year Ulbricht was his usual tactless self: "When the West German militarists talk about commercial relations with Poland, they have in mind the tearing of Poland from the rest of the socialist camp." The SED's theoretical monthly *Einheit* (Unity) warned that Bonn was threatening bloc countries with "economic blackmail, political pressure, and ideological subversion." All the unwanted advice was ignored. Poland even seemed to enjoy its peril and began negotiating with Krupp and several other West German firms on agreements for jointly owned factories in Poland to produce for European and overseas markets. Premature publicity as well as the ideological scruples of the older Polish communists scuttled these efforts, but in September 1965 a joint trading company was set up to organize cooperation between Polish and West German plants in planning, production, and sales of construction machinery and food-processing equipment. The company is controlled by a Polish state trading agency. A Frankfurt mail-order house is now advertising Polish motor scooters in the Federal Republic under an arrangement that may make possible the sale of low- and medium-priced West German cars in Poland.

While Poland cultivates economic ties with West Germany, its commercial relations with the DDR remain unsatisfactory. Poland incurred a deficit of more than 71 million dollars in 1965 on trade with the East Germans, whose total volume was just over 400 million dollars. The wily Poles make up some of the gap by imposing heavy transit charges on Soviet-East German trade conducted across Poland.

The East Germans retaliate by making Poland route its oil shipments to West Berlin via Helmstedt, 110 miles to the west on the East-West German border. East Germany is ready to accept payment for its exports to Poland in the form of more Polish coal and coke, but Warsaw prefers to sell in the West. The East Germans consider themselves ill-requited for the long term loan they made in the late fifties to enable Poland to modernize her coal industry. "We warned them against relying on Western markets," an SED economist told me, "but they went ahead and expanded to meet Western European demand. Now that has dried up, and the Poles are in trouble. They have serious unemployment and lots of idle capacity. But we're not going to bail them out again."

The SED could overlook Poland's pursuit of trade with the West if the Poles would at least hold the ideological front. The "Polish October" in 1956 ruled that out. The following year the leader of reformist East German intellectuals, Wolfgang Harich, was charged with having obtained support from "Polish circles." Some of his accomplices were accused of planning to flee to Poland "to propagate the aims of the group from there." At closed SED meetings Ulbricht bitterly reproached Gomulka for opening the floodgates to revisionism.

In February 1958 another SED heretic, Politburo member Karl Schirdewan, was accused of advocating the use of the "safety-valve technique" used in Poland and Hungary during the high tide of de-Stalinization. The Polish regime has now reverted to a more orthodox ideological line, but the DDR still keeps its intellectual traffic with Warsaw to a minimum. "We know so little about each other," a theater critic in *Neues Deutschland* lamented, "hardly more than that there exists a yearly cultural agreement. How far is it after all from Berlin to Warsaw?"

The distance might be reckoned in light-years. Poles dislike Russians, but they abhor Germans—East or West. When Ulbricht paid a long-delayed state visit to Warsaw in 1963, he rode through streets lined by silent crowds. He returned the compliment by devoting a third of his farewell speech to the glories of the DDR's collectivized agriculture, a system abandoned seven years earlier in Poland. Ulbricht neglected to mention the privately grown Polish potatoes that saved East Germany from an acute post-collectivization potato shortage in 1962. When the potato famine was over, the SED sent Karl Mewis, the apostle of agricultural collectivization and former Chairman of the State Planning Commission, as DDR ambassador to Warsaw. The Polish government kept him waiting a month before accepting his credentials.

Poland and the DDR are supposed to be united in defending what the communists call the "frontier of peace" on the Oder-Neisse line. The East German regime says it has accepted the loss of the German territories east of the Oder-Neisse, but the Poles have not forgotten the late Wilhelm Pieck's remark on the subject in October 1946: "We will do everything to see to it that the Allies review the frontier question and carry out a serious rectification of the present eastern border." The present West German government takes approximately the same stand as Pieck did then. It argues that Germany's 1937 boundaries are legally valid until they are defined in a peace settlement.

When Foreign Secretary Michael Stewart of Britain was in Warsaw in September 1965, his Polish counterpart, Rapacki, told him that Poland was not opposed to German reunification "in principle" but feared that "old expansionistic tendencies" prevalent in West Germany might spread to the DDR.

When I visited the "frontier of peace" at Wilhelm-Pieck-Stadt (formerly Guben) on the Neisse, I found armed East German and Polish guards staring at one another across a deserted bridge over the river that marks the boundary in that area. "They're friends over there," a young East German soldier told me with a smile, but the atmosphere hardly bore out his words. Like all the DDR's other frontiers, "the frontier of peace" is closed. It will stay closed so long as the Poles refuse to extradite East German refugees, including some of the DDR's most talented painters.

Czechoslovakia is the only communist state that borders

on both East and West Germany. For a long time the Czechs steadfastly ignored the Federal Republic. Since the mid-sixties they have been increasingly interested in developing trade and other relations with Bonn, even at the expense of their "fraternal" ties to the DDR. In September 1965 a high Prague official said that Czechoslovakia desired normal relations with West Germany "more than with any other European country." The stumbling block is Bonn's refusal to declare the Munich Pact, by which Hitler extorted the Sudetenland from Czechoslovakia, legally null and void. Chancellor Erhard's assurances that his government has no territorial claims on Czechoslovakia have not satisfied the Prague regime. Czech fears of German "revanchism" have been fed by Bonn's demagogic Transport Minister, Hans-Christoph Seebohm, leader of the Sudeten German expellees, who once proclaimed: "Home to the Sudetenland without Czechs or communists!"

Resentful of Bonn's attitude on the Munich Pact and reluctant to alienate the DDR, Czechoslovakia has so far refused to sign a trade agreement in which the Federal Republic would be allowed to speak for West Berlin. Nevertheless, even without a formal agreement, West Germany has already supplanted Britain as Czechoslovakia's main Western trade partner, and West German tourists are flocking to Prague and Brno in ever larger numbers. Lufthansa, the West German airline, opened its first regular service to any Soviet bloc country with a flight to Prague in April 1966. Krupp's Bertold Beitz is a welcome guest at Czech trade fairs and the Prague radio recently broadcast a glowing appreciation of his firm, which the DDR still depicts as the most notorious purveyor of death.

Despite these differences, Czechoslovakia and East Germany share the misfortune of being the two perennial food importers in Comecon, the Soviet bloc economic cooperation organization, whose difficulties are compounded by the fact that Poland, Bulgaria, Hungary, and Rumania, the bloc's food exporters, are far more interested in earning hard capitalist currency than in aiding their socialist allies. When the Soviet grain harvest falls short, as it does with depressing frequency, the Czechs and East Germans must disgorge their own small reserve of foreign exchange to import food from capitalist producers. With some reason, therefore, they regard themselves as the aggrieved members of Comecon and often present a united front at meetings of the organization.

Food is by no means the only reason for coolness between the SED and the Rumanian regime. When Moscow still hoped to subjugate the Rumanians in an integrated Comecon, Ulbricht denounced the renegades in Bucharest for insisting on having their own heavy industry and upbraided the late Gheorghiu-Dej for buying capital goods in the West instead of in the DDR and other bloc countries. SED economists were commissioned to produce learned articles proving that Rumania was violating the "socialist division of labor." The Rumanians evened the score by exchanging trade missions with Bonn in December 1963 after signing the now classic trade agreement with West Germany, including West Berlin. Ulbricht assailed Bonn's "double-dealing policy" at the Rumanian party congress in July 1965, but Bucharest continued to patronize Ruhr suppliers. West Germany is now Rumania's second largest trading partner (after Russia). A further increase in exchanges was foreshadowed by the Rumanian foreign trade minister's visit to Bonn in May 1966. The same month the Rumanians granted consular status to the West German mission in Bucharest in exchange for similar privileges accorded the Rumanian trade office in Frankfurt. At a Warsaw Pact meeting, Moscow, June 1966 Rumania's foreign minister reportedly refused to sign a statement branding Bonn a "troublemaker" despite charges of "treason" from his DDR colleague.

The DDR has inherited little of Germany's traditional prestige in Hungary and Bulgaria. Both countries are "fraternal socialist allies," and both offer natural markets for East German goods, but neither has shown any particular desire to develop its relations with the "first German peace state." On the contrary, Hungary and Bulgaria have each signed trade agreements with Bonn incorporating the infamous Berlin clause and have exchanged trade missions with the Federal

Republic. Under a supplementary agreement signed in November 1965, Hungarian trade with West Germany was due to
rise twenty percent to a volume of 150 million dollars the
following year. Hungary also signed an agreement with Krupp
for the production of machine-tools designed jointly by Krupp
and Hungarian engineers. The Hungarians are already co-
operating industrially with the West German Rheinstahl company and negotiating with other Ruhr concerns.

The "Intermetal" project, formed in July 1964 for joint
administration of steel-rolling plants in Hungary, Czechoslovakia, and Poland, notably omitted the DDR, one of the bloc's
main metal producers, at the inception of the scheme.

Far worse, from the SED's viewpoint, was Kadar's
dictum: "Who is not against us is with us." Budapest has been
a much livelier place than East Berlin for many years now.
The Hungarians have also tactlessly underscored the Wall's
grotesqueness by removing some mines and other barriers
along their border with Austria. So far as Ulbricht is concerned, there are at least as many rotten eggs in Budapest as in
Prague.

Sofia is the nearest thing to an ideological refuge the SED
chief would find in the Soviet bloc today, but even there the
atmosphere would not be completely congenial. West Germany is now Bulgaria's main trading partner in the capitalist
world, and Todor Zhivkov, the local party boss, talks enthusi-
astically about "mixed ventures" with Western concerns to
develop Bulgaria's manganese and other resources. More Bulgarian fruits and vegetables, sorely needed in the DDR, will be
winding up in West German markets under an agreement to
boost trade between Bonn and Sofia by more than thirty percent over the 1964 level. West German firms are already making deep inroads in working out cooperation agreements with
the Bulgarians.

It is notable that although Brezhnev had set the stage at
the Twenty-third Soviet Communist Party Congress in the
spring of 1966 with a vicious attack on "Bonn revanchists," the
Rumanian, Hungarian, and Bulgarian party chiefs ignored the

subject and Novotny, the Czech boss, devoted only one sentence to criticizing the Federal Republic's foreign policy.

Such, in outline, is the picture of Eastern Europe and the Soviet Union that one might get from the top floor of the DDR State Council building in East Berlin. It mocks the Stalinists as well as the reformers. It is a study in political decomposition. A generation after the triumph of the Red Army, Eastern Europe is subject to more severe nationalist chills and fevers than at any time since the breakup of the Austro-Hungarian Empire. Ideological loyalties are thrown overboard in the unrestrained pursuit of hard currency and good bargains. New socialist man behaves like old capitalist man. The DDR is not immune to these currents. An embryonic nationalism is being spawned in East Germany. Old feelings of Germanic superiority are already evident in what one analyst calls "the posture of the prescient, ever-correct party leadership" now assumed by the SED. As befits Germans, the party is gradually transforming itself from a malleable instrument of Soviet policy into an assertive mentor of the entire bloc, including the Motherland of Socialism. The DDR still lacks the power to drive its lessons home, but Germans have a way of accreting power.

[10]

Two Minds,
Two States

■

DAWN CAME SLUGGISHLY over central Germany on
November 2, 1964. At Helmstedt on the East-West German
border it rained during the night, and the Red Cross women
shivered as they brewed big kettles of coffee in tents set up on
the station platform. The tents also sheltered nurses, first-aid
medical equipment, and stretchers. Black-uniformed railway
police stood among a milling throng on the platform. Some
women wept quietly. Everyone kept peering anxiously down
the tracks that disappeared in the morning mist to the east. A
stranger might have supposed that the Helmstedt station was
about to receive the victims of a major disaster. He would
probably not have suspected that the disaster had taken place
almost a generation before when Germany was divided.

The train that Helmstedt waited for that morning was
nothing unusual. Its hoary steam locomotive pulled half a
dozen decrepit passenger cars. The same train had been passing through Helmstedt for years. But that morning the passengers were different; they were all elderly East German

pensioners—men over sixty-five and women over sixty—fore-
runners of the first large-scale migration permitted from the
German Democratic Republic since the building of the Wall
more than three years before.

"Welcome to the Federal Republic of Germany," a loudspeaker blared as the train ground to a halt and the crowd on
the platform surged forward.

"Welcome to our fellow countrymen from the Zone," the
voice continued. Red Cross workers handed out coffee and
cigarettes to the travelers. Nurses attended those in distress.
Reporters and cameramen clambered onto the cars or shoul-
dered their way through the crowd to record tearful reunions.
Some of those who had waited on the platform were lucky;
they found their relatives. Others dashed from car to car, scan-
ning every face they saw.

The train's occupants surveyed the scene with mingled
awe and bewilderment. It was as if the Walpurgis Night were
being enacted before them. They were accustomed to the hush
that pervades a communist country; now their pallid faces
twitched with excitement.

A whistle blew. The train lurched forward, carrying its
passengers deeper into a strange new world.

Today the pensioners arrive without fanfare. They have
become another commonplace in an uncommon situation. But
each trainload of East Germans that reaches the West testifies
to the fact that Germany is now two minds as well as two
states. The divided country has a divided conscience. It is not
primarily ideology or political loyalty that divides Germans.
Time and circumstances have produced two societies, two
ways of life, two Teutonic worlds. Both societies speak German, but the words no longer mean the same things. Each way
of life professes to glorify man, but each defines him in its own
terms. A magnetic field still exists between the two German
worlds, but they are now in different orbits.

The communists believe time is on their side. Prolonged
separation becomes estrangement. The West is striving to pre-

serve the human ties between the two German states without
giving them a new political sanction. The result is ambivalence.

Since 1949 the federal German government has concluded
more than 150 separate agreements with a state whose legal
existence it continues to deny. West German editors are en-
joined to use the expression "Soviet Occupation Zone" or "Central Germany" (implying that the Oder-Neisse territories are
really Eastern Germany) whenever they refer to the DDR.
Audacious spirits who use the initials DDR must enclose them
in cushioning quotation marks or justify themselves to Bonn's
Ministry of All-German Affairs. When the *Frankfurter Rundschau* headlined "DDR Wins World Handball Championship"
on a story from Switzerland, the ministry sent a letter to in-
form the paper that "legally as well as according to the political will of the German people there is no state called the
'DDR.'" With the letter came a brochure entitled "Instructions
on Nomenclature of Territories and Delineation of German
Frontiers in Maps and Texts," including a section on how to
refer to places in the former German overseas colonies. Dr.
Rainer Barzel, the majority leader in the Bundestag, once
argued for half an hour on television that the West was losing
ground to the communists because people forgot to call East
Germany the "Soviet Occupation Zone." In fact, the term
"Zone" has become anathema to East Germans. "We're fed up
with being referred to as the 'Zone' twenty years after the
war," an anti-communist Dresdener told me. "This is a state,
whether you like it or not." Ritual use of the phrase "Soviet
Occupation Zone" in Western broadcasts to the DDR induces
a feeling of ghettolike isolation in East Germans. Enlightened
West German newspapers like *Die Zeit* of Hamburg are no
longer afraid to call the DDR by its name, but the politicians
still cling to the old nomenclature.

While the bureaucrats in Bonn quibble over names, the
DDR has succeeded in establishing official representation in 34
countries, signing 900 international treaties and agreements,
and joining more than 200 international organizations. More

than 100 countries now import goods marked "Made in DDR." Forty-eight countries have signed formal trade agreements with the East German regime.

The Federal Republic government, however, still boasts that it returns any official communication from the DDR unopened. More than once, however, West German officials have made the mistake of commenting on the contents of allegedly unopened letters from East Berlin before they were published by the East Germans. Presumably, the only federal office authorized to peek at missives from the other side is the special department in West Berlin responsible for negotiating "interzonal" trade agreements. Even invitations to international conferences are subject to being pigeonholed if there is a chance that DDR representatives will be present. Every year the West German Transport Ministry politely turns down an invitation to the annual conference of the European Railway Federation because the DDR is also invited. But every year the story ends happily. Both German states are represented at the conference. West German transport officials sit behind a nameplate inscribed "German Federal Railways." The East Germans' sign says "German Reich Railways." The trains still run on time in both countries.

The DDR has been a member of the League of Red Cross Societies since 1954, but since West Germans are not supposed to sit at the same table with DDR emissaries, the Red Cross roster lists Germany twice, once with "Federal Republic" in parentheses, once with "Democratic Republic" in parentheses. In Moscow, Cairo, New Delhi, and other capitals where both German states are officially represented, the West Germans go to elaborate lengths to avoid running into DDR emissaries. Even the Russians seem affected by this antic behavior; they tactfully kept Ulbricht and his retinue out of Moscow in September 1965 while Rolf Carstens, Bonn's Deputy Foreign Minister, was holding talks with Soviet officials. When East Germany was allowed to sign the Partial Nuclear Test Ban Treaty in 1963, the federal government agonized for weeks over its own adherence to a treaty that seemingly put the **two**

German states on a par. Before the great debate began, Foreign Minister Gerhard Schroeder rashly assured an interviewer that Bonn would sign the test ban treaty without delay. He almost lost his cabinet seat in the ensuing furor. By the time Bonn finally made up its mind to sign, it had succeeded in emphasizing the DDR's importance more effectively than Ulbricht could possibly have done. The West Germans themselves brought about the dreaded *Aufwertung* (upgrading or enhancement) of the DDR that they had striven to avert.

The fiction that government representatives of the two German states never sit at the same table or affix their signatures to the same document was threadbare long before the Partial Nuclear Test Ban Treaty. Since 1950 when officials of the two sides first met to work out what Bonn calls "interzonal" trade agreements, the value of goods exchanged between East and West Germany has risen eightfold to the present rate of 625 million dollars a year, more than the DDR's trade with all other members of the Common Market and the European Free Trade Association combined. To facilitate trade and win political concessions, Bonn has repeatedly extended credit to East Germany, guaranteed premium prices for DDR agricultural products, and authorized tax-free imports of DDR synthetic fuel oil. Major Ruhr firms are again exhibiting their products at the Leipzig fairs. The NSU motor works has awarded a license to the state-owned East German automobile trust to build the Wankel rotating combustion engine developed by NSU and the Wankel Company in West Germany. West German businessmen flock to Weimar for the annual "economic colloquium" organized by the East Germans. Their interest is understandable. As one of the largest West German banks reported to its clients in October 1965, "The white spot on our political map turns out, from the economic viewpoint, to be an area that has gained a front-ranking place among world exporters."

Bonn takes a different stand when other countries, especially its NATO allies, show commercial interest in the DDR.

The federal government has protested the presence of East German trade representatives in London and Paris and regularly complains when British or French parliamentarians visit the Leipzig fair. In 1965 when American firms were again authorized to exhibit at Leipzig, Bonn clucked loudly. It also objected when two American companies received Department of Commerce permission to sell synthetic-fiber manufacturing equipment and technology to the East Germans. Rainer Barzel has urged West Germany's allies to impose an economic boycott against the DDR while Bonn continues increasing "interzonal" trade. Bonn argues that if it is the DDR's only Western supplier, it can extract political concessions from Ulbricht by cutting off deliveries of West German goods, as it did in the fall of 1960 in retaliation for restrictions on freedom of movement from West Berlin. This doctrine is invalidated by the fact that East Germany now does less than nine percent of its foreign trade with West Germany, compared with sixteen percent a few years ago. Bonn's economic leverage is now almost nil. When I visited the Schwarze Pumpe lignite-processing combine in 1965, it was working overtime to eliminate East Germany's need for manufactured gas from the Federal Republic. Helmut Wiedmer, technical director of the big industrial instrument trust in East Berlin, told me: "We don't depend on West Germany for critically needed imports of equipment or supplies because they could be cut off any day. We'd rather buy anywhere else than in West Germany." The terms of trade may be less favorable elsewhere, but the East Germans are willing to pay more, even in hard currency, rather than be subject to political pressure from Bonn. As René Bayer of *Die Zeit* noted after Ulbricht returned from Moscow in September 1965, "It may now be too late for West German economic initiatives that go beyond the fringe of the East German economy." The hardliners in Bonn find such facts unpalatable.

"The federal government will do everything in its power," Chancellor Erhard told the Bundestag on November 10, 1965, "to consolidate the inner cohesion between the two parts of our divided people but—let this be clear to everybody—we will not pay any political price for it."

How Bonn can refuse political concessions while demanding them from the other side has never been satisfactorily explained. The compulsion to appear to be getting something for nothing in dealing with the East increasingly dictates Bonn's tactics and distorts its policy. On September 4, 1964, after negotiating a Berlin Pass Agreement for almost eight months, the federal government abruptly ordered the West Berlin Senate not to sign until "improvements" had been incorporated in the arrangement. Bonn stalled for three weeks. Stories were leaked to the West German press about the Erhard government's "tough" stand on the pass issue. On September 24 the West Berlin representative, acting on Bonn's orders, signed an agreement with the other side permitting West Berliners to visit relatives across the Wall during four holiday periods in the coming year or when a family emergency arose. This agreement, as published by both sides, was identical with the September 4 draft and little different from what the communists had offered back in January.

The same performance was repeated the next year. The East Germans refused to renew the 1964 agreement but offered to allow West Berliners to cross over at Christmas time as they had done both previous years. Prolonged talks reached a deadlock. In August, one month before the West German elections, Bonn rejected "brusquely and decisively" (as the *Süddeutsche Zeitung* of Munich put it) the communist offer. Erhard had shown he could be firm. There was the expected murmur of approval from the conservative West German press and public. Three months later, having failed to obtain any improvements, Bonn reversed itself and accepted the original communist proposal.

The cabinet was said to have acted unanimously, but most CDU and CSU ministers made no secret of their fears that Bonn had embarked on a process that was bound to lead to permanent contacts with the DDR and, possibly, to the joint commissions proposed by the East Germans. There were also serious divergences between the federal government and the Brandt government in West Berlin. Ulbricht had won another tactical success.

The SED chieftain fared less well in a bid for "cooperation" with the West German Social Democrats in the spring of 1966. The SPD replied that no cooperation was possible as long as refugees were shot down trying to leave East Germany. *Neues Deutschland*'s circulation passed the million mark for the first time when it printed the full text of the SPD letter to Ulbricht. The SED countered by proposing public debates between spokesmen of the two parties in East and West Germany. Brandt promptly agreed for the SPD and, after the usual hesitation, the Erhard government announced that it also favored "a continuation of the argumentation with the opponents of a democratic order of society." Eight days later Ulbricht declared that SPD-SED debates scheduled to be held in Karl-Marx-Stadt (formerly Chemnitz) and Hannover in May would have to be put off at least until July. He blamed the postponement on provincial West German elections, although *Neues Deutschland* had said in March that contacts should be arranged regardless of local political considerations in either German state. Ulbricht had clearly retreated under pressure from the SED's hard-liners, apparently led by Erich Honecker, who signed the message informing Brandt of the postponement and took charge of the government when Ulbricht left on "vacation" the next day.

The SED's clumsy handling of the debates, coupled with its earlier rejection of a West German proposal for television discussions among politicians from both sides, gave Bonn and the SPD new confidence in dealing with the East Germans. On the other hand, at least part of the SED leadership obviously feared an open confrontation with West German spokesmen. Ulbricht's own position appeared to have been compromised by the dissension in his party.

SED policy on cultural contacts with West Germany has also blown hot and cold. During the hot phases when even recalcitrant East German writers and artists have been permitted

to appear in the West, the communists have achieved some notable successes. Younger members of the SED realize that unorthodox emissaries of the DDR are often the best advertise-
ment for their regime beyond the Wall.

There is much wooly talk in West Germany about poets
inspiring "inner reunification" so long as the politicians are
unable to achieve the real thing. "It seems very German," as
Die Zeit observed, "to turn to poets when statesmen have
failed."

The poets usually get no further than the statesmen in
healing the German schism. Meetings of East and West German literati have a habit of degenerating into political donny-
brooks. Billboard listings of participants in East-West gather-
ings in West Berlin proved so touchy that the organizers ended
up identifying each author by the East or West German currency symbol after his name. Even this seemingly foolproof
method provoked violent political argument.

Audiences in West Germany and West Berlin inevitably
ask about the Wall and inevitably get the standard East German retort. "Most of their questions about DDR literature,"
says a young East Berlin broadcaster, "are hackneyed and can
be dismissed with a smile. They miss the real problems here."
The novelist Christa Wolf told me that West Germans always
used to ask her why the DDR did not publish Kafka. "Then we
finally did, and that particular question stopped," she sighed.
East German writers have complained to me that loaded questions from West German audiences put them in an embarrassing position because they are strictly accountable to the SED
for what they say outside the country. To avoid the emotionally charged atmosphere of East-West "poets' olympics," East
German writers are now being invited simply to read from
their works and to answer nonpolitical questions. Since everything is political in a communist society, it is hard for the DDR
representatives to avoid stepping on the SED's toes or insult-
ing the intelligence of their Western audiences.

Such "cultural evenings" are nonetheless intensely popular, especially among young people, in West Germany and

West Berlin. Part of the interest stems from ignorance. A survey in 1965 showed that only 15 percent of West German university students of Germanic languages could name as many as two contemporary East German authors. Several put down the name of Bertolt Brecht, apparently unaware that he had died in 1956. Ignorance of modern West German literature, it should be said, is almost as abysmal in the DDR. There is no lack of popular interest on either side. The governments are to blame. The SED bans anything that would make West Germany appear in a good light. Bonn's policy is more ambivalent. Officially, the federal government is committed to expanding contacts among Germans. In fact, it has vacillated between grudging acceptance of exchanges and outright rejection of anything that might contaminate the Federal Republic with "communist propaganda." Never were Bonn's hesitations more painfully apparent than when Ulbricht offered in 1963 to allow the import of a number of copies of *Die Zeit* of Hamburg and the *Süddeutsche Zeitung* of Munich in return for permission to sell *Neues Deutschland* in West Germany (no East German publications are available on newsstands in the Federal Republic). It would be hard to underestimate the demand for *Neues Deutschland* outside the DDR. On the other hand, as an East German doctor told me later, "If *Die Zeit* and the *Süddeutsche Zeitung* were sold here, the supply would never catch up with the demand. They'd be sold out if they cost a mark a copy." Although Bonn had inveighed for years against the intellectual isolation of Ulbricht's subjects, his offer created consternation in the West German government. At first there was official silence. Then the federal government's spokesman announced that the law forbade the import of "anti-constitutional" communist material. A few days later Bonn changed its tune and expressed an interest in discussing a newspaper exchange, but only at the "technical" level. The communists countered by insisting on negotiations at "government" level. Bonn balked. Ulbricht could afford to gloat after casting Bonn in the role of archspoiler. West German officials consoled themselves later with the thought that

Ulbricht's offer had never been "sincere," which would mean, of course, that there was all the more reason for West Germany to have exposed the SED chief's hypocrisy to the world by taking him up on the newspaper exchange offer.

Ulbricht renewed his proposal on newspapers early in 1966. After the SPD administration in Hamburg had decided on its own to allow the sale of East German papers, the Bonn cabinet finally got around to approving a bill lifting many restrictions on the import of communist publications in the Federal Republic. An actual exchange of newspapers had still to be worked out.

By mid-1966 cautious moves were also underway in Bonn to liberalize the section of the Criminal Code that makes it a punishable offense for any West German to engage in public discussion with East German spokesmen. As the law stands now, the *Süddeutsche Zeitung* observed pointedly: "Journeys [to East Germany] become an incalculable risk, especially if the visitor opens his mouth." Even if a West German willing to engage in public argument with the SED is not subjected to legal prosecution, he runs the risk of being ostracized by his fellow citizens, to say nothing of the Ministry of All-German Affairs. The conviction has been officially expressed that spokesmen for the communist-run Free German Youth (FDJ) would be better prepared and therefore able to out-talk West German youth. Such misgivings were never warranted; that they were seriously entertained for many years by the government of the richest nation of Western Europe strains credulity.

Bonn is often betrayed by self-doubt when it deals with the DDR. The famous Gewandthaus Orchestra of Leipzig has performed Bach compositions before enthusiastic audiences all over West Germany, but the federal government hesitates to send a West German symphony orchestra to East Berlin. It might be interpreted as a sign of recognition of East Germany as a state. When the East Germans arranged at the end of 1964 for West German authors to read selections from their works over the DDR radio, Bonn put roadblocks in the way. The liberal-minded young cultural editor of DDR Radio on a visit to the Federal Republic taped hours of conversations with West German writers with the intent to broadcast them on the East German radio upon his return. On his way out he was questioned by West German police, and some of his recordings were confiscated. Taped readings by several West German authors were delayed so long by federal customs officials that DDR Radio was obliged to cancel part of the scheduled programs.

Such harassment naturally strengthens the diehards in the SED who insist that all cultural exchanges should be regularized by a formal agreement between Bonn and East Berlin at "government" level. The federal government professes to be horrified by the suggestion. Actually, apart from the recognition issue, the SED can disseminate more cultural propaganda in West Germany without a cultural agreement. The interministerial committee in Bonn that licenses the showing of East German and other communist-made films in West Germany has not distinguished itself for catholicity of taste. State and local governments in the Federal Republic often adopt an even more crabbed approach. In the summer of 1965, for example, the Augsburg City Council asked Erfurt and Leipzig to lend several paintings from their collections to a special Holbein exhibit in Augsburg. The East German cities agreed, but Augsburg refused to mark the paintings "from the DDR," and the project fell through. On the other hand, when government officials can be kept out of things, cultural exchanges between East and West German theater managers have enabled each country to see performances by the other's dramatic ensembles. East German artists, including a conductor and seventeen orchestra members, took part in the Bayreuth Wagnerian Festival for the first time in 1965 under an agreement between Wolfgang Wagner and the Staatsoper management in East Berlin.

The SED has exploited Bonn's hesitations about cultural contacts so effectively that even anti-communist East Germans doubt the Federal Republic's motives. A Leipzig schoolteacher says: "Bonn talks a lot about contacts but does nothing to bring them about." The same reproach could have been directed at the SED after December 1965 when the party reverted to a hard line in cultural matters, forbidding all but a handful of East German intellectuals to visit the West and demanding sterner measures against the spread of "bourgeois" ideas in the DDR.

In the realm of sports the SED's self-confidence has been boosted by the International Olympic Committee's decision in October 1965 to allow East Germany to field its own team at future Olympic Games. The all-German team that performed at previous Olympic Games has been dissolved despite strenuous West German efforts to maintain it. There will henceforth be two German Olympic teams, designated as "Germany (Federal Republic)" and "East Germany." The East German National Olympic Committee, granted provisional nonvoting status in 1955, has now achieved complete equality with other members of the International Olympic Committee. The IOC's decision shocked West Germans, not only because it enhanced the DDR's status, but also because it opened the way for the communists to press their demand for a third German Olympic team representing West Berlin.

The recognition of a separate East German team is the result of chicanery by communist sports officials and hard training by DDR athletes. The East Germans never missed an opportunity to convince the IOC that an all-German team was unworkable. When Juergen Kissner, one of the DDR's top bicyclists, defected before an elimination meet for the 1964 Olympic Games in Tokyo, the East Germans charged that he had been drugged and kidnapped in "one of the most inhuman scandals of West German slave-trading practices." Ulbricht has accused West German sports officials of "abusing" DDR athletes. Whenever the two national Olympic committees met, the East Germans raised objections over the most trifling details. They also fought ruthlessly to win a majority of berths on the all-German team. At the Tokyo games an East German captained the team for the first time. Bonn did little to promote the cause of West German athletes until it was too late. By 1965 international Olympic officials had had their fill of inter-German wrangling. Even the IOC chairman, Avery Brundage, originally a strong supporter of an all-German team, voted to grant the DDR separate representation. Polls showed that forty-three percent of West Germans considered it a "very bad" decision, but there was nothing they could do. Bonn had lost another round to the East German communists, who now look forward to fielding their own team at the 1968 Olympic Games in Mexico City and the 1972 Games in Munich.

The Olympic rebuff and the muddle in cultural relations illustrate what is regarded by many as the federal government's primary failing: it is long on legalism and short on imagination. Its good intentions are often blurred by poverty of conscience. Unlike Goethe's Mephistopheles, the West German leaders may always will the good, but they often work the evil. Few regimes have gone to such lengths to undo a hateful past; few have reaped such a harvest of hatred and suspicion for their pains. In the beginning, the German authorities in the Western occupation zones cooperated as zealously in the Allied de-Nazification program as the German communists cooperated in bolshevizing the Soviet Zone. After the founding of the Federal Republic in May 1949, West German courts continued trying accused Nazi criminals, and Bonn began paying billions of dollars to the victims of Hitler's barbarism. Meanwhile, East German courts were already focusing their attention on more inviting political targets, and the DDR regime paid no indemnities. Bonn's mistake was to drop war crimes trials for almost a decade after 1953 and, simultaneously, to allow former SS officers and other servants of the Nazi regime to return to positions of importance, especially in the police and the judiciary.

The fact that Hans Globke, Adenauer's former State Secretary and for years the highest-ranking civil servant in the federal government, had held a prominent post in the Nazi Interior Ministry and had produced a legal commentary on the anti-Semitic Nuremburg laws did not improve Bonn's image abroad. Using material available to them in the Potsdam archives, the East German communists have driven several federal cabinet ministers from office by well-timed disclosures of their Nazi past. Despite the pressure from the East, Bonn has reacted sluggishly. A central office for investigating Nazi crimes in occupied Europe was not established until 1958. After the East Germans released incriminating documents in 1965, the head of the investigation center, Dr. Erwin Schuele, was forced to admit he had joined the Nazi Party in 1937, but he denied having committed war crimes in Russia. Then a few hours after Bonn's Prosecutor General dropped his investigation of Schuele, Moscow announced it could produce eyewitnesses to mass executions he had ordered of Russian civilians.

West Germany resumed prosecutions of suspected Nazi mass killers only a few years before new investigations were to stop under Bonn's twenty-year Statute of Limitations in murder cases. As the deadline neared, a worldwide outcry forced Erhard's government to sponsor a law authorizing new prosecutions until 1970. This grudging and graceless compromise satisfied no one inside Germany or abroad.

The impression is widespread that West Germany is a haven for unrepentant Nazis. Nowhere does this have more important political effects than in East Germany, where memories of the war and its brown-shirted instigators are still fresh. A Schwerin businessman with no love for the communists told me: "The old Nazis got back too cheaply in West Germany." A University of Leipzig professor (and SED member) echoes the same thought: "What we really object to over there is the number of former Nazis in high positions." Robert Reuman, the Quaker international affairs representative in Germany, who travels widely in the DDR, has noted that even East Germans who thoroughly reject the SED's domestic policies often support the party's criticisms of Bonn, especially on the Nazi issue.

Such attitudes are a remarkable tribute to SED propaganda in view of the employment of scores of former Nazis in important positions in East Germany. The well-informed Free

Jurists investigating committee in West Berlin reported in 1964 that "at least" thirteen former National Socialists sat on the SED Central Committee and that five held cabinet-level positions in the government. Among those named by the Free Jurists were former Culture Minister Hans Bentzien (SED), Hans Reichelt of the satellite Democratic Peasants' Party, now Deputy Chairman of the Agricultural Council, and Kurt Blecha (SED), longtime head of the DDR Press Office and chief government spokesman. In January 1963 the SED Party Congress promoted Professor Karl-Heinz Bartsch to the rank of Candidate Member of the Politburo and Chairman of the newly created Agricultural Council. Two days later the Free Jurists in West Berlin disclosed his previous membership in the Nazi SS, and Bartsch was out. The Free Jurists say that Ulbricht's chief bodyguard, Franz Gold, joined the Nazi Party in 1938. He now holds the rank of major general in the East German Ministry of State Security. The London *Daily Telegram* reported in the fall of 1965 that 53 of the 434 members of the DDR Volkskammer ("People's Chamber") are ex-Nazis.

The Nazi past is as contemporary in the DDR as it is in the Federal Republic. The difference is that it casts a shorter shadow east of the Elbe. And in politics, shadows are often the most important realities.

The Nazi past has now been joined in Germany's hall of infamy by a more recent communist past—and present. Since the founding of the DDR, West German prosecutors have been collecting evidence of crimes committed by the communists and their helpers. A central office was established after the Wall went up in 1961 to register acts of violence against would-be refugees or West Germans traveling through the DDR. More than 5,700 such cases have already been registered by the West German investigators, who are said to have "clarified" seventy percent of the refugee killings on the Wall and the East-West German border. Several border guards who defected to the West have been sentenced to prison terms by federal German courts for killing people trying to flee. West German judges usually take the view that obedience to orders is not a sufficient excuse for shooting a refugee, although they have often exonerated former SS killers on the same grounds. The border guards' experience in West Germany has not notably reduced the number of killings on the Wall, but it does deter other servants of Ulbricht from defecting. The specter of de-communization in the DDR (if Germany is ever reunified on Western terms) gives all SED members pause and makes most of them partisans of permanent division. Even noncommunist East Germans who have cooperated at all with the regime fear a latter-day version of the Nuremburg Trials engineered by the "revenge-seekers" in Bonn. West German officials deny such intentions, but their assurances are weakened by pronouncements, such as that made by *Die Welt* of Hamburg in April 1966, that after reunification "thousands of [East German] people would be convicted, and tens of thousands of relatives and friends would be directly involved."

Although the DDR is democratic only in name, there are enough flaws in the Federal Republic's political system to provide ample ammunition to the communists. Democracy in West Germany is crocheted onto an imported constitution that fits the Germans like an evening gown on a prize fighter. Since the notorious "Spiegel affair" in 1962, a series of scandals has cast doubt on the Bonn government's devotion to civil rights. "Tell the people in Bonn when you go back," an anti-communist East German university professor told an English correspondent in 1963, "that what they have over there is a real political pigsty." West Germany is the only NATO country besides Portugal, Greece, and Turkey in which the communist party is banned. In West Berlin the party leads a twilight existence under the eyes of Mayor Brandt's police and Allied counterintelligence. The arrest and detention without trial in 1963–4 of Günther Hofé, an East German publisher enroute to the Frankfurt Book Fair, was one of several cases in which West German police have seized DDR visitors on what later proved to be flimsy evidence. Those arrested quickly achieve martyrdom in the East German press, which depicts the Federal Republic as a country in the grip of a reign of terror. The

SED's picture of West Germany has been made more credible by Bonn's inept handling of proposed legislation that would drastically curtail civil liberties and parliamentary government if a state of emergency were declared in the Federal Republic.

Even without such inviting targets as the Emergency Law, the East German communists would feel an obsessive need to vilify Bonn and all its works. The torrent of abuse from the SED exceeds in volume and violence any propaganda coming out of other Eastern European countries or from the Soviet Union. On a typical day *Neues Deutschland,* the main SED organ, will devote as much as two thirds of its white space to attacks on the Federal Republic. Stories datelined Düsseldorf, Essen, or elsewhere in West Germany (but usually concocted in East Berlin) report protest marches by workers, police reprisals, mass arrests, and other signs of mounting discontent. No mention is made of the fact that the number of unemployed in West Germany has shrunk to microscopic proportions, forcing Bonn to import more than one million foreign laborers. The SED press also harps endlessly on Bonn's alleged connections with American monopolists, South African racists, Israeli expansionists, and anyone else deemed in ill repute. In the manner of American high-school newspapers, *Neues Deutschland* publishes banner headlines exhorting readers to "stop Nazi-style terror wave in West Germany," or it will pose rhetorical questions such as "Herr Erhard, when will you tell the voters the truth?" As the paper's chief foreign editor told a *New York Times* correspondent not long ago: "We do not regard ourselves as a source of information. It's not that we have anything against free information. We simply do not have the space for it." But then, with admirable objectivity, he admitted: "We are not interested in being objective." It is true that much West German news about the DDR is biased against the communists, but it does not approach the SED's morbid fascination with defaming the foe.

However excessive DDR propaganda may be, it has undoubtedly influenced East Germans, including those who dislike their own regime intensely. "Neither German government is optimal," a Leipzig physician says with a shrug of the shoulders. "Our students don't dare speak their minds," a religious leader in East Germany admits, "but apart from England and America, where is there freedom of speech? How free is West Germany?" Many East Germans are not only alienated from their own government; they are alienated from Bonn and politics in general. "DDR not good, West Germany not good, USA not good," an old Leipzig man muttered in broken English when I told him I was an American. He said America discriminated against Negroes. The race problem, incidentally, provides the East German communists with their most effective anti-American propaganda. Those most sympathetic to the United States raised this question more often than any other when I was in the DDR. A Leipzig radio engineer expressed admiration for President Kennedy (almost universal in East Germany), then asked me anxiously: "What about the race question in your country? The African students here always talk about it. Is it true that there's discrimination against blacks?" A successful East German industrial manager recalls his days as a prisoner of war at Camp Kilmer, New Jersey, with fondness, but he also remembers a Negro GI who told him: "You're prisoner number 1 here; every Negro is prisoner number 2." Despite such blots, America's prestige is high in East Germany, and Americans are popular.

The same, unfortunately, cannot be said of all West Germans who visit the DDR. In 1965 more than 2,800,000 West Germans visited East Germany, a sizeable increase over any previous year. This number does not include hundreds of thousands of West Berliners who went to East Berlin on holiday-period passes. All the West Berliners and most of the West Germans go ostensibly to visit relatives in the DDR. Their reaction on first entering East Germany is often paranoid terror in the presence of communist officialdom. I remember an episode involving a young West Berliner who unquestioningly surrendered his identity card in East Berlin to an imposter posing as an East German policeman. The West Berliner was arrested later the same day when he tried to leave without identification. Weeks passed before the matter was finally straightened out. It would never have happened if the young West Berliner had not been so blindly afraid of what he mistook for communist officialdom.

Once West Germans or West Berliners realize that communists don't necessarily arrest and torture visitors, their pent-up feelings of antagonism find expression. They often become arrogant and overbearing. They pilot their Mercedes or Opels at high speed past East Germans who must walk to work. They complain loudly about the food in East German restaurants. They distribute largesse to their poor relatives in the "Zone" as a grandee would dispense alms to his serfs. Most of the visitors now know enough not to offer potatoes, but even when their gifts are welcome, the manner of giving often leaves much to be desired. Not all West Germans behave so gauchely, but enough of them do to inspire unkind feelings east of the Wall. "The West Germans have lost their ethical values in the pursuit of prosperity," an East German industrial executive told me bitterly. "We're tired of being pitied," says a Dresden dentist. "The West Germans will make much of our pensioners when they first come out," a Leipzig teacher told me in 1964, "but they'll ignore them once the novelty has worn off." Her words were confirmed by an old East German at the end of his visit to relatives in Munich. "It's good to be going home," he told an American reporter. "Everyone's been nice to me, but it didn't come from their hearts."

Even churchmen from opposite sides of the Wall find it difficult to communicate. East German Christians detect a certain smugness in their co-religionists in the Federal Republic. Roland Warren, the former American Quaker international affairs representative in Germany, who knows both parts of the country well, says: "East German Christians are real do-or-die Christians. Most Lutherans in both East and West Germany are convinced that the East German church is much healthier, much less materialistic, and more realistic in its approach to basic issues than the church in West Germany or in the United States."

Churchmen, like other East Germans, may be less materialistic simply because they have fewer material goods, but the fact that even they resent West Germans shows how the two peoples have grown apart.

Germany is two minds as well as two states. Melvin Croan of Harvard considers resentment the dominant characteristic of what he calls the "East German public mind." It is certainly a strong undercurrent. Among older East Germans, many of whom are unalterably opposed to their regime, resentment sometimes takes the form of a reversion to traditional German nationalism or even racism. An elderly gentleman in Weimar told me that German officers had been brutally mistreated by Jewish guards in American POW camps. A Leipzig resident says: "Those Jewish fur merchants who used to have open-air stalls here are sitting pretty in Frankfurt today. If they ever come back, we'll know for sure things are better here."

Many East Germans focus their resentment on the Federal Republic. Ironically, it is often based on an exaggerated idea of West German opulence. Describing East German attitudes, a London *Times* correspondent has written: "West of the Harz Mountains, California begins. Everyone is rich, happy, drives a Mercedes to the Riviera, culture and learning flourish." A doctor from a small town outside East Berlin told me: "Our drugs are good, but patients always want Western drugs because they're sure they are better. In most cases the only real difference is that the West produces dozens of different brands of the same drug whereas we produce only one." An old lady dressed entirely in black bustled up to my wife in a Leipzig park and murmured: "They have everything over there. There's no hope here, not with the DDR."

Practically all East Germans watch Western television. Those who get to see the reality behind the flickering screen are often disappointed by what they find. A Leipzig pensioner just back from a visit to Hamburg told me: "I paid six marks for a veal cutlet over there. The same thing would cost me four marks in the best restaurant here." He overlooked the fact that the cutlet was undoubtedly better in Hamburg. High rents in West Germany also shock many East Germans used to the DDR's subsidied housing. Only 0.20 of one percent of the 1,700,000 East German pensioners who visited West Germany and West Berlin in 1964–5 stayed in the West, in part, as Germans say, because "old trees don't transplant easily," but also because they simply could not afford life on the other side.

The elderly are not alone in eschewing the pleasures of the Federal Republic. Every day from ten to thirty people of all ages and conditions of life leave West Germany or West Berlin to settle in the DDR. Few are convinced communists. Many are former refugees returning to their homes in East Germany after failing to make a go of it in the West. Others are lawbreakers seeking to elude the federal police. Hardened criminals and anyone else likely to cause the DDR more trouble than good are often pushed back across the border by the communists.

East German refugees who stay in the West often send back discouraging reports. "Our son has had a more difficult time adjusting to Hannover than he expected," a professor's wife in Rostock told me. Their eldest son had fled the year before. "He misses his close circle of friends in Rostock," she explained. "Young people here are very close to each other. Our son also dislikes the student societies at the Technical College in Hannover. They invited him to join, but he doesn't want to." (Many West German student "corporations," as they are called, are notoriously reactionary.)

The young man in Hannover is no exception. Many of the 3,700,000 East Germans who have gone West since 1950 feel lost in the atomized, impersonal society of West Germany. They miss the close human relationships that help East Germans survive. I was always amazed in East Germany at how quickly I could establish rapport with total strangers. The readiness of most East Germans to help, to share, and to understand is remarkable. It is as if they have found release from political bondage by freeing their minds of many of the conventions and inhibitions that still encumber human relations in West Germany. The communists insist that "new socialist man" is responsible for the difference. If I could ever have found him in East Germany, I might agree. But there, as in other communist countries, "new socialist man" is a rare creature.

One emotion I found among the alienated majority as well as the converted minority was pride in what East Germans have achieved since the war. Sometimes it is based on a politically inspired misconception of the differences between East and West Germany. For example, a young schoolteacher from the Erzgebirge told me: "Our school system in the DDR is better because in West Germany only children from certain social strata can go to school." A Dresden architect in his early thirties spent most of an evening explaining to me why he prefers to stay in East Germany and design schools. "If I were over there," he said, meaning West Germany, "I'd have to earn my living building villas for the Krupps and the Thyssens."

"The West Germans are the real materialists," says a broadcaster in East Berlin. "Our youth doesn't swallow any ideology. They're leery of all systems of thought. It's part of the reaction to Nazism, carried over against socialist ideas."

There is also pride in tangible achievements. "In terms of hospital beds per thousand inhabitants," a Rostock physician observes, "the DDR is one of the most advanced countries in the world." "The real economic miracle is here," a plant manager told me as we sat in the Auerbachskeller in Leipzig. "We didn't choose this damned system, but we've made a success of it. Look at the new industry in Schwerin and along the Oder." Ulbricht calls this "socialist consciousness." I would call it "Teutonic consciousness."

Resentment, envy, compassion, pride, and defiance! What mixed emotions swell in the East German breast! Wars not only begin in the minds of men; they end there. Mentally, the East Germans are still at war on many fronts. Ulbricht once said that the late President Kennedy did not want nuclear war with the Soviet Union but that he would "not mind if Germans

were to fight Germans." This remark was aimed at disrupting
the American-West German alliance; in fact, it betrayed the
SED's own hopes that, with Soviet backing, it can induce East
Germans to dig an unbridgeable chasm between themselves
and West Germans.

"Those people in Bonn should admit we not only lost a
war; we began one," a well-educated lady in Rostock told me
bitterly. "We in the DDR, who pay the heaviest price for the
war, concede this. Why can't the West Germans?"

Bonn's refusal to acknowledge the loss of the Oder-Neisse
territories to Poland puzzles many East Germans. The federal
government reminds them of a wife who insists that her dead
husband is alive because his death certificate has not been
issued. East Germans know it is fear of West German irredentism that helps tie Warsaw to Moscow and inhibits liberaliz-
ing influences in Poland that could help the DDR.

"Are the West Germans really interested in reunification?"
is a question I have been asked dozens of times by East Germans. "The West Germans had a chance to get concessions
from our government before 1958," an East Berlin newspaper-
man told me, "but they refused to talk. They always do."
When Erhard succeeded Adenauer as Chancellor, East Germans hoped for a thaw in relations. "Let's wait and see," a
research scholar at the Goethe Museum in Weimar told me not
long after the change-over in Bonn. "Erhard seems to show
somewhat more movement." Such hopes were soon disappointed. Erhard proved to be nearly as rigid and unimagina-
tive toward East Germany as his predecessor. "In some ways,
Erhard is worse than Adenauer," a high-ranking SED man in
Leipzig told me. "He makes you think something is going to
happen, then does nothing. Regardless of what he personally
wants, Bonn's policy is still dictated by people who oppose
understanding with the DDR and relaxation of tensions." Such
people, it should be said, are by no means all in Bonn. The
SED has repeatedly reneged opportunities to broaden all-
German contacts or ease tensions. The ambivalence in East
German policy was particularly apparent in the spring of 1966

when the communists first proposed a public debate with the West German SPD and then backed away from the idea. Bonn, on the other hand, continues to delude itself that all noncommunist East Germans crave nothing more than a political boycott of their state. Letters purportedly written by people in the "Zone" expressing violent opposition to their regime play a major part in perpetuating West German myths about the DDR. One such letter, quoted with obvious approval in the news bulletin of the West German embassy in Washington for November 15, 1965, reads as follows:

> The agreement on visiting passes [in Berlin] spells acceptance of the Berlin Wall, and the sanctioning of the shots which have fallen there. What we want are not visiting passes through the Wall, but a forest of huge crosses whose long shadows would fall upon the faces of the criminals. Agreements on visiting passes, trips for old-age pensioners, and efforts toward alleged humane arrangements for life in the Zone are all excellent means of accustoming people to the Berlin Wall. No, this wound must remained unclosed.

Another letter reproduced in the same issue says:

> We are sitting here in a cage and cannot escape. Visiting passes for West Berliners are of no help to us. . . . We reject even the slightest concession to our oppressors.

In the course of months of travel through East Germany, I have heard torrents of criticism of the regime—much of it profane or even obscene—but I never found anyone who demanded to be completely cut off from the outside world, as the writers of the two letters quoted above appear to demand. Fanatic anti-communists are almost as small a minority as fanatic pro-communists in the weary land between the Elbe and the Oder. Intelligent West Germans know this, but they have not yet been able to stop Bonn from picturing East Germany as a big concentration camp peopled by pitiable helots who dream only of being reunited with their prosperous federal cousins. The West German government not only deludes itself about present realities in the East; it also hinders their evolving to the West's advantage. A shrewd Yugoslav diplomat in East Berlin told me: "A great deal here depends on how Bonn treats the DDR. A strong anti-policy by Bonn strengthens conservative elements in the SED." A Czech correspondent who is severely critical of the East German regime says: "Bonn's refusal to recognize the DDR or to have anything to do with it keeps the SED on the defensive. This means the party is reluctant to shelve even old comrades who are clearly ready for their pension because the West Germans would immediately seize on such a move as evidence of weakness in the SED. So the old guard remains, the old lineup is kept intact, and change becomes more difficult." A young SED member in Leipzig told me: "The West German press always plays up our differences. They rejoice at the slightest sign of disunity. You can imagine the effect of this in our party."

In his excellent study *Offensive Relaxation of Tensions* the West German writer Peter Bender argues for an end to Bonn's political warfare against the East German regime so as to permit internal changes in the DDR and eventual German reunification. He believes the West should grant full diplomatic recognition and extensive credits to the SED to enable it to consolidate its position. I think Bender goes too far, but Bonn could certainly contribute to a more relaxed and possibly more liberal atmosphere in East Germany by tempering its polemics against the SED and dropping the pretense that it never deals with the DDR regime on political matters. The federal government's present strategy gives the East German communists an unassailable argument. The longer the DDR exists, the more hollow Bonn's contention that there is no such state. Barring some unforeseen catastrophe, time means economic progress in the DDR, further undercutting the notion that the country is nothing more than a huge slave-labor camp. Time also means a new generation of East Germans, perhaps no more enamored of their regime than the present generation, but acutely aware of what divides it from West Germany. The real gravediggers of Germany are those who help deepen the cleavage that already exists everywhere except on Bonn's maps. The federal government could find no better advice than that offered by Theo Sommer of *Die Zeit* in his little book *Journey to a Distant Land,* written after he and two other editors of the paper returned from East Germany:

> We need have no fear of an imaginative, dynamic contact offensive. Everything is in our favor. The spirit of doubt is at work over there [in the DDR] in any case; the laws of the market will also demand an easing up. The longest lever is in our minds. What we need is more self-confidence for the long pull.

(11)

The Dragon
and the Gnat

∎

LEIPZIG AT FAIR TIME puts on a smiling face. Windows are washed, park benches painted, and new propaganda slogans appear on every building front. A special flower stand blossoms near the railroad station. Lebanese oranges and Cuban pineapples are available for a few days in grocery stores, and new television sets adorn shop windows. The white Meissen tiles in the lobby of the modern opera house are as highly polished as the party buttons of the SED functionaries who throng the city during the fair. Hotels are crowded with Indian traders, Swiss exporters, British booksellers, and Ruhr steelmakers. Even the most reactionary capitalist is welcome. Flatulent hospitality is the order of the day.

Press conferences organized by the fair's sponsors offer lavish buffets but little news. When the DDR's Foreign Trade Minister and his chief deputy invited reporters on September 3, 1963, Western and communist newsmen expected to eat well and be bored by the usual recitation of the fair's statistical triumphs. Everything went according to plan until an alert Western reporter asked the two officials to elaborate on a DDR government statement issued six weeks earlier accusing Communist China of seriously harming the East German economy by canceling shipments. Obviously embarrassed, Erwin Kerber, Deputy Foreign Trade Minister, acknowledged that there had been "certain difficulties" caused by the cutoff of Chinese raw materials but said that they had been "largely overcome." His soft answer left Western newsmen unsatisfied and enraged one of their journalistic colleagues.

"The Chinese people have always supported the struggle of the DDR," a small man shouted from the back of the room. "China never caused any harm to the DDR. The accusations made in the statement are entirely false."

The irate voice belonged to Li Y, East Berlin correspondent of the communist New China News Agency. As his tirade continued, Kurt Blecha, the chief DDR press spokesman, broke in to remind Li that he should put his remarks in the form of a question.

"I have a question," the Chinese shot back. "Do you know the recent development of trade between China and the DDR? Then you must know that it [the DDR government statement] is baseless. You must know that trade developments are based on the needs and possibilities of both countries."

Angry and flustered, Kerber said that his comments referred to the period 1958–62, that he had dealt only in facts, and that it had not been "easy" for the DDR to issue its statement on trade with China. He added that he was optimistic about prospects for expanding Sino-East German exchanges as a result of negotiations then underway. The DDR was even ready, "as an exception," as he put it, to double the level of trade with China.

Li Y sat down, clearly convinced he had won the argument.

That public altercation at the 1963 Leipzig autumn fair showed what a precarious tightrope the DDR walks between Russia and China. No communist country, with the possible exception of North Vietnam, suffers more acutely from the clash of titans. The problem is ambivalence. Like Communist

China, whose regime was also founded in October 1949, the DDR is a state with territorial ambitions, multiple grievances, and a pervading sense of insecurity. Like China, it relies on rigid discipline and the suppression of dissenters to maintain conformity at home. But unlike China, East Germany is a highly industrialized European state occupied by Soviet troops and intimately linked with Russia in every sphere of national life. If, as someone has suggested, the DDR were moved to southeast Asia, its policy toward Moscow might be markedly different. But the facts of geography are not so easily modified. Nor is the SED's present dependence on Soviet bayonets to stay in power.

To say that Ulbricht and Mao Tse-tung are both Stalinists is to conceal a multitude of differences. In fact, during China's "hundred flowers" period in 1957, Ulbricht's "revisionist" opponents in the SED drew inspiration from Mao's policies. Karl Schirdewan, ousted the following year as Ulbricht's deputy in the Politburo, praised the Chinese for their "creative" adaptation of the softer line introduced at the Twentieth Soviet Communist Party Congress. Another admirer of the "hundred flowers" campaign was Paul Wandel, a Moscow-trained party veteran, who was dismissed in October 1957 as Central Committee Secretary for Culture and Education because of his indulgence toward "revisionist" East German intellectuals. He later served as DDR ambassador to Peking and became a champion of the "people's communes." During Mao's "hundred flowers" phase, as Carola Stern has written, "advocates of thorough de-Stalinization within the SED, like those in Poland, began to follow events in China with growing interest and were much inclined to see in Peking a mecca of revisionism."

For Ulbricht, Peking became a mecca when the hundred flowers withered. He delightedly imitated Mao in stamping out all noxious growth in the SED's backyard, including the Schirdewan-Wollweber "revisionist" group. By the second half of 1958, the SED was ready to attempt a "great leap" of its own toward annexing West Berlin and surpassing West Germany in per capita consumption of food and consumer goods.

The East German version was no more successful than was the Chinese, but Ulbricht continued extolling Mao's "ideological contributions" as late as October 1959. Applying Chinese concepts of "social consumption," the SED experimented in at least one city with distributing wage premiums in the form of subsidized rents, utilities, and public services.

Following the forcible collectivization of East German agriculture in 1960, the provincial SED press began printing officially inspired reports about the establishment of communal kitchens in the countryside. Farmers were advised to "eat out of the same big pot," commune fashion. Several years later I asked a young engineer in Dresden about the brief heyday of commune ideology in East Germany.

"They talked a lot about communal kitchens," he told me, "where each housewife would have her own corner. They also built other communal facilities such as crèches. That reflected pro-Chinese sentiment in the SED at the time. But they found the crèches were expensive to build and trained staff was hard to find. Then when one child got ill, they all came down with the same thing, which meant all the mothers were absent from their jobs twenty percent of the time. This caused big periodic contractions in the work force. So the plans handed down from the top were dropped because of practical considerations."

Unlike Grotewohl, Hermann Matern, and several other high SED leaders, Ulbricht had noted Moscow's significant silence on the subject of the Chinese communes and discreetly ignored them in his public utterances. By June 1960, when the Sino-Soviet split had become open, the SED chief forbade further talk of communes in East Germany. *Neues Deutschland* echoed the same line a few days later in an editorial that expressed open disagreement with the Chinese communists for the first time. The collectivized East German farmer, it turned out, would still be free to eat where he pleased.

Whatever they said at the time, the overwhelming majority of SED members have always opposed communes in any form. A party leader in Leipzig told me late in 1964: "There's absolutely no possibility of applying Chinese communes here or in any European country. I understand the Chinese may have felt it necessary to adopt such a system under conditions of war communism, but they should have made clear that the communes are a transitional form suitable only to Asian conditions. They should never have held up the communes as the universal norm for socialist countries."

In June 1960, when ordinary East Germans were getting their first inkling that all was not well in the communist bloc, Soviet and many East German engineers and technicians were already trekking home from China. The rift was affecting state as well as party relations. All the Russians reportedly departed by the end of the year, but even today China and the DDR maintain a small-scale exchange of specialists, reflecting the SED's reluctance to sever economic ties with Peking. During the period of "fraternal friendship," according to *Neues Deutschland,* the DDR had helped to put up more than fifty industrial plants in China, including an electronics factory, a plant to produce industrial regulating devices, an artificial silk mill, and assorted sugar refineries, cement mills, and power plants. Almost 500 Chinese scientists and technicians had received training in the DDR, and 214 Chinese attended East German universities and colleges.

It was the SED's misfortune to be chosen by Khrushchev as the Soviet bloc's barking dog in the dispute with the Chinese at the East German party congress in January 1963. Until that time Ulbricht had consistently sought to play down differences within the bloc. At the SED congress the Chinese delegate was hooted down, and his speech was heavily censored by the East German press. The works of Mao and other Chinese communist leaders had already disappeared from DDR bookstores.

On a visit to Warsaw later that year Ulbricht excoriated Peking's policies while Wang Ping-nan, the German-educated Chinese ambassador, listened impassively. Kurt Hager, the SED's chief ideologist, had already had the temerity to blame Chinese "deviations" on Confucianism and "idealistic philosophic tendencies." As East German propaganda against China reached a peak of intensity in the fall of 1963, Peking unexpectedly assumed the role of guardian and spokesman for the interests of the DDR. It charged that Moscow's acceptance of the Partial Nuclear Test Ban Treaty amounted to "obliterating the international position of the DDR in order to curry favor with United States imperialism." *Neues Deutschland* retorted that Peking was guilty of "blatant lies" and "boundless arrogance."

The dragon was not deterred by the gnat's ingratitude. Accusations of "ignoble betrayal" of the DDR by the Russians continued to emanate from the Chinese propaganda machine. Peking did not confine itself to the test ban treaty. It cast suspicion on Moscow's entire German policy, recalling Khrushchev's 1958 ultimatum against West Berlin and the failure to unite Germany under communism.

The SED has reacted to such "support" much as a man on the gallows reacts to the hangman's supporting noose around his neck. Chinese solicitude is far more unnerving for the East German comrades than Chinese hostility.

The DDR leadership at first reacted sluggishly to Peking's new tactics. *Neues Deutschland* accused the Chinese of "pouring water on the mills of West German militarists" and trying to poison relations between the DDR and the Soviet Union. Moscow found that the SED's rebuttal lacked the requisite Bolshevik bite. The SED was told to try harder. Politburo Candidate Member Horst Sindermann was assigned the job of making manifest the East German party's alignment with Moscow in the great communist schism. In February 1964 he rejected "with outrage" Peking's running comments on the Soviet Communist Party's "Open Letter" of the previous summer. He accused the Chinese of making "the vilest attack to date on the general line of the international communist movement." To many, however, Sindermann's indignation sounded contrived. The SED was clearly more worried about revisionism in its own ranks than vileness among the Chinese. Sindermann devoted most of his report to the SED Central Committee to upbraiding "fraternal" Czechoslovakia where the once-Stalinist administration of President Novotny was allow-

ing the weeds of liberalism and reformism to sprout in what
was dubbed the "Prague spring." The Chinese could not fail
to notice that the East German diatribe against Czech "revisionism" could have been written in Peking and directed
against that archrevisionist, Nikita Khrushchev.

Ulbricht's sensitive antennae and his friends in the Soviet
hierarchy told him that a change of strategy was imminent
in Moscow in October 1964. He ordered a cease-fire in the
attacks on the Chinese, beginning on the Peking regime's
national day, October 1. He had always tried to straddle
the ideological fence without impairing his essential ties with
the Russians. When Khrushchev fell, Ulbricht adopted a pose
of statesmanlike moderation toward the broils in the communist camp. He minimized the extent of differences and played
up the slightest sign of reconciliation between Moscow and
Peking. *Neues Deutschland* reacted sharply the morning after
the Chinese nuclear explosion of October 16, but Professor
Gerhart Eisler, the former Comintern agent who jumped bail
in America to come to the DDR in 1949, broadcast a considerably more sympathetic reaction over the East Berlin radio:
"It might perhaps have been better," he said, "if the Chinese
communist party had coordinated its policy with the policies of
the other socialist states, which would have made this explosion completely superfluous. . . ."

A day later, Eisler was even more circumspect. He said
merely that he did not wish to discuss what "our Chinese
friends" had done. In another broadcast he insisted the
DDR had been "forced" to engage in polemics with Peking.
The truth of his remark was evidenced by the speed with which
the SED adopted the new line of moderation laid down by the
Kremlin in the ideological conflict. Even before Khrushchev's
successors acted to try to paper over the cracks in the communist front, Ulbricht had anticipated their tactics. The exchange
of abuse was stopped. Three weeks after Khrushchev's removal,
the SED boss had a sudden attack of humility in answering a
question about China at a public meeting: "Of course, the
Chinese People's Republic will make decisions and will de-

velop politically and economically according to its conditions. But I say very frankly, our knowledge does not suffice to comment in detail about these questions. It is enough for us to master the tasks in the DDR."

A year before, Ulbricht had accused the Chinese leaders of risking war to make "big leaps" into a communist never-never land and of squandering "great economic powers and resources for the development of Chinese nuclear weapons," instead of promoting industry and agriculture "to give the people more food and clothing." In the post-Khrushchevian euphoria, these sins seemed to have been forgiven. But it takes two to settle a quarrel. China soon renewed its broadsides against Soviet revisionism, and the SED was impaled on its familiar dilemma.

Late in 1964 I asked the director of the Institute for Marxism-Leninism at the University of Leipzig how the SED assessed the situation. His answer reflects the party's thinking to this day: "We doubt the dispute can be settled," he said, "but we hope it will be debated in more objective fashion. It was inevitable that it would take on personal overtones as the quarrel got hotter. So long as Khrushchev was there, this couldn't be helped. Now, at least, personalities may be kept out of it."

I asked if the SED would reply to Peking's latest sallies.

"That's always our problem," he said, "to reply or not. If we don't answer, it looks as if we are conceding the Chinese arguments. If we do, the dispute gets more violent. We want a calm discussion."

That of course is the last thing the East German party will get. The Chinese have intervened for good in European politics, including the German problem. They will keep harping on Moscow's failure to carry out its threats against West Berlin or its promise to sign a separate peace treaty with the DDR. After the West German Bundestag ignored Soviet protests and met in West Berlin in April 1965, a Chinese Politburo member demanded caustically why Khrushchev's successors "continue to pursue Khrushchev's policy of selling out the German Democratic Republic?" Peking also practices more subtle forms of harassment. By insisting that no country has ever made a peaceful transition to socialism, the Chinese in effect say socialism was imported into East Germany on Soviet bayonets, not by dint of the efforts of the German working class led by the SED. This strikes a sensitive nerve. Historical fictions are vital to a party that rules against the will of most of its subjects.

While it demolishes some of the SED's most cherished myths, the Chinese party is appealing covertly to those East German comrades who still dream of communizing all Germany. Kurt Hager hinted at the existence of a Chinese clique in the East German party when he accused Peking in July 1963 of "the worst Trotskyism," "fractional activities," and "inciting the members of individual parties against their leadership." The following year Peter Florin, Central Committee Secretary in charge of relations with other parties, accused the Chinese of spending lavishly to form splinter communist parties from "Trotskyite, nationalist, and petty bourgeois forces and from morally depraved elements in Western countries." Although he neglected to mention the DDR, the country seems to offer an abundance of human material to fit Florin's description and Peking's purposes. At about the same time Erich Mueckenberger, Politburo member and party boss in the Frankfurt-on-Oder district, denounced "former comrades who crawled onto the Trotskyite platform of the leader of the Chinese Communist Party." He censured SED district leaders for failing to deal with such reptiles more promptly and announced the expulsion of one pro-Chinese deviate. How many other SED members have been excommunicated for pro-Peking sentiments is a closely guarded secret, but the party's visceral reaction to the dissemination of any Chinese propaganda in the DDR seems to reflect continuing anxiety on this score.

The only thing that seems to frighten the SED hierarchy more than China's professed sympathy for the DDR is Chinese interest in trade and other relations with West Germany. As Carola Stern has observed, "The SED's own criticism of the Chinese . . . began only when the possibility of a *rapproche-*

ment between Peking and the Federal Republic appeared to arise." The most ominous form of *rapprochement* is implied in Mao's thesis of a "second intermediate zone" between the United States and the communist world. Countries of the "second intermediate zone," including West Germany and other capitalist nations outside the United States, are reckoned to have "something in common" with genuine Marxist-Leninists in the struggle against U. S. imperialism. For the SED, the main enemy is not America but West Germany. Commenting on Mao's grandiose concept, *Neues Deutschland* observed ruefully in 1964: "The question must be asked, against whom this 'third force' of the Chinese People's Republic and the Allied NATO comrades, i.e., the members of imperialist war blocs, is to be directed?"

The SED mouthpiece hardly needed to answer its own question. The "third force" is to be directed against the United States, the Soviet Union, and their remaining allies.

While they hopefully await the day of discord between Bonn and Washington, the Chinese have shown remarkable flexibility in their approach to the German problem. Almost fifteen years after the establishment of diplomatic relations between the DDR and the Chinese People's Republic, Peking's Foreign Minister Ch'en Yi told Western journalists that China desired the peaceful reunification of "both parts" of Germany, thus ignoring the Soviet-SED gospel of two sovereign German states. *Neues Deutschland* fumed that Ch'en had "slandered" the DDR. Mao was even more brutally outspoken in his now famous interview with a Japanese socialist delegation in July 1964 in which he accused Russia of having "detached part of East Germany" and given another part of East Germany to Poland as compensation for Polish territory occupied by the USSR. The Chinese autocrat is clearly not impressed by the Oder-Neisse "peace frontier." As the SED noted with an audible shudder, Mao's remarks put him squarely in the camp of those who want to undo the results of the Second World War.

At the same time that the leader of Chinese communism

was casting his shadow over the Soviet-imposed frontiers of Eastern and Central Europe, Peking quietly let it be known that it was prepared to sign a trade agreement with Bonn that would include West Berlin. The Chinese offer was the culmination of a campaign of political pressure that had reduced Peking's trade with the DDR to less than fifteen percent of its 1958 volume. As late as 1959, according to West German sources, the DDR had held second place (behind the Soviet Union) in China's foreign trade. The SED later accused the Chinese of exerting economic pressure beginning in 1961 in an effort to split East Germany from the Soviet Union. The pressure failed to achieve its object, but, as one high SED official exclaimed, "Economic cooperation between the DDR and China has been strangled." Meanwhile, unofficial trade relations between China and West Germany continued to expand. By 1963 Peking was doing more business with the Federal Republic than with its "fraternal allies" in the DDR. The Chinese offer to include a Berlin clause in a trade agreement with Bonn was designed to pave the way for the exchange of trade missions between the two countries. The West Germans were delighted at the chance to get the second strongest communist power to recognize their right to speak for West Berlin and would gladly have concluded an agreement with Peking had President Johnson not intervened personally in June 1964 with Chancellor Erhard to warn him of the effect of expanded trade between China and the Federal Republic while the Vietnam fighting continued. The Bonn government reluctantly announced that it would not enter into a formal trade pact with Peking, and the Chinese promptly concluded a new commercial agreement with the DDR. By the spring of 1965, Peking and East Berlin had signed another accord providing for an increase in exchanges. At the same time, the Chinese returned in force to the spring Leipzig trade fair.

Notwithstanding the slight thaw in DDR-Chinese economic relations and the continued absence of any formal agreement governing trade between Peking and Bonn, the Federal Republic more than doubled its exports to Communist

China in 1965 to just under 80 million dollars. Imports from China rose more than forty percent to 72.5 million dollars. In March 1966 Bonn announced it would guarantee a credit of 87.5 million dollars to finance the West German share in a two-million-ton steel complex to be built in China by a consortium of European firms. The project was said to be the largest industrial undertaking by Western firms in China since the communist regime came to power. Secretary of State Rusk and several senators voiced American displeasure at the deal. The SED hid its chagrin behind a curtain of silence. After all, it was not the first time that West German firms found an attractive market in China. West German engineers have supervised the construction of a large synthetic-fiber plant in China, and West German firms have supplied chemical factories, hardwood mills, and machinery to Peking. West German businessmen are now welcome visitors at the annual Canton trade fair, and the Chinese commercial office in Berne sends frequent purchasing missions to the Federal Republic. DPA, the West German press agency, has become the third Western news service (after Reuters and Agence France-Presse) to be permitted to maintain a regular correspondent in Peking. Li Y and a colleague from the East Berlin bureau of the New China News Agency have in the meantime established themselves in Bonn. Chinese propaganda against West Germany has been resumed, particularly in Asia and Africa, but Ch'en Yi was careful in September 1965 to leave the door open for the eventual establishment of official trade relations between Bonn and Peking. The Chinese leaders are willing to wait for a falling out between Bonn and Washington akin to the Franco-American rift under de Gaulle.

Meanwhile, DDR-Chinese relations are in uneasy suspense. Chinese tea has disappeared from East German grocery shelves (to be replaced by Indian and Russian brands), and other Chinese goods are rarely seen except at the Leipzig fairs. East German trade unions have stopped organizing tourist excursions to China, and few East Germans now visit that country. "People here have no conception what China is like," a professor in Rostock told me. Only Berlin and Leipzig universities now offer courses in Chinese. The Chinese embassy in East Berlin is shuttered and forbidding. Its denizens are rarely seen in public. In Peking, DDR diplomats and the ADN correspondent are viewed with the same suspicion as the most reactionary capitalists.

After a lull during most of 1965 the East German press was ordered to resume polemics against China toward the end of the year. Vietnam was the issue. *Neues Deutschland* denounced Peking for allegedly blocking the shipment of Soviet aid to Hanoi and for seeking to embroil Russia in war with America "during which the Chinese side would abstain in order to take over the role of the laughing third party." But Ulbricht still strove to find a high perch somewhere above the bitter Sino-Soviet conflict. Without much hope that anyone was listening, the SED press urged tripartite consultations among the Soviet, Chinese, and North Vietnamese parties and "unity of action" in world communism.

The East German party's pious hopes for communist unity belie the real feelings of most of its members. They make little effort to conceal their dismay at Peking's advocacy of war as an instrument of national policy. "China—that's becoming a real problem," one well-informed SED member remarked as I sat talking with him in East Berlin. "The thing is, they don't accept peaceful coexistence," he went on with genuine shock in his voice. "They want war. How many of them are there? Six hundred million? Seven hundred million? Maybe more."

Noncommunist East Germans are even more apprehensive about China. They blame Peking for much of the trouble in Vietnam and are skeptical of the regime's charges of American "aggression" in that country. In private even SED members occasionally sympathize with the United States' predicament in Southeast Asia.

Despite the revulsion that their policies arouse in most East Germans, the Chinese have succeeded in sowing doubts in the minds of many SED members about the "credibility" of Soviet retaliation in the event of a Western effort to swallow the DDR. The spectacle of American bombers over North Vietnam while Moscow discusses cultural exchange with Washington is not reassuring to an East German communist who has thrown in his lot with the regime. There may well be a faction in the East German army that shares Peking's distrust of Russian intentions and its contempt for Moscow's methods of dealing with the United States. But China is too weak and too remote to offer a practical alternative to the SED's present dependence on the Soviet Union. Not only in geography are China and East Germany a world apart.

East Germans are Europeans, and Western Europeans at that. The Chinese are Orientals. Their affinities are few. Few SED members harbor illusions about China's true feelings as (in Carola Stern's apt phrase) "they cringe in Peking's stifling embrace." Despite its flirtations with Maoist theory, the SED has adopted little from Chinese communist practice except the concept of relatively small mixed concerns where the state allows private entrepreneurs to maintain a minority interest in order to exploit their managerial skills during the transition period. In other respects, China's rocky road to communism has held little attraction for the East German party, especially its more pragmatic members.

The SED has reason to deplore the split in world communism, even though its own freedom of action has been widened as a result. Living on what *Neues Deutschland* calls "the boundary line between two world systems," the East German communists feel each convulsion on their side with particular intensity. If communist unity should disintegrate entirely, Moscow might be so weakened and distracted that it would be unable or unwilling to come to the aid of its most exposed European ally.

Without allies of its own, the DDR would dissolve in the morning mists. Confronted with the categorical imperative of political survival, the East German communists will continue groping their way between the crags of ideology and power politics.

[12]

Red on Gray

■

T*HE MOST POPULAR BOOK* in East Germany has
never been sold in the country's bookstores. It consists of a
series of lectures, innocuously entitled "Natural Scientific Aspects of Philosophical Problems," delivered by a professor of
physical chemistry at East Berlin's Humboldt University between October 1963 and February 1964. More than 1,200 students, including many from distant parts of the DDR, jammed
into a small auditorium off Unter den Linden to hear the lectures. Their notes were later incorporated into a stenographic
transcript that was clandestinely reproduced and passed from
hand to hand. It soon became the most sought after document
in East Germany.

Dr. Robert Havemann, the cause of all the excitement, is
no longer at Humboldt University. At the moment, in fact, he
is jobless. After a lifetime of distinguished service to communism, he has been expelled from the party, barred from the
university, ousted from the East German Academy of Sciences,
and denounced by the Politburo itself. The views that sealed
his fate seem almost banal except in the airless intellectual atmosphere of the German Democratic Republic. "Human be-
ings," Havemann had said, "can be told to do many things but
not what to think. Man's thought is the one thing that is really

beyond any kind of orders. The only way to influence thought is to be prepared to submit one's own viewpoint to criticism." At another point he told his students: "Throughout history reactionary regimes have tried to keep the people in ignorance. . . . They have tried to prevent people from knowing the real conditions and have also closed their own eyes, so as not to see what in the end everyone was able to see." Sometimes he was more specific: "What is indispensable to socialism, and what was lost in the Stalinist period, is democracy. Socialism cannot be realized without democracy."

It would have been easy to silence and discredit the lean, nervous professor if he had simply advocated transplanting Western democracy to the DDR. He could then have been branded an imperialist agent and given an exit visa to the West. But Havemann is the most dangerous kind of critic because he believes in communism's professed goals. Moreover, his credentials as a communist are impeccable. In 1932 at the age of twenty-two he joined the KPD. When Hitler came to power he refused to flee Germany or recant his faith. He was imprisoned and sentenced to death by the Nazis, but the sentence was commuted to forced labor to enable the Wehrmacht to utilize Havemann's scientific talents. After the war he served the party loyally, first in West Berlin where he was jailed for agitating against American nuclear policy, and later in East Berlin where he was awarded a National Prize for his ideological contributions.

Like many other communist intellectuals, Havemann began to have doubts when he realized how deeply the movement had been contaminated by Stalinism. It was not enough to blame everything on the paranoid personality of the late Soviet dictator. He began to champion the right of dissent and open discussion as the only reliable landmarks on the road to a new society.

There was a time not too long ago when anyone propagating such heresy would have been whisked to oblivion in East Germany or any other communist country. Today things are different. The Minister of State Security can no longer pick up the telephone and have a troublemaker arrested within the hour. Even if he is arrested, it is now more difficult to dispose of him. There are judicial procedures to be observed. Charges must be brought. Most important of all, each heretic is no longer an island unto himself in a sea of terrified humanity.

In March 1966 the SED failed to get the required three quarters of the members of the East Berlin Academy of Sciences to vote for Havemann's expulsion from that body. Despite strong official pressure, many members abstained or actually voted against the expulsion motion after Havemann had again refused to recant his heresy. The party was not to be thwarted. *Neues Deutschland* reported a week later that the rebellious professor had been "struck off" the membership roll because "the required prerequisites for actually remaining a member of the Academy have been eliminated." There was no mention of another vote as required by the Academy statutes.

The SED's "victory" was quickly soured by an eloquent defense of Havemann from another quarter of the communist movement. Through its central organ *l'Unità,* the Italian Communist party accused the SED of practicing Stalinist dogmatism, declaring: "In our opinion, no persecutory measures should intervene in the confrontation of opinions." The Italian party had already called Havemann a "great communist."

The SED says it expelled Havemann from the party and the East German Academy of Sciences because he "slandered" the DDR in the columns of West German news media. The party could ignore the professor's calculated defiance if he were alone, but he is not. Thousands of East Germans have begun a long march to intellectual freedom. As Stefan Heym, one of the main targets of the SED's 1965–66 cultural crackdown, has written: "We're on the track of something new; we've got hold of it, and we won't let go." Their tenacity is fed by new currents entering the DDR from the rest of European communism. The appeal for cultural freedom contained in Togliatti's testament has been repeatedly cited by Havemann, who was also encouraged in his heresy by liberal Soviet intellectuals. The Politburo's indictment accused Havemann of try-

ing to propagate the "weeds of revisionism" in the DDR
from seed spawned in Prague's "cultural spring." Two years
after Kafka was "rehabilitated" in Czechoslovakia, his works
were published for the first time in East Germany. A Russion-
language edition of *One Day in the Life of Ivan Denisovich*
was bought out overnight in East German bookstores. The
Hungarian savant Georg Lukacz created a sensation when he
advocated a new approach to literature in a speech in East
Berlin. Polish films are still shown only to select East German
film-club audiences, but even in *Neues Deutschland* the question has been asked why the best works of the Polish stage
are not performed in the DDR. By December 1965 the SED's
cultural isolation was so menacing that Alfred Kurella, a senior
Central Committee official demanded an all-out fight against
"the massive revisionist tendencies among our socialist and
communist brothers." As Professor Alfred Kantorowicz, a brilliant communist intellectual who fled East Germany in 1957
has said, "The danger for the SED has been coming for years
not so much from the West as from the East, from Poland,
Hungary, and Prague, but also from the Soviet Union." No
wall can permanently deflect the winds of change.

For sixteen years the intellectuals, like other East Germans, had a twenty-pfennig way out of their dilemma. They
voted with their feet even more emphatically than other groups
in the population. Now the elevated railway no longer stops at
freedom. The East German intelligentsia must fight or surrender.

The first to fight were the lyric poets whose esoteric
weapons spread alarm in the ranks of the SED's cultural functionaries. "Hostile political aims are being disguised in the
form of dreams," the Politburo ideologist, Kurt Hager, complained in 1963. "Criticism of the present is dressed up in the
trappings of history or in parables, and new symbolism is
rampant." The party could forbid physical flight; it was more
difficult to keep imagination earth-bound. Poetic silence, which
the writer Peter Huchel called the "last legacy," was the most

eloquent protest. "We are not going to put up with silence any more," the Humboldt University party satraps thundered angrily in the days before Robert Havemann made them wish they had settled for silence.

In contrast to the optimism that accompanied the brief thaw in 1956, many East German poets felt despair after the building of the Wall. Helmut Richter expressed their feelings (the following translations are mine):

> I often feel a yearning
> For a shot,
> That will take me back
> For later.
> Perhaps—are we
> Always born too early?

In a poem called "To my Friends, the old Comrades" Rainer Kirsch lamented the lost illusions of earlier days:

> For it's easy to dream about happy schooldays;
> But happiness is hard in this land.
> We must love in different ways from yesterday
> And with sharper understanding.
> And call all dreams by their real names,
> And know the whole truth.

The anguish of the young lyric poets soon found its way onto the East German stage, long reserved for the machine-loving heroes and heroines of socialist realism. Peter Hacks, a dedicated communist who left West Germany in 1955 to settle in the DDR, wrote *The Cares and the Power,* in which one of his characters delivers a biting monologue:

> Colleagues, if you want to imagine communism,
> Then cast your eyes
> On what is now, and take the opposite;
> For the road is little like the goal.
> Imagine as many joys as you now have cares,
> As much abundance as there is want today,
> And paint with today's gray hues
> The bright picture of the future.

The dissemination such scandalous truths from the stage of East Berlin's Deutsche Theater outraged the cultural commissars. The "Hacks case," as it came to be known, figured prominently at the Sixth SED Party Congress in January 1963. Ulbricht accused Hacks and like-minded writers of trying to "smuggle in petty bourgeois ideology" under cover of the preposterous claim that "everyone has the right to determine what he does." Alfred Kurella, the SED culture warden, was more pointed: "From a view of the present as 'gray on gray,' from a view of the party's policy as a chain of failures . . . it is not far to the next step: one feels confined . . . and from there one goes on quickly to the cry for freedom, freedom from this confinement, freedom for artistic inspiration without being supposed to be bound by understanding our life, freedom from control of publishing by the state and from control of cultural life by our party."

Hacks was removed as chief dramatist of the Deutsche Theater, whose gifted general manager Wolfgang Langhoff also quit after performing the required "self-criticism." The SED had again demonstrated that nothing approaching "absolute freedom" would be tolerated. The lesson was clear to all except those for whom it was intended—the rebellious intellectuals. Before the year was out, Hacks was back on the stage of the Deutsche Theater with an adaptation of Aristophanes' *Peace* that bristled with sardonic allusions to the DDR.

At the Fifth Congress of Creative Artists in March 1964 the national prize-winning sculptor Professor Fritz Cremer joined the writers' revolt: "In the realm of culture and art we need more differentiated and more open behavior patterns toward experimental tendencies of development, both in the practical and theoretical fields. And we do not need behavior patterns that confront the smallest move toward something new or unknown with political suspicion. What we really need is the elimination of this dogmatic devil. . . . We do not need artists, critics, and art theoreticians who, due to their lack of artistic knowledge, attempt to change that which they cannot grasp into political defamation and hostily toward the party.

. . . We need a sort of Twentieth or Twenty-Second [Soviet] Party Congress in the realm of culture."

Ulbricht himself rebutted this dangerous heresy: "If certain resolutions of the Twentieth Party Congress are interpreted in the sense of 'absolute freedom,' these resolutions have been misinterpreted. . . . We need an open creative atmosphere that must not be disturbed by revisionist subversion. . . . The fact that some people do not correctly understand the dialectical relation between freedom and responsibility is borne out by their request for absolute freedom of information. . . . Absolute freedom of information? But this is unrealistic. . . . Information for the sake of information, without concrete conclusions concerning our life and work, this does not correspond to the necessities of socialist man."

Ulbricht's warnings went unheeded. By the end of 1965 the flood of critical novels, plays, films, and television programs had reached the proportions of what one SED cultural commissar called "counter-revolution." Ulbricht demanded "corrective measures" and strict adherence to the canon that "art is a weapon of class struggle." Culture Minister Hans Bentzien was dismissed and replaced by an old-line communist. A novel by Stefan Heym about the June 17, 1953, uprising was suppressed. Nonconformist youth groups were broken up and "beat" music temporarily proscribed. East German writers were forbidden to accept invitations to visit West Germany or America. The executive board of the DDR Writers' League sent a groveling message to Ulbricht:

> In a spirit of self-criticism, we writers will tackle our tasks as set forth in the long-range plan of the party in the awareness of our responsibility. We thank the Central Committee and you, Comrade Ulbricht, for your help in this matter. We are happy that you have recovered and wish you full working ability.

Not all East German intellectuals were so supine. One novelist resigned in protest from the League's executive board. Others temporarily retreated into what Dorothy Miller of

Radio Free Europe has called "the exile of silence."

The principal scapegoat of the new crackdown was the popular lyric poet and ballad singer Wolf Biermann, whose political satire had often offended the SED's "office elephants" (as he called them). He was accused of refusing to "fulfil the pleasing and lofty social obligation of every writer in our republic: to depict in terms of literature the creation of a new and equitable social order." Although he had sung before West German audiences the year before with the party's permission, Biermann was now forbidden to perform in public or publish his work in the DDR. There were reports that he had been briefly arrested. *Neues Deutschland* may have foreshadowed a new tactic toward refractory writers when it accused Biermann of producing pornography and declared: "Whoever is perverse politically must be perverse sexually."

Such periodic contractions in the official limits of artistic expression only intensify the pressure for liberalization. The SED can no longer plug all the leaks without provoking an explosion among the intellectuals. Brigitte Reimann wrote the first East German novel about sensual love even before the party formally lifted its taboo against sex in literature. Christa Wolf's *Divided Sky*, published in the spring of 1963, marked the first time an East German author had been allowed to deal frankly with the reasons that prompted some 3,700,000 DDR citizens to flee to the West before the Wall was built. Despite some initial criticism in the party press, it quickly became the country's top best seller and went through a dozen editions. *Divided Sky* is the tragic love story of a young East German chemist who becomes disgusted with communist bureaucracy and escapes to West Berlin before the Wall went up. His nineteen-year-old fiancée follows him there for a day, vainly entreats him to come back, and finally returns by herself because in West Berlin she feels "more foreign than a stranger in a foreign land." The girl's decision fits the party line, but her fiancé and a number of lesser characters in the novel are distinctly off-beat. The author, who was thirty-four when she wrote *Divided Sky*, makes it clear that incompetent and unscrupulous party hacks, not the bright lights of West Berlin, were responsible for the chemist's decision to leave the DDR. The book is notably free of anti-Western propaganda.

With the help of friends in East Berlin, I made contact with Christa Wolf and drove out with my wife to see her at Klein-Machnow near Potsdam one frigid day in December 1964. She and her husband, a lyric poet, occupy an old house almost within sight of the barbed-wire border with West Berlin. We were ushered into a comfortably furnished sitting room where we were served the traditional German Christmas cakes and the best coffee I have every tasted in the DDR. Even the finely granulated sugar was of much better quality than one usually sees in East Germany. The rewards are substantial for any East German writer whose work pleases the public without offending the party.

Christa Wolf is an attractive dark-haired young woman, serious-minded, and deliberate in speech. She answered most of my questions while her husband listened and nodded.

"I wasn't really concerned in *Divided Sky* with the problem of physical emigration," she said. "I was trying to describe the 'inner emigration' of many of our people—their unwillingness to take part in life here. The Wall has actually reduced this. So long as people had an easy way out, they didn't bother to think things through and come to terms with themselves and society. Now they know they have to face a difficult situation."

I asked why no writer on either side of the Wall had yet produced a major novel on Germany's partition.

"We have done more on this subject than West German authors," Christa Wolf replied, a bit defensively, I thought. "Of course, you always come up against the question of how the division is to be healed. The fact is that the cultural ties between the two parts of Germany were broken long before the physical links were. The result is that writers here and in West Germany have developed in completely different ways. Except for the war, their experiences are completely different. My youngsters, for example, regard West Germany as a foreign country."

Christa Wolf is no enemy of the DDR regime. An expellee at the end of the war, she joined the SED in 1949 and is now a Candidate member of the Central Committee. She has been allowed to make frequent speaking trips to West Germany. Without violating the canons of party discipline, she manages to avoid doctrinal cant.

"We'd like to see more West German writers come here," she told me. "It helps to remove prejudices about the DDR. The reserve is on their side, not ours. Bonn fears their coming here would imply recognition of the DDR. It means that more of us go over there than West Germans come here. Still, our professional relations are good. We understand one another, although our arguments sometimes sound like the story about the American visitors who asked why there were so few trains in the Moscow metro and were asked in return, 'How many lynchings were there in Mississippi last year?' "

Christa Wolf laughed, and her husband joined in. Our conversation turned to the DDR's cultural relations with the rest of the Soviet bloc. I asked why Solzhenitsyn's novel of prison-camp life in Stalinist Russia has never been published in East Germany. The question evidently touched a sensitive nerve.

"We haven't published it," Christa Wolf said, "because the German people are not so politically mature as the Russian people. The petty bourgeoisie is still dangerous here. Don't forget it was the petty bourgeoisie who supported Hitler."

When I followed up by inquiring why the DDR had not until then published any of Kafka's works, Miss Wolf and her husband laughed nervously, and she said, "Of course we've all read Kafka. He's available in university libraries although not in local libraries. There was a question of foreign exchange. The Czechs wanted a lot for the copyright." Her answer ended in another embarrassed laugh.

I had the feeling it would have been more rewarding to talk to Christa Wolf before she became a celebrity. As we stood up to leave, she looked at me searchingly and murmured: "Remember, the fight here is still against dogmatism."

A year later Christa Wolf found herself in the thick of that fight when she clashed with the powerful Margot Honecker, Minister of Popular Education and wife of Politburo member Erich Honecker, during a Central Committee session devoted to castigating "revisionist" intellectuals. The young novelist held her ground.

A few months after *Divided Sky* was published, another novel riled the stagnant waters of East German literature. *Ole Bienkopp* by Erwin Strittmatter, long-time party member and former SED cultural functionary, is the story of a dedicated communist who persuades the farmers in his village to form the first collective after 1945. But narrow-minded bureaucrats frustrate the villagers' hopes for a better life, and Bienkopp, the hero, dies tragically after telling them: "You make it sound as if original people were the plague of our century."

Not all East German authors are so fortunate as Christa Wolf and Erwin Strittmatter in skirting ideological pitfalls. Youthful Erik Neutsch, one of the SED's favorites, produced a best seller about his days in the Hitler Youth, but when he finished a second autobiographical volume dealing with the postwar period friends advised him not even to submit it for official "review."

"For a year after that, he was in a state of shock and wrote nothing," a young writer in East Berlin told me. "Then he came up with a new manuscript that pleased the officials but completely failed as autobiography."

Neutsch's dilemma illustrates the conflict between writers who regard their work as primarily a means of self-expression and the party which considers literature as another channel of indoctrination. The struggle is embittered by the anti-intellectual bias of the present generation of SED leaders. Ulbricht is as much a philistine in his approach to the arts as Khrushchev. Whenever the SED boss visits an exhibition of paintings, he asks such questions as "But what does the working class get out of this?" or "How does this art help our workers in their struggle?"

The SED's cultural policy is really an extension of its education policy, and education is big business in East Germany. The DDR spends more than twice as much per capita on education than the Federal Republic. If one includes students enrolled in correspondence courses, East Germany has nearly twice as many university students as West Germany on the basis of population. There are now about 125,000 undergraduates studying at seven East German universities and thirty-eight college-level institutions.

The figures mean little, of course, without some idea of the quality of education. In technical fields it tends to be high. The humanities and social sciences are oppressed by the dead weight of Marxist-Leninist orthodoxy.

Indoctrination begins in the kindergartens where working mothers are encouraged to leave their children for as much as twelve hours a day. There, according to law, they are introduced to "socialist life" and "familiarize themselves with the creative activity of the working people." Despite their obligations to society, East German kindergarteners whom I have seen are as natural and unspoiled as children anywhere. They and the inmates of old people's homes are, in fact, the only wholly uninhibited people you find in the DDR. I suppose this is because the very young and the very old are alike in being unafraid of the regime.

The SED has abolished the traditional German school system. Since 1964 youngsters up to the age of sixteen have been legally required to attend the so-called "ten-year general poly-technical high school" which combines elementary and secondary instruction. West German pupils are still required to complete only nine years of schooling. In the DDR, however, polytechnical training begins in the seventh grade and basic vocational training in the ninth grade. Ulbricht has left little doubt about the nature of the curriculum: "Instruction in general technology, which begins in the seventh grade, must impart to the pupils the fundamentals of mechanical technology and production and labor economy by the end of the eighth grade. From the ninth grade onward, instruction is systematically continued in machinery and in the fundamentals of automation and electrical engineering, including techincal electronics."

Most pupils get technical training by working at nearby factories or collective farms one day a week or one week out of every three. The aim, according to Ulbricht, is to inculcate respect for "every kind of work and working people." In fact, the new system is primarily designed to overcome East Germany's acute labor shortage.

A pupil's choice of vocational training is restricted by the kind of economic activity in his area. A professor's son in Rostock who wants to be a journalist had to choose between working as a waiter, cook, or gardener. He became a waiter. To make up for time lost in "production," youngsters are saddled with as many as nine hours of classroom work and an hour and a half of homework every day. "Everybody's tired all the time," a Leipzig schoolteacher and mother of two children told me. "They're up at 6:30 every morning and can't get to bed before midnight." Slow pupils are allowed to drop out after the eighth year, but teachers are held accountable if the proportion of dropouts rises above fifteen percent. Gifted youngsters are obliged to take time off from their own studies to assist lagging "partners." The academic community in East Germany makes no secret of its opposition to the new educational system. "We don't know how it's going to work out," a Dresden professor says. "We'll give it a try, but I suspect you'll see the universities teaching students things they should have learned in secondary school."

Technical training may overburden students and lower the general academic level in East Germany; it will never displace political indoctrination. Until they are fourteen, children get their ideological education in the Thaelmann Pioneers, a replica of the Soviet Young Pioneers organization; thereafter, they belong to the Free German Youth (FDJ), the East German Komsomol, which serves as "active helper and reserve of the SED." Promising FDJ members are given an opportunity to become candidates and later full members of the party.

The FDJ has never been popular among East German young people. In September 1963 the Politburo issued a communique expressing "confidence" in the youth and promising less regimentation of their free time. The consequence was an upsurge of what the party calls "rowdyism" and "beat-behavior."

In view of the ideological content in all but purely technical instruction, the introduction of Marxism-Leninism as a required course in all schools beginning in 1963 would seem redundant. Indoctrination starts early. A new third-grade primer, for example, relates the story of a former East German estate-owner (given a ludicrous-sounding name to make the children laugh), a count now living in exile in West Germany, who writes his erstwhile tenants a peremptory letter warning them against dismantling the old castle wall to obtain stones for a new barn. The now happily collectivized peasants meet to express their indignation at the count's threats. Younger farmers are advised to enlist in the "People's Army" to make the count think twice before he goes to war to get his land back. At length it is decided to write a collective letter telling the count that his land is now owned by the "working people" and will never belong to him again. One elderly peasant woman asks to be allowed to sign the letter from her sickbed because she remembers the bad old days when her first-born died for want of a roof over their hovel.

Such clumsy propaganda puts many East German parents on the spot. "What can I tell my children," a Leipzig mother says, "when they want to know if this kind of thing is true? If I tell them it isn't, that creates doubts in their minds and trouble for them at school. And yet we know it isn't true." Such conflicts may also jeopardize the youngsters' chances for admission to a university.

By law children of workers and collective farmers (including anyone who enjoyed that status before 1945) are given preference for admission to institutions of higher learning. They also receive monthly stipends of 190 marks a month instead of the 140 marks paid to students from other occupational groups. Children of "bourgeois" parents were especially handicapped in the early postwar period when competition to enter universities was severe. Now, however, East Germany's low birth rate has so reduced the number of applicants that they hardly exceed the available places.

Ninety-five percent of all university students in the DDR get some financial support from the state. A number of "performance stipends" are awarded to gifted students who also achieve what party officials call "clarity" in their political thinking. Every student receiving such a grant must undergo an annual evaluation by a board, which includes the secretary of the party committee in the university. The pursuit of ideological clarity is also encouraged by two hours a week of compulsory instruction in Marxism-Leninism every semester.

Students at Dresden's Technical University, one of the largest in Europe, spend one of the eleven semesters necessary for a degree working in the kind of enterprise in which they will be employed after graduation. At least one year before graduation they are required to sign a contract with their future employer.

Nowhere is the cleavage between SED activists and other East Germans more glaringly evident than in the universities. Many professors who wear the party button scorn the party line. Even those whose entire education has been under a communist regime are often outspokenly critical of the political system. The academic community and the DDR's new technical and scientific elite now increasingly make common cause against Stalinism and the old guard. Robert Havemann symbolizes their alliance. Their objective is not a return to capitalism but a humanized and more democratic form of socialism with ties to the West as well as the East. The DDR's massive investment in education is already yielding dividends that can never be ploughed back in straight and narrow furrows. Ulbricht and the old guard have reason to distrust the educated.

(13)

Waiting at Wartha

∎

MOST FOREIGNERS who visit East Germany enter
and leave through Checkpoint Charlie in Berlin. They walk
a block from one world to another. The change is abrupt.
I prefer to go through the little crossing point at Wartha where
the DDR's Thuringian border bellies out against Hesse in West
Germany. Wartha is practically the westernmost point of
communist penetration in Europe. The watchtowers are there
and the cleared death strip and the barbed wire, but they are
blurred or concealed by the pine forests. The villages on both
sides of the frontier seem deserted. The roads are potholed.
Perhaps because so few people pass through Wartha, the East
German guards and customs officials are exceptionally polite,
even friendly. When you enter the DDR at Wartha a guard
lifts the familiar candy-striped steel barrier and directs you to
a clapboard shack by the unused railroad tracks. Once inside,
you find yourself in a tiny vestibule facing two closed doors,
one marked "DDR Travel Bureau," and the other "Visa Office."
Behind the first door sits a man at a bare desk, staring out the
window. A radio blares communist propaganda. As you enter,
he turns it down. After explaining where you want to go in
East Germany, you get hotel vouchers, gasoline coupons, and a
supply of East marks at the artificial rate of one to one for

West marks or four to one for American dollars. Then you go
back through the vestibule to the visa office. A pot-bellied
stove stands in one corner, and the inevitable official portrait of
Walter Ulbricht frowns from the wall. A solitary functionary
shuffles his papers at a desk at the far end of the room. As you
enter, he turns down his radio (which is tuned to the same
program), mutters a curt greeting, and inquires which cities
you will be visiting. He carefully writes the name of each on
the visa which is stamped in your passport. As he returns the
passport, the official wishes you a pleasant sojourn in "our
republic." The first time I went through Wartha I asked the
visa officer when his bureau was open. "Oh, we're always
here," he said. "You can get a visa whenever you come, day or
night." A tourist visa, that is. Other kinds must be arranged in
advance, but they too are now usually granted without difficulty. The communists are no longer afraid to let outsiders see
East Germany, especially outsiders with hard foreign exchange in their pockets.

When you leave Wartha's 24-hour visa office, you proceed
to the customs and immigration shed on a slight rise overlooking the railroad tracks. A guard inspects your car and asks if
you are carrying firearms or Western publications, presumably
regarded as equally dangerous contraband. If not, your luggage is passed with barely a glance. Another guard stamps
your passport. You pass two more candy-striped barriers
(showing your passport at each). Then you are in the German
Democratic Republic.

Going out through Wartha is quicker. You produce your
passport, convert any East marks still in your possession into
Western currency, submit to another car inspection, answer a
few perfunctory questions about your baggage, and drive
through the last two barriers. It's easy—if you have the right
color passport. Brecht was right when he said man is nothing
without his passport.

To me Wartha symbolizes the institutionalized tragedy of
Germany, the grotesque become commonplace. Checkpoint
Charlie is dramatic and showy, almost like a Hollywood set. At

Wartha the two German states meet without benefit of klieg lights. There the man-made ironies are muted by the lonely forest. The visa officer waits in his little office to admit anyone with a passport; the guard waits in his watchtower to shoot anyone without a passport. In the dead zone on either side of this unnatural border the wilderness is encroaching on crumbling roads and silent houses. The weeds are rank amid the tracks that used to carry the Frankfurt-to-Berlin express. All signals on that line are in "stop" position. They will remain in that position so long as Germany is a house divided.

Winds of change are blowing on both sides of the German frontier today, but they are still too weak to uproot the barriers and the barbed wire. A generation will pass before they begin to blow with hurricane force. Then trains may again pass through Wartha.

In the meantime, the two great powers primarily responsible for drawing a boundary through Wartha and the rest of Germany will continue to dominate the destiny of the divided country. No book like this one would be complete without some reference to what the Soviet Union and the United States would like to bring to pass—or to avert—in the heartland of Europe.

The Russians have long proclaimed with more fervor than sincerity the goal of uniting Germany under the Red banner. Their experience with a unified China under centralized communist rule augurs ill for its Teutonic equivalent. Stalin foresaw what anguish the Chinese comrades could cause Russia once they had inherited the Middle Kingdom. He gave them bad advice for what he probably considered good reasons. Stalin's aim was to keep China weak and divided. He was thwarted by what the West mistook for a triumph of international communism. In fact, it was a triumph of Chinese nationalism in communist colors.

Stalin's successors are old enough to have seen Germans change colors more than once. When the East German communists tell their people the DDR is the new Prussia, the message also reaches Moscow. Those goose-stepping soldiers in

Prussian battledress on Unter den Linden look more German than communist. And among Russians they evoke infinitely more painful memories than the American GI's on the other side of the Wall. The DDR's new "Scharnhorst Order," created on March 1, 1966, to mark the tenth anniversary of the East German army, is (to quote the East German news service) "named after the Prussian general and progressive military theoretician who carried out the army reform in Prussia and laid the foundations for a people's army." The Russian has yet to be born who relishes the prospect of sharing a continent with a Germany reunited under "progressive" Prussians. Fortunately for Moscow, it is now clearly impossible to communize all of Germany, short of war.

The West, especially the Bonn government, professes to believe the Russians will eventually perceive that it is in their own interest to permit the peaceful reunification of Germany under noncommunist auspices. As they become increasingly preoccupied with China and the rest of Asia, according to this argument, the Soviet leaders will willingly sacrifice the DDR to secure their European flank. The arrangement is to be made even more attractive by German promises of good behavior and Western guarantees of Soviet security.

It is difficult to understand how anyone can seriously believe that the Kremlin should embrace this benign vision. The Russians' memory of the Nazi attack in June 1941 would argue forcefully against basing policy on German promises. Nor would surrendering the DDR solve the problem of the former German territories east of the Oder and the Neisse. For the sake of reunification, an all-German government might sincerely renounce all claims to the eastern territories, but would a politician like Franz-Josef Strauss always remain deaf to the demands of expellees' associations for recognition of their "right to the homeland" in parts of the old Reich now incorporated in Poland and the Soviet Union? More to the point, is it reasonable to expect the Russians to assume such benevolence? Only by dismembering Poland and the western marches of the Soviet Union itself could Moscow bury German irredentism. It is a price no reasonably strong Soviet regime would be willing to pay.

The first installment of the price Russia would have to pay for German reunification would be the liquidation of the Soviet economic stake in the DDR. Times have changed since Beria and Malenkov considered abandoning the attempt to build communism in one third of old Germany. Most East Germans may still dislike their regime, but they are no longer rebellious and impoverished. From being Moscow's heaviest international liability, the DDR has become since 1960 the Soviet Union's leading trade partner and its main supplier of chemicals and equipment. A river of Soviet crude oil now flows through the longest pipeline in the world to the new Schwedt refinery on the Oder. The DDR is a mainstay of Comecon. No all-German government, however well disposed to Moscow, would allow itself to be systematically defrauded in trade with the Russians as the SED has done. No matter what concessions the Russians make to the SED on this score, a fully independent German government would still consider them hopelessly inadequate. The conclusion is inescapable that reunification on any terms acceptable to the West would upset Moscow's most cherished plans for modernizing and diversifying the Soviet economy with the help of East German resources.

The prohibitive economic price would be only a foretaste of the final cost to the Kremlin of Soviet withdrawal from Germany. There would also be an ideological price, reckoned in Peking but payable to every communist party in the world. Moscow is bound by treaty to uphold the integrity of the DDR. Reunification on Western terms would amount to scuttling the first communist state in the homeland of Marx and Engels. A surrender of such epic proportions would cast doubt on Moscow's commitments to other communist states. In the eyes of communists everywhere, it would confirm the Chinese charge that Russia is now ruled by a new bourgeoisie intent on seeking an accommodation with the United States at any price. The damage to Moscow's already tarnished prestige in the world communist movement would be incalculable.

Such would be the cost of German reunification to the Soviet Union in terms of territorial concessions, economic disruption, and ideological disaster. What benefits, if any, would such heavy sacrifices bring the Soviet state? Two answers are generally given in the West. The first and more common is that a reunited Germany would be "neutralized" and, therefore, no threat to Russia and no help to NATO or the United States. The second, and more adventurous, answer is that an all-German government would be an invaluable Soviet ally in the struggle to contain China.

As for "neutralizing" 75 million Germans in the middle of Europe, it would be preferable to try sopping up the Atlantic with a hand sponge. Germany is a political fact that cannot be covenanted out of existence. To assume that Germany could go the way of neutral Austria is tantamount to pretending that France will become another Switzerland. Even if some magic potion were found to benumb Germans' political instincts, German markets, German jobs, and German technology would still exert a magnetic attraction on Moscow's crumbling empire in Eastern Europe. The effect would be explosively political.

It is sometimes argued that a reunited Germany could be rendered harmless to Russia by being integrated into a united Europe. Such a European community is not now in sight. If it ever does become a practical possibility, the other partners are not likely to welcome a massive infusion of Teutonic blood. From Moscow's point of view, it would seem that Europe had been integrated into Germany, with even more baleful consequences than a "neutralized" Germany standing in splendid isolation.

The quarter million American troops now in West Germany come nearer to neutralizing that country than any number of paper agreements among high contracting parties. The U. S. Seventh Army is the most effective guarantee yet devised that neither Bonn nor its Bundeswehr will seek to reunify Germany by force. Any neutralization agreement of the kind discussed in the West would in effect de-neutralize Germany by removing the restraining presence of American forces. The

American military presence in West Germany has the added advantage that it justifies a Soviet military presence in East Germany and elsewhere in Eastern Europe. Whatever role Bonn is eventually accorded in NATO's nuclear strategy will be infinitely less dangerous to Moscow than the power of a reunited and nonaligned Germany to break its own vow of nuclear abstinence. After all, the Germans are not Albanians. These facts are not lost on the Russians, however much they inveigh against MLF and its successor schemes. Soviet policy is no longer primarily directed to driving America out of Europe, certainly not out of West Germany. The Russians would much rather see the larger part of Germany in the confining embrace of the United States than all Germany chafing under an imposed and illusory "neutrality."

The thesis that Moscow would trade the DDR for German help against China is at least more ingenious than the neutralization formula. Such an alliance might allow the Russians to shift some troops from Europe to the Far East, but it is unlikely that the Kremlin would ever denude Eastern Europe and Russia's own western provinces of forces. It is also hard to see what more aid a reunited Germany could give Moscow against China than the Russians already get from the DDR. More German experts are not required for the Soviet nuclear program. Russian rockets are presumably more than adequate to deal with Peking and Shanghai without a German contribution. And if Russia were engaged with China and the United States at the same time, the outcome would hardly be affected by German assistance, assuming it were forthcoming.

The word "Rapallo" is used so often and so loosely to describe a possible German-Soviet alliance that it has lost practically all meaning. The Pact of Rapallo signed in 1922 was an alliance of outcasts, both weakened by war and revolution. The Soviet Union and the Weimar Republic were young, unstable regimes that cooperated to survive in a hostile world. Today the Soviet Union is one of two superpowers, and West Germany enjoys the protection of the other. The only thing that could now induce the Federal Republic to forsake its trans-Atlantic protector and align itself with Moscow would be a Soviet offer of reunification.

If the Russians ever made such an offer and then made good on it, they would soon find that the "German problem" was far from being solved. The natural ally for a reunited Germany still seeking redress for territorial losses in the East would be not Russia, but another victim of Russian imperialism. Demands for a Bonn-Peking axis directed against Moscow are already being voiced in West Germany. So long as the Federal Republic prospers behind the American shield and pins its hopes for reunification on American power, such demands will be ignored. But if the Russians relinquished the DDR, the resulting German state would no longer depend on America or anyone else in the pursuit of its national interests, including "rectification" of the Eastern frontier. A reunited Germany could afford to alienate the United States by joining China in a gigantic pincers movement against Russia. A Sino-German entente would be an alliance of the disgruntled and the aggrieved. Mao Tse-tung has already advanced the notion of a "second intermediate zone," including West Germany, France, Britain, and Japan, joined with China against America and Russia. Absurd as this vision seems today, it intrigues many Germans. It frightens Russians.

It would be interesting to know what frightens Russians and their rulers most: Germany reunited under communism or under capitalism, Germany allied with the Soviet Union or with Russia's enemies, or Germany decked out in the finery of a "neutral." All options are repugnant so long as Russians dread Germans. Therefore, Moscow opts for the *status quo*. The difficulty is that the *status quo* in Germany is not static. As this book has tried to show, both parts of Germany are in flux. While they do their best to control the flux in East Germany, the Russians will not try to suppress it because they realize that the DDR must evolve if it is to play its full part in Comecon and as a magnet for Western trade. The most striking evidence of Moscow's acceptance of the *status quo* in Germany is its refusal to sign a separate peace treaty with the

DDR despite intense SED pressure. Although it now prefers to avoid a confrontation between Allied and East German forces on the Berlin Autobahn or in the air corridors, the Kremlin is by no means averse to exploiting its own control of the access routes to demonstrate Soviet power or to warn Washington and Bonn against tampering with the situation in West Berlin. There will be more Berlin "crises" in years to come, but they are not likely to involve a frontal attack by Moscow on the Western position in the former German capital. The Russians now show little sign of believing they can alter the *status quo* in Berlin by threat of force. In accordance with the same policy, the Russians will maintain politically frigid but commercially warm relations with the Federal Republic. The intermittent dialogue between Moscow and Bonn will never be broken off for good.

The struggle for Germany is now many-sided. Britain, France, and the United States have been directly involved since the end of the Second World War. Despite his flamboyance, General de Gaulle does not seem to have the power to affect the outcome decisively. Nor do the British. The United States bears the brunt of the burden for making good on the Allied commitment to reunite Germany in something approaching freedom. A few words about American policy in Germany, therefore, may be in order.

No one who has visited West Berlin can doubt that the United States has come to stay in Central Europe, at least so long as there is such a thing as the Cold War. Washington officially deplores the *status quo* in that part of the world but will not wage war to alter it. American and Soviet policies in Germany are hostile but congruent. Moscow approves the *status quo;* Washington accepts it. The most important difference is that America's special relationship to Bonn is now the core of NATO. The Soviet Union is economically, but not militarily, dependent on the DDR. West Germany demands more of its principal ally than simply being defended against external threats. The federal government ceaselessly importunes Washington to take some "initiative" to break the deadlock over German reunification. Bonn offers few ideas of its own. Unwilling to use force and unable to evict the Russians from East Germany by any other means, every postwar American administration has felt obliged to make repeated protestations of devotion to the cause of German unity. Like an aging mistress, the Federal government is increasingly dubious of such expressions of constancy.

To allay German suspicions, the United States has given Bonn what amounts to a veto power over important elements of American policy in Europe. Washington refuses to recognize the Oder-Neisse line in deference to Bonn. The Kennedy Administration dropped its proposal for an international Berlin-access authority when the Federal Republic objected to East Germany's inclusion on the body. The United States shuns any suggestion for thinning out forces or setting up observer posts in Central Europe that could be construed to "discriminate" against Germany. The Pentagon maintains an oversize army in West Germany to reassure nervous leaders in Bonn. The most trifling reduction in that force is the subject of prolonged consultations between the two capitals.

One reason that America has no policy toward the DDR almost twenty years after the founding of an East German state is that the Federal Republic insists that it alone speak for all Germans. Accordingly, official American contacts with the DDR are conducted almost furtively. When an American is arrested in East Berlin, diplomats from the U. S. mission in West Berlin quietly get in touch with the DDR Foreign Ministry. Whenever they enter or leave East Berlin, they show their passports to East German guards. During the height of the Berlin crisis in 1961, it was found that the U. S. Army had been routinely dealing with the East Germans on several technical questions connected with the Autobahn.

On the other hand, Washington has made no secret of its wheat sales to East Germany. Despite protests from Bonn, it has licensed the export of synthetic-fiber manufacturing equipment and radio isotopes to the DDR and lifted the ban on American participation at the annual Leipzig trade fairs. An

ADN correspondent is accredited to the United Nations in New York, and the Department of State no longer makes any effort to discourage American newsmen from traveling in East Germany. But when the American ambassador to Germany visits East Berlin, he calls on the Soviet ambassador, not Ulbricht. The fiction is maintained that Washington has no dealings with the DDR government. The United States also declines to recognize Peking, but the ambassadorial talks in Geneva and Warsaw have ensured a channel of communication with the Chinese communists that does not exist with the East German regime.

The time has come for Washington to reflect if it should continue denying itself regular access to the Soviet Union's most important ally. The aim of policy is, after all, to influence events, not simply to perpetuate legal fictions. The United States has never shared Bonn's anxieties over "recognition by inadvertence." The American administration should, therefore, be able to approach this question without the neuroses that afflict West German policy. Actual diplomatic recognition of the East German regime would probably be a mistake from all points of view. It would cause an earthquake in Bonn and demolish whatever remains of four-power responsibility for Berlin. Nor is there any evidence that such a costly gesture would soon strengthen the SED's hand in dealing with the Russians. Trade is another matter. It can be conducted without diplomatic relations. Even a small increase in their dollar earnings would give the East Germans more bargaining power with Moscow. Trade would relieve the DDR's dependence on Russia and help to overcome East German feelings of isolation and subjugation to Moscow. In the long run, it would accelerate the movement toward a more independent SED policy. Commerce with the West would encourage reformers like the late Erich Apel to persevere in dismantling the structure of Stalinist economic and political controls. The SED would naturally claim credit for any benefits that accrued to the East German people from such trade. The party might even win a measure of popularity. But the United States has correctly discounted such drawbacks in deciding to pursue a more co-operative policy with Poland and Yugoslavia and, more recently, with Rumania. The same approach should be applied to East Germany.

In his *Alternative to Partition* Professor Zbigniew Brzezinski of Columbia University urges the West to improve relations with all Eastern European countries except East Germany. If the DDR can be isolated, he believes, it may eventually become a "Soviet Mozambique—a source of irritation to the east Europeans and embarrassment to Moscow." The Russians might then be persuaded to liquidate East Germany, allowing Germany and the rest of Europe to unite again after "fifty years of continental civil war."

This view overlooks the DDR's pivotal economic, strategic, and ideological importance to Moscow. Professor Brzezinski undercuts his own argument when he rejects the "assumption that a policy of pressure and isolation would somehow prompt the entire communist structure (in eastern Europe) to dissolve . . . or, if the dissolution should take place in an individual communist state, that the Soviet Union would not be able to restore the status quo ante (as in Hungary in 1956)." The assumption is no more valid for East Germany than it is for the rest of Eastern Europe. Professor Brzezinski proposes "a firm definition of the East German regime as a tool of the Soviet occupation forces" after he has already pointed out that Soviet military power is a depreciating political asset in Eastern Europe.

Even if it were possible to make the DDR a pariah among communist states, such a policy would only cement the division of Germany. Unrelenting Western hostility toward East Germany would help the Russians avoid making concessions there of the kind they have already made elsewhere in Eastern Europe. Instead of trying to ignore the DDR and hoping it will somehow disappear, we should quietly begin applying to East Germans the policy of bridge-building successfully pursued by the Kennedy and Johnson Administrations in other parts of the former Soviet empire. Such a policy has nothing to do with the discredited 1952 Republican campaign slogan of "rollback" or "liberation." East Germany, like the rest of Eastern Europe, will remain communist but not bolshevik. The difference is important, as the example of Rumania demonstrates. We should not be blinded to all possibilities by Bonn's apprehensions. Many West Germans already appreciate the need for bridges of all kinds to the DDR.

The federal German government itself is beginning to realize that Washington is unable and Moscow unwilling to deliver German unity. This situation must eventually lead to a direct approach by Bonn to the DDR. A dialogue among Germans will not produce a unitary state based on free elections. Some form of confederation or association is probably the most that can be expected in this century, barring a cataclysm in the Kremlin. Ironically, the outcome is unlikely to please either America or Russia. The United States is committed to German reunification by all-German elections, but it will probably accept whatever form of association the Germans work out among themselves. In the long run, we can neither extinguish the impulse toward unity nor determine its expression. "Confederation" has been a favorite word in the Soviet lexicon on Germany, but Moscow has never been genuinely interested in seeing Germans gathered too closely around one table. By the time that comes to pass, Moscow may rue the day it first championed a German confederation.

If the SED ever agrees to open serious talks on confederation, it will no longer need Soviet tanks to stay in power. It will then have reliable tanks of its own. Communist governments do not talk themselves out of business.

If an agreement is ever worked out, it will have to include some restrictions on East German immigration into the Federal Republic. Bonn now insists that any German has the right to reside anywhere in the country. A few West German politicians, including Ewald Bucher when he was Justice Minister, have suggested imposing curbs on freedom of movement in exchange for removal of the Wall. If conditions continue to improve in the DDR and fewer East Germans want to leave, such ideas might become politically acceptable in the Federal Republic.

A confederation based on reciprocal concessions will be as provisional, and therefore probably as lasting, as everything else connected with the German problem. The DDR and the Federal Republic both began life as expedients and continue as institutions. They are stopgaps that have acquired the respectability of age. No one can foretell how the Germans will finally heal their twentieth-century diaspora. I venture only the prediction that the denouement of this great human epic will fit no pattern, fulfill no prophecy, and confirm no theory. By then it will be enough to say that a remarkable and contradictory race that almost suffered biological extinction in 1945 has endured, which is to say, prevailed.

Currency Equivalents

■

The East German mark is artificially pegged at parity with the West German mark (DM) and at approximately 4 to 1 with the U. S. dollar. The purchasing power of the East mark is generally less than these rates indicate, but since DDR currency is legally traded only inside the country there is no valid way of estimating its free market value. In this book I have therefore stated most wages, prices, and other amounts in terms of East marks, only occasionally converting them to dollars at the 4-to-1 rate to give a rough order of magnitude.

Glossary of Abbreviations

■

CDU—*Christlich-Demokratische Union*—Christian Democratic Union, the party that has controlled the Bonn government since the founding of West German Federal Republic.

Comecon—Council for Mutual Economic Assistance—Soviet bloc organization for economic and technical cooperation.

CPSU—Communist Party of the Soviet Union.

CSU—*Christlich-Soziale Union*—Christian Social Union, Bavarian affiliate of the CDU.

DDR—*Deutsche Demokratische Republik*—German Democratic Republic.

FDJ—*Freie Deutsche Jugend*—Free German Youth, East Germany's communist youth organization.

HO—*Handelsorganisation*—DDR's state-run retail and service combine.

KPD—*Kommunistische Partei Deutschlands*—German Communist Party, founded December 30, 1918, renamed Socialist Unity

Party of Germany (SED) after merger with the SPD in the Soviet occupation zone on April 20, 1946.

LPG–*Landwirtschaftliche Produktionsgenossenschaft*–agricultural production cooperative; East German term for a collective farm.

MLF–Multi-Lateral Force–inter-Allied surface fleet armed with nuclear missiles championed by United States in early 1960's; abandoned in 1965.

MTS–*Maschinen-Traktoren-Station*–machine-tractor station; one of state-run facilities set up on Soviet model in East Germany after 1945 to service collective farms; now disbanded.

SED–*Sozialistische Einheitspartei Deutschlands*–Socialist Unity Party of Germany; the name assumed by the German Communist Party in the Soviet Occupation Zone after it merged with the East German SPD in April 1946; now the ruling party of the DDR.

SPD–*Sozialdemokratische Partei Deutschlands*–Social Democratic Party of Germany; principal opposition party in West Germany.

SSD–*Staatssicherheitsdienst*–East German secret police organization.

VEB–*Volkseigener Betrieb*–People's-owned Enterprise; designation for state-run concern in the DDR.

VEG–*Volkseigene Gut*–People's-owned Estate; East German state farm in which all land, livestock, and tools belong to the government.

VVB–*Vereinigung Volkseigener Betriebe*–Association of People's-owned Enterprises; one of the state-run trusts or holding companies given broad autonomy to manage a particular branch of industry under the DDR's new economic system.

Volkspolizei or *Vopos*–East Germany's "People's Police."

Index

◼

A Note about the Author

Welles Hangen has reported the news for NBC since 1956 from the Middle East, India, and Germany. He was born in New York City in 1930 and is a graduate of Brown University, where he was elected to Phi Beta Kappa. Mr. Hangen was with the Paris edition of the New York *Herald Tribune* (1948–9), served as a staff correspondent for *The New York Times* from 1949 on except for a military leave of absence from 1951 to 1953. He was awarded a Council on Foreign Relations Press Fellowship for 1965–6. Mr. Hangen is the author of *After Nehru, Who?* (1963) and has published articles in *The New Yorker, The Saturday Evening Post, Harper's Magazine,* the *Yale Review,* and other magazines. He is married and the father of one son.

A Note on the Type

The Text of this book is set in Caledonia, a typeface designed by W(illiam) A(ddison) Dwiggins for the Mergenthaler Linotype Company in 1939. This new typeface was inspired by the Scotch types cast about 1833 by Alexander Wilson & Son, Glasgow type founders, and Dwiggins chose the Roman name for Scotland—Caledonia. There is a calligraphic quality about this face that is totally lacking in the Wilson types. Dwiggins referred to an even earlier typeface for this "liveliness of action"—one cut around 1790 by William Martin for the printer William Bulmer. Caledonia has more weight than the Martin letters, and the bottom finishing strokes (serifs) of the letters are cut straight across, without brackets, to make sharp angles with the upright stems, thus giving a "modern face" appearance.

W. A. Dwiggins (1880-1956) was born in Martinsville, Ohio, and studied art in Chicago. In 1940 he moved to Hingham, Massachusetts, where he built a solid reputation as a designer of advertisements and as a calligrapher. He began an association with the Mergenthaler Linotype Company in 1929, and over the next twenty-seven years designed a number of book types for that firm, of especial interest are the Metro series, Electra, Caledonia, Eldorado, and Falcon.